"With close attention to the text's rhetorical features, Michelle Stinson's use of food as a lens for reading Psalm 78 provides a rich and nourishing banquet. Stinson opens up important dimensions of this psalm while also integrating it more fully into other parts of the Psalter. Taste and see, for this is good!"

—DAVID G. FIRTH, Tutor in Old Testament, Trinity College Bristol

"Over the past two decades, there has been growing academic interest in meals within the Hebrew Bible. By and large, study has been largely archaeological and historical in nature. Michelle Stinson's work fills an important void by offering a literary and rhetorical analysis of the function of food within Psalm 78. This study is a welcome contribution to the field and hopefully paves the way for future studies on the function of meals within biblical texts. Highly recommended."

—ANDREW ABERNETHY, Professor of Old Testament, Wheaton College

"Michelle Stinson offers a methodologically sophisticated and literarily sensitive analysis of Psalm 78. Her focus on the multidimensional aspects of food language and its rhetorical potential results in a rich and compelling explanation of this complex poetic presentation of Israel's story, accounting for its structure, imagery, and connections with other psalms."

—MICHAEL A. LYONS, Senior Lecturer in Hebrew Bible and Old Testament, St Mary's College, University of St Andrews

"Stinson argues that food language is the key to unlocking the 'enigmas' of the strangely under-examined poem that stands—not by coincidence—at the precise center of the Hebrew Psalter. Through lucid rhetorical, sociological, and agrarian analysis, she shows how a great poet, reflecting on the most basic human need, discloses the pattern of Israel's experience of God and place, through blessing and bane, across the long course of history. The topic is as urgent as the exegesis is exemplary."

—ELLEN F. DAVIS, Amos Ragan Kearns Distinguished Professor of Bible and Practical Theology, Duke Divinity School

"Stinson's volume does much more than simply remind the reader of the significance of food in an agrarian culture; she explores 'the multi-dimensionality of food' and how those various dimensions are employed to great rhetorical effect in the biblical text. Stinson's methodological approach opens new vistas for reading Psalm 78, but even more, her work charts an exciting path for future research on the rhetoric associated with food in the Hebrew Bible. An insightful and engaging work!"

—W. DENNIS TUCKER JR., Professor of Christian Scriptures, Truett Seminary, Baylor University

A Table in the Wilderness

A Table in the Wilderness

The Rhetorical Function of Food Language in Psalm 78

MICHELLE A. STINSON

Foreword by J. Clinton McCann Jr.

PICKWICK *Publications* • Eugene, Oregon

A TABLE IN THE WILDERNESS
The Rhetorical Function of Food Language in Psalm 78

Pickwick Publications
An Imprint of Wipf and Stock Publishers
199 W. 8th Ave., Suite 3
Eugene, OR 97401

www.wipfandstock.com

PAPERBACK ISBN: 979-8-3852-6228-1
HARDCOVER ISBN: 979-8-3852-6229-8
EBOOK ISBN: 979-8-3852-6230-4

Cataloguing-in-Publication data:

Names: Stinson, Michelle A. [author] | McCann, J. Clinton, 1951– [foreword writer].

Title: A table in the wilderness : the rhetorical function of food language in Psalm 78 / Michelle A. Stinson ; foreword by J. Clinton McCann Jr..

Description: Eugene, OR: Pickwick Publications, 2026 | Includes bibliographical references and index.

Identifiers: ISBN 979-8-3852-6228-1 (paperback) | ISBN 979-8-3852-6229-8 (hardcover) | ISBN 979-8-3852-6230-4 (ebook)

Subjects: LCSH: Psalm seventy-eight. | Bible Psalms—Criticism, interpretation, etc. | Food in the Bible | Food habits—Social aspects—Israel.

Classification: BS1450 S75 2026 (paperback) | BS1450 (ebook)

04/16/26

In grateful memory of
Gordon J. Wenham
(1943–2025)

Bless us, O Lord,
and these thy gifts
which we are about to receive
from thy bounty,
through Christ our Lord.
Amen.

Contents

Analytic Table of Contents

Foreword

Ever since James Muilenburg in 1969 issued his famous call for biblical studies to move beyond form criticism, the scholarly study of the Psalms has been on the move—beyond form criticism to rhetorical criticism (as Muilenburg suggested), beyond rhetorical criticism to sustained attention to the shape and shaping of the Psalter, and most recently, beyond the shape and shaping approach to interpreting the Psalms from an agrarian perspective, building upon the ground-breaking work of Ellen F. Davis, especially her volume entitled *Scripture, Culture, and Agriculture: An Agrarian Reading of the Bible* (Cambridge University Press, 2009). Michelle Stinson has been and is at the forefront of this latest move, and this volume is a prime example of an agrarian approach to the Psalms. To be sure, movement beyond does not mean leaving behind, as Stinson demonstrates. Stinson carefully considers Psalm 78 among the other historical psalms (form criticism); she attends closely to the literary features and persuasive force of Psalm 78 (rhetorical criticism); and she discusses Psalm 78 in relation to the rest of the Asaph collection (shape and shaping). Students of the Psalms will recognize these dimensions of Stinson's work as important connections to previous scholarship, but what is unique and new in Stinson's work is the consistent agrarian concern. For agrarian thinkers, two closely related things are of paramount importance—land and food. While land has received a good deal of attention in biblical studies, food has not; and Stinson aims to address this deficiency. Since biblical scholars have not often thought in a sustained way about food, Stinson devotes major attention to defining "food language"; and she carefully analyzes the rhetorical function of food language in Psalm 78, especially in vv. 13–53 that recount the divine provision of food in the wilderness and the dismantling of Egyptian food supplies as part of the plagues against Egypt. As Stinson clearly demonstrates, the use of food language in Psalm 78 (and elsewhere) is not coincidental or haphazard;

rather, it is carefully chosen and arranged to maximize its persuasive (rhetorical) force. And furthermore, this persuasive force has not only literary significance but also theological significance, since for a postexilic audience—Stinson assumes that Psalm 78 is a postexilic creation—the remembrance of divine provision of food in the past would invite trust in the promise of divine provision in the present and future.

Evidence of the timeliness and cutting-edge dimension of Stinson's work is the fact that other scholars have recently begun to interpret the Psalms and other biblical material from an agrarian perspective. In fact, the SBL Press is currently preparing for publication a volume of essays on the Psalms and agrarianism, edited by W. Dennis Tucker, and it will include an essay by Stinson. My hope (and expectation) is that the SBL Press volume and Stinson's current volume will provide even further impetus for the study of the Psalms and other biblical material from an agrarian perspective, which will have the potential to enrich our understanding of the Bible rhetorically, theologically, and ecologically.

J. Clinton McCann Jr.
Eden Theological Seminary
St. Louis, MO

Acknowledgments

THE STORY OF HOW this book came to be is a long and winding and harrowing one that gratefully has a very happy ending. Like a good epic tale, it involved great heartache but also the gift of rightly timed guides, faithful traveling companions, and profound moments of grace. If you have been a part of this journey from the beginning, you know how the tale unfolded and thus know why this book in your hands is a testament to a long journey of confident trust in the God who held Israel's story and holds our own.

I owe a tremendous debt of gratitude to Professor Gordon Wenham (1943–2025) for believing in the viability of a PhD thesis focused on food, especially before this area of exploration had gained the recognition it has at the present. This book began as that PhD thesis completed through Trinity College Bristol/University of Bristol and written under the supervision of Professor Gordon Wenham (2011–17) and finished under the direction of Dr. David Firth (2017). Dr. Ellen Davis served as a second supervisor throughout the process (2012–17). I am deeply grateful for the ways that these scholars added their gifts to this project. My thanks also goes out to the examiners of my thesis, Dr. J. Clinton McCann Jr. and Dr. Peter Hatton, for their gracious reception of my work.

While a successfully defended PhD thesis will earn you a degree, moving this manuscript into a book has also had its own rambling journey. I am truly grateful to Wipf and Stock for publishing this revised work in their Pickwick Publications imprint. A special thanks to Dr. Robin Parry for answering this new author's seemingly endless questions, all with grace and good humor. And a huge thank you to Elisabeth Rickard and Savanah N. Landerholm for their work behind the scenes to bring this manuscript to press.

With a project that has spanned almost fifteen years, the list of individuals, communities, and institutions that need to be thanked has continued to grow. I first need to celebrate the memory of Dr. Gordon Wenham, who passed away in May 2025. His initial kindness in taking me on as a PhD student was just one of many ways that he responded to life with generosity, collegiality, humility, and grace.

I also owe great thanks to the Trinity College Bristol community of faculty, staff, and fellow students for the ways that they built into my life while I was a PhD student (2011–18). I began my studies on site at Trinity College during the autumn 2011 term. I carry with me the memory of a Eucharist on campus where the bread for the service was carried directly from the oven to the altar, driving home the rhetorical force of the sensory dimension of food.

I am also grateful to the warden, librarians, and staff at Tyndale House (Cambridge). During the past two decades now, I have been warmly welcomed as a "reader" at the library for summer research trips and an extended sabbatical stay. Thank you to the many individuals who have grown dear to my heart through the years. It was an early summer afternoon sitting in the Tyndale House back garden where I felt the nudge to finally send off this manuscript to a publisher.

I am also deeply grateful to my former colleagues and various administrators at Simpson University (Redding, CA) for their support during the completion of my PhD, especially the late Stanley Clark for his faith in and support for me when I was a newly hired faculty member. I am grateful for the research support provided through the Rev. Charles Dale Scholar Grant and the Francis Owen Distinguished Scholar Award. And to my former colleagues in the Theology and Ministry department, I couldn't have asked for a better group of guys to work alongside.

More recently, I owe a debt of thanks to the individuals and institutions that have encouraged and supported my research and writing the past few years as I have journeyed this odd road of being an independent scholar. Thank you to Denver Seminary—in particular Dr. Don Payne and Dr. Rick Hess—for offering me an institutional home. I am honored to be a visiting scholar at a place that so deeply formed me as a graduate student. I am grateful to the Meals in the Hebrew Bible/Old Testament and Its World SBL unit who warmly welcomed me and offered me a context to continue to lead and serve in the academy. To Calvin Institute for Christian Worship and their "Vital Worship, Vital Preaching" grants that have helped to fund this season of research and writing. To my writing-group friends, John Ayabe and Philip Fox: I don't think this book would be here without your faithful commitment to journeying these pandemic and post-pandemic years together. And to the Downing House community who offered me "the gift of place" during this past season. I remain profoundly grateful.

And to Dr. Clint McCann who served as an external examiner on my PhD thesis and who kindly agreed to write the foreword to this book. Thank you for the many ways that you have celebrated and advocated for conversations about food, land, and justice in classrooms and conferences. I owe you a debt of thanks for adding your voice in support once again in the form of this foreword.

And finally, to all of you—family, dear friends, and even strangers—who fed me, housed me, supported and encouraged me through the years of the writing of this book. I wish I could name you each here, but you know who you are. I remain forever grateful.

Abbreviations

AB	Anchor Bible Commentary Series
ABD	*Anchor Bible Dictionary*
ABib	Academia Biblica
ACOT	Apollos Commentary of the Old Testament
ANE	Ancient Near East
AOAT	Alter Orient und Altes Testament
AOTC	Abingdon Old Testament Commentary
ASTI	*Annual of the Swedish Theological Institute*
BBR	*Bulletin for Biblical Research*
BCOTWP	Baker Commentary of Old Testament Wisdom and Poetry
BDB	Brown, F., S. Driver, and C. Briggs. *Brown-Driver-Briggs Hebrew and English Lexicon.* Peabody, MA: Hendrickson, 1999.
Bib	*Biblica*
BibSac	*Bibliotheca Sacra*
BIS	Biblical Interpretation Series
BN	*Biblische Notizen*
BTB	*Biblical Theology Bulletin*
BZAW	Beihefte zur Zeitschrift für die alttestamentliche Wissenschaft
CBQ	*Catholic Biblical Quarterly*
CC	Continental Commentaries
CHANE	Culture and History of the Ancient Near East

ET	English Translation
FAT	Forschungen zum Alten Testament
HALOT	*The Hebrew and Aramaic Lexicon of the Old Testament*
HCOT	Historical Commentary on the Old Testament
HeBAI	*Hebrew Bible and Ancient Israel*
HUCA	*Hebrew Union College Annual*
IBC	Interpretation: A Bible Commentary for Teaching and Preaching
ICC	International Critical Commentary
Int	*Interpretation*
JBL	*Journal of Biblical Literature*
JBQ	*Jewish Biblical Quarterly*
JNSL	*Journal of Northwest Semitic Languages*
JPS	Jewish Publication Society
JPSTC	Jewish Publication Society Torah Commentaries
JSOT	*Journal for the Study of the Old Testament*
JSOTSup	Journal for the Study of the Old Testament Supplement Series
LHBOTS	The Library of Hebrew Bible/Old Testament Studies
LSTS	Library of Second Temple Studies
LXX	Septuagint
MT	Masoretic Text
NCB	New Century Bible
NCBC	New Cambridge Bible Commentary
NICOT	New International Commentary of the Old Testament
NIDOTTE	*New International Dictionary of Old Testament Theology and Exegesis*
NIVAC	New International Version Application Commentary
NRSV	New Revised Standard Version
NSBT	New Studies in Biblical Theology
OTL	The Old Testament Library

SBL	Society of Biblical Literature
SBLDS	Society of Biblical Literature Dissertation Series
SBLMS	Society of Biblical Literature Monograph Series
SJOT	*Scandinavian Journal of the Old Testament*
SJT	*Scottish Journal of Theology*
TOTC	Tyndale Old Testament Commentary
UF	*Ugarit-Forschungen*
VT	*Vetus Testamentum*
VTSup	Supplements to Vetus Testamentum
WBC	Word Biblical Commentary
WUNT	Wissenschaftliche Untersuchungen zum Neuen Testament
ZKTh	*Zeitschrift für Katholische Theologie*

I

Introduction

Engaging the audience through its artful construction and didactic—yet enigmatic—nature, Psalm 78 provides a captivating composition for reflection and study. As Klaus Seybold remarks, here in this poem, "poetic art and pedagogical intent come together."[1] This wedding of pedagogy and poetry becomes apparent from the psalm's opening exhortation (vv. 1–2):

> Give ear, O my people, to my teaching (תורתי); incline your ears to the words of my mouth. I will open my mouth in a parable (במשל); I will utter enigmas (חידות) from of old.[2]

These introductory verses make clear the instructional nature of this psalm.[3] However, the psalmist is equally clear that the form of this instruction will be opaque, requiring the audience to work to uncover

1. Seybold, *Introducing the Psalms*, 48.

2. Biblical quotations are the author's own translation, unless otherwise noted. In addition, verse numbering will follow the MT; English numbering, when different, will appear in brackets with the notation ET.

3. This instructional intention is also supported by Psalm 78's superscription, which identifies the psalm as a *maskil* (משכיל). Because of the close resemblance with the *hiphil* form of the root שכל "to be wise, skilled," Kraus proposes that the term refers to "a poem that is intellectually and artistically conceived or that produces an intellectual or artistic effect." Kraus, *Psalms 1–59*, 25. The classification משכיל appears in the headings of twelve other psalms (Pss 32, 42, 44, 45, 52, 53, 54, 55, 74, 88, 89, 142). Regarding Psalm 78, Hossfeld concludes: "This psalm, then, is not a prayer, but a narrative addressed to the nation; to that extent the superscription, with its title, 'instructional poem,' strikes the right note, especially since it also indicates the poetic form of the psalm." Hossfeld and Zenger, *Psalms 2*, 286.

its secrets. As Greenstein observes: "The audience had better pay close attention because, the psalmist warns, his teaching will be presented not in a straightforward manner but rather in a puzzling or mysterious form—in 'riddles' (*hidot*, v. 2)."[4] And as the introduction continues, the purpose of the psalm is revealed. For the psalmist proposes that it is through the generational recital of YHWH's deeds and statutes (vv. 5–6)—perhaps a self-reverential nod to the use of *this* particular recital—that Israel would come to "put their confident trust (כסל) in God and not forget the works of God, but keep His commandments" (v. 7).[5] With the psalmist's stated goal in mind, this study seeks to consider how the selection, depiction, and arrangement of material within this psalm helps to create the context for the realization of this desired outcome of Israel's "confident trust" in God.

The body of Psalm 78 (vv. 13–72)[6] takes the guise of a historical recital, an extended narrative "re-presentation" (*Vergegenwärtigung*)[7] of YHWH's work in the history of Israel. This recital includes a recounting of the exodus event, the wilderness wanderings, the entry into the land, and the establishment of the Davidic monarchy. And yet this litany of events is more than a review of history, as the opening lines announce. Westermann observes the didactic trajectory of the psalmist's presentation of this history: "What is here so precisely and clearly enunciated is that the 'traditioning' of the events of past history within the contemporary scene has a meaning that is forward looking."[8] For here in Psalm 78, the artful construing of the past becomes paradigmatic of the concerns of the present and hope for the future. As Westermann continues: "By

4. Greenstein, "Mixing Memory and Design," 197.

5. Psalm 78 employs a variety of terms for the divine. Even within the psalm's opening verses (vv. 1–12), the psalmist employs three different terms: יהוה (v. 4), אלהים (vv. 7, 10) and אל (vv. 7, 8). In translations, I will use the designation that appears within each section of the psalm. However, for the sake of sentence clarity, I may at times use an alternative term in discussions. Translations of the Hebrew text will retain the MT's use of the masculine pronoun for God.

6. There are differing views regarding where the introduction ends and the historical recital begins (see extended discussion in ch. 2). The dominant view—put forward by Richard Clifford—is that the psalm opens with an introduction (vv. 1–11) followed by two historical recitals (vv. 12–39, 40–72). Clifford, "In Zion and David a New Beginning," 129. In this study, I consider v. 12 as part of the introductory material of the psalm. Clifford does, however, acknowledge v. 12's "transitional" nature, noting the fact that it looks back to v. 11b and forward to the second recital, in particular, v. 43 (128).

7. Westermann, "'Re-Presentation' of History in the Psalms," 236–42.

8. Westermann, "'Re-Presentation' of History in the Psalms," 238.

recounting the glorious deeds of God, the future is opened."[9] A future, according to the psalmist, that is directed by a God who has proven—time and time again—worthy of Israel's trust.

PURPOSE OF STUDY

The majority of Psalm 78's historical recital focuses on Israel's experience leaving Egypt and its journey in the wilderness (vv. 13–53). Within this "wilderness frame,"[10] two central events are showcased: the provision of food in the wilderness (vv. 15–31) and the plagues in Egypt (vv. 43–51). If the purpose of the psalm is to build confident trust in YHWH, several significant questions arise. First, why does the psalmist invest so much of the recital on Israel's departure from Egypt and their time in the wilderness?[11] Second, why does the recital slow its pace to describe in detail the provision of food in the wilderness and the destruction of food supplies in Egypt by divinely initiated plagues? Third, as one considers the recital as a whole, why does food language appear as the dominant motif for narrating Israel's history?

This study argues that the psalmist's use of food language in the recital of Israel's past is a rhetorically driven means to instill confident trust in the possibility of YHWH's renewed intervention in the psalmist's present. Food language provides a rhetorically powerful medium to facilitate this goal through its ready availability, literary flexibility, and multidimensionality.

METHODOLOGY

This study considers Psalm 78's use of food language by employing literary and rhetorical analysis, as well as considering the psalm and its key

9. Westermann, "'Re-Presentation' of History in the Psalms," 238.

10. In this study, I will use the designation "wilderness frame" to refer to the frame created by the opening (v. 13) and closing (v. 53) of the Red/Reed Sea that bookend the wilderness events.

11. This section of the psalm, what I refer to as the "wilderness frame" (vv. 13–53), covers a period of a little over forty years and yet its description accounts for almost 70 percent (68.33 percent, forty-one verses) of the recital. In contrast, the depiction of Israel's life in the land makes up only slightly more than 30 percent of the recital (31.16 percent, nineteen verses) but covers a period that spans centuries.

food events within the larger context of the Hebrew Bible. By doing so, a clearer picture of the psalmist's rhetorical strategies emerges.

Literary and Rhetorical Analysis

While many past studies of Psalm 78 have used the terms "literary" and "rhetorical" almost interchangeably, in this study I will differentiate these approaches.[12] I will use the term "literary analysis" when I refer to the literary features of a text that contribute to the meaning or significance of a passage.[13] I will reserve the terms "rhetorical" or "rhetoric" for discussions of the passage's persuasive force. I find the description provided by the "Committee on the Advancement and Refinement of Rhetorical Criticism of the National Development Project in Rhetoric" particularly helpful in clarifying a rhetorical approach: "The critic becomes rhetorical to the extent that he studies his subject in terms of its suasory potential or persuasive effect. So identified, rhetorical criticism may be applied to any human act, process, product or artifact which, in the critic's view, may formulate, sustain or modify attention, perceptions, attitudes, or behavior."[14] This definition of a text's rhetorical function moves beyond Muilenburg's concern with primarily the stylistic and literary features of a text.[15] While literary features contribute to a text's rhetorical force, I use

12. This distinction has not always been made in the study of Psalm 78, especially in the early years of the resurgence of literary studies within the field of biblical studies (see ch. 2). In his 1979 essay "In Zion and David a New Beginning: An Interpretation of Psalm 78," Richard Clifford asserts that past scholars have failed to acknowledge "the rhetoric of the work, i.e., how the psalm works as a piece of liturgical poetry" (127). He equates rhetoric with the overall arrangement of the psalm, specifically its use of "repetition of key words and phrases, chiasm, paronomasia or word play, and especially in the parallel structure of the two historical recitals" (127). Of the scholars who explicitly employ some version of rhetorical analysis (as understood as persuasive intent) in their study of Psalm 78, I follow most closely the approach of Greenstein, "Mixing Memory and Design," 197–218.

13. In this study, the sections entitled "literary analysis" consider the specific literary features of a text. As will be seen in chapters 3, 4, and 5, Psalm 78 employs a variety of techniques to create literary cohesion across the composition—most notably literary scaffolding through the use of intra-textual links.

14. Bitzer and Black, *Prospect of Rhetoric*, 220. Noted in Fox, "Rhetoric of Ezekiel's Vision," 2.

15. Muilenburg uses the term "rhetorical" to describe his method, but his approach falls short of considering a text's persuasive intent. "What I am interested in, above all, is in understanding the nature of Hebrew literary composition, in exhibiting the structural patterns that are employed for the fashioning of a literary unit, whether in poetry

the term "rhetorical" only when I am considering the persuasive power of texts to influence an audience's attitudes, actions, or behaviors.[16]

The rhetorical intent of Psalm 78 becomes apparent in the opening lines of the composition (vv. 1–2). By introducing the composition as a "parable"/"enigmas," the psalmist cues the audience that the material that follows may depart in some way from what one might expect. It is a call to be attentive, not just to which events are included in the composition, but also to how these events are presented. For within the historical recital (vv. 13–72), one finds that Israel's past is recounted not as an orderly sequence of historical events but, as I will argue, a series of comparisons and contrasts. For these reasons, rhetorical analysis becomes a useful lens to consider the psalmist's compositional choices.

Defining "Food Language"

This study expands the discussion of food beyond actual food events to consider the broader category of "food language." In order to understand the rhetorical uses of food within biblical texts, one needs to consider a whole range of processes associated with food. In his study *Cooking, Cuisine, and Class: A Study in Comparative Sociology*, Jack Goody introduces a classification system that identifies five categories for talking about food—its production (including various processes and aspects of agriculture and husbandry), distribution (involving storage, transport, and exchange of foodstuffs), preparation (processing and cooking of food), consumption (serving, eating, and clearing away of food), and disposal

---

or in prose, and in discerning the many and various devices by which the predications are formulated and ordered into a unified whole. Such an enterprise I should describe as rhetoric and the methodology as rhetorical criticism." Muilenburg, "Form Criticism and Beyond," 8.

16. Within biblical studies, so-called rhetorical studies continue to display wide diversity in approach and method. Trible offers a helpful set of categories for distinguishing some of the major trends. Trible, *Rhetorical Criticism*, 55–62. Within psalms studies, reserving the term "rhetorical" for a consideration of the text's persuasive force has been championed by Foster and Howard. And yet they observe: "It seems to us that the landscape of Psalms research has yet to benefit fully from rhetorical analysis as a way of understanding the psalms and their effects." Foster and Howard, *My Words Are Lovely*, vii–viii. Their collection of essays offers a helpful corrective. See also Miller, "Prayer as Persuasion," 356–62; Bellinger, "Psalm 61," 379–88; Cook, "Prayers That Form Us," 451–67; Cook, *Rhetoric of Praise*. Adele Berlin's essay on Psalm 145 offers a concise and illuminating exercise in rhetorical analysis. Berlin, "Rhetoric of Psalm 145," 17–22.

(the disposal of the leftovers from the meal).[17] This five-fold classification system offers helpful categories for discussing food in its broadest sense.[18]

In everyday speech, the term "food" is often reserved for solid nourishment, distinguishing it from "drink" as liquid nourishment. However, the *Oxford English Dictionary* defines food as "any nutritious substance that people or animals eat or drink in order to maintain life and growth."[19] This definition broadens the category of food in two key ways. First, it expands the definition of food to include not only solid but also liquid nourishment; second, it includes water as a "food" source.

The discussion of food in this study will also move beyond food-focused events to include food-based language used within the biblical text. In addition, both literal and figurative descriptions of food will be considered within the term "food language." In summary, "food language" in this study refers to the full range of processes associated with both solid and liquid food used in either a literal or figurative sense.

CONTEXTS FOR ANALYSIS

In order to understand the rhetorical purpose of a text, it is essential to consider it within the context of other texts that depict similar material. In this study, I will consider the selection, depiction, and arrangement of material in the wilderness frame of Psalm 78 compared with other biblical texts that record the same events. Psalm 78's "wilderness frame" (vv. 13–53) includes two central food-based events: the provision of food in the wilderness and the dismantling of food supplies in the plagues in Egypt. Within the psalm, three distinct food elements are provided in the wilderness: "water from a rock," vv. 15–16; "manna," vv. 23–25; "meat," vv. 26–28. In Psalm 78's depiction of the Egyptian plagues (vv. 43–51), three food arenas are affected by the plagues: water (v. 44), agriculture (vv. 46–47; possibly v. 48), and livestock (v. 48; possibly vv. 49–50). Each

17. Goody, *Cooking, Cuisine, and Class*, 44–49.

18. Goody's categories have been used in a variety of food-related studies, including Shafer-Elliott, *Food in Ancient Judah*; Wilson, *For I Was Hungry and You Gave Me Food*. Stephen Reed's 1987 dissertation "Food in the Psalms" only considers the categories of food consumption and production.

19. *Oxford English Dictionary*, "Food," https://www.oed.com/dictionary/food_n?tl=true. Don R. and Patricia Brothwell expand on this definition: "Strictly speaking, food may be defined as all solid and fluid substances which permit the human organism to grow and maintain its health throughout life." Brothwell and Brothwell, *Food in Antiquity*, 13.

of the six food elements/arenas will be considered in light of other depictions in the Hebrew Bible in order to establish any common vocabulary and descriptions before investigating the unique literary features in Psalm 78's account of the event. In addition, this study also considers Psalm 78 in the context of the collections in the Psalter with which it is most closely identified. Psalm 78's rhetorical distinctives become apparent when considered with other "historical psalms" (Pss 105, 106, 135, 136). This collection of psalms relates to Psalm 78 through their *content*, namely, psalms with an extended historical recital. Psalm 78 will also be considered in light of the Asaph Collection (Pss 50, 73–83), a set of psalms that are related to Psalm 78 through occupying the same immediate literary *context* (Pss 73–83) and/or through the common designation לאסף (Pss 50, 73–83).

In this study, I work under the hypothesis that Psalm 78 is a postexilic composition.[20] And yet, I am fully aware of the differing opinions on this issue. I appreciate Brettler's candidness: "It is difficult to analyze the relationship between any psalm and related Torah traditions. The dates of various psalms are highly debated, as are the dates of composition of the Torah sources. Even in cases where it is clear that one text knows the other, there are often debates concerning which is the earlier text."[21] While some of my suggestions are based on the psalmist's proposed awareness of Pentateuchal material, I have attempted in this study to present the evidence in such a way that scholars who hold a differing view may still find this study helpful for their own work.

Israel's experience in the wilderness would have been all too poignant for a postexilic audience, as Israel asked: "Can God set a table in the wilderness?" (v. 19). I will argue that the psalmist's intention within this

20. No consensus view has emerged in the past 150 years on the dating of Psalm 78. While I recognize that this proposed date is impossible to prove beyond doubt, I believe that this view gains additional strength in light of the research that will be presented in this study. This includes (1) the psalmist's selection of material for the recital, (2) the psalm's shared similarities (and its concurrent placement) to other more widely agreed upon postexilic psalms (i.e., historical psalms and its nearest Asaph psalms), and (3) the psalm's food-based rhetorical strategies. I also stand in the company of a wide range of scholars who assign a postexilic date for the psalm. Gunkel, *Psalmen*, 342; Kraus, *Psalms 60–150*, 123–24; Hossfeld and Zenger, *Psalms 2*, 290–92; Witte, "From Exodus to David," 39; Wagner, "Recounting חידות מני־קדם in Psalm 78," 19; Gärtner, "Historical Psalms," 382; Ramond, "Growth of the Scriptural Corpus," 440. Scholars who date Psalm 78 as exilic include Berlin, "Psalms and the Literature of Exile," 65.

21. Brettler, "Poet as Historian," 21–22.

composition is to persuade the original audience that the answer remains the same—yes, God can and God will.

OVERVIEW OF CHAPTERS

In the chapters that follow, I will establish the uniqueness of this study of Psalm 78 (ch. 2), explore the rhetorical force of food language (ch. 3), analyze its specific use in Psalm 78 (chs. 4 and 5), compare Psalm 78's use of food language to two associated psalms collections—association through *content* in the historical psalms (Pss 105, 106, 135, 136) and association by *context* in the Asaph Collection (Pss 50, 73–83)—and argue for the specific function of food language in Psalm 78 (ch. 6). What follows below is a detailed summary of each chapter.

In order to situate this study of the literary and rhetorical function of food language in Psalm 78, chapter 2 surveys the historical trends in scholarship on Psalm 78 over a span of 150 years. This survey moves chronologically. This chapter is particularly helpful for those interested in trends and movements within the history of scholarship on Psalm 78, in particular, and the Psalms in general. Depending on their interests, readers may choose to move directly to chapter 3's discussion of food language and return to chapter 2 only if questions arise in later chapters about how this present study fits within a longer arc of scholarship on Psalm 78.

Chapter 3 explores the multidimensionality of food language and considers its rhetorical potential. This chapter introduces five central dimensions of food—its physical, sensory, social, locational, and patterned dimensions—and then illustrates these dimensions with examples from historical narratives and individual psalms. The chapter closes with a discussion of the rhetorical potential of food language, asking the question: "Why might the biblical authors be drawn to use the language of food?"

Chapter 4 addresses the psalmist's presentation of the divine provision of food in the wilderness ("water from a rock," vv. 15–16; "manna," vv. 23–25; "meat," vv. 26–28). Each food element is studied alongside other depictions in the Hebrew Bible in order to establish any common vocabulary or descriptions before investigating the unique literary features in Psalm 78's account of the event. Each of the three food elements is examined within its immediate literary context within the psalm and then within the literary frame around the food account as a whole (vv.

13–31). A particular focus of this chapter is to analyze the literary and rhetorical strategies at work in the retelling of these food events, identify the food dimensions present in the passage, and highlight the rhetorical use of these food events within the psalmist's argument.

Chapter 5 addresses Psalm 78's portrayal of the Egyptian plagues (vv. 43–51) by analyzing the three food arenas described in the account—water (v. 44), agriculture (vv. 46–47; possibly v. 48), and livestock (v. 48; possibly vv. 49–50). Each element is studied alongside other depictions in the Hebrew Bible (i.e., Exod 7–11; Ps 105:26–38) in order to establish any common vocabulary and descriptions before investigating the unique literary features in Psalm 78's account of the event. Following the analysis of the plagues that affect agriculture (vv. 46–47), the psalmist's description and positioning of the plagues of flies and frogs (v. 48) are examined as possible ways to link them to the agriculture-affecting plagues. Following the analysis of the plague that affects livestock (vv. 48), the psalmist's description of general destruction in vv. 49–50 is considered as a possible depiction of the plague of cattle pestilence. In light of the psalmist's specific presentation, I argue that the psalmist's selection and arrangement of the plagues is rhetorically motivated in order to show a systematic dismantling of food supplies in Egypt. The chapter then turns to explore the rhetorical use of various dimensions of food within the passage. The chapter concludes by considering the psalmist's presentation of the Egyptian plagues after the wilderness food events as a rhetorically motivated decision within the wilderness frame (vv. 13–53).

Chapter 6 expands the study of Psalm 78 by exploring the composition as a whole, as well as its place within two key collections—the "historical psalms" (Pss 105, 106, 135, 136) and Asaph psalms (Pss 50, 73–83). The chapter begins with a summary of Psalm 78's rhetorical uses of food language in the wilderness frame (vv. 13–53) and then extends the study into the land-based section of the psalm (vv. 54–72). Next, Psalm 78 is considered in the midst of and in light of the historical psalms (Pss 105, 106, 135, 136). The purpose of this investigation is to identify similarities and differences in the use of food language in other historical recitals within the Psalter. Finally, Psalm 78 is considered in the midst of and in light of the psalms in the Asaph Collection that also employ food language (Pss 50, 74, 75, 79, 80, 81). The purpose of this investigation is to identify similarities and differences in the use of food language within the Asaph Collection.

In the chapters that follow, I will argue that the psalmist employs food language in Psalm 78's remembrance of divine provisions in the past in order to instill confident trust (v. 7) in the possibility of YHWH's renewed intervention in the present. As will be shown in a variety of ways, food language becomes a rhetorically powerful medium to facilitate this goal.

2

Historical Trends in the Study of Psalm 78

INTRODUCTION

Defying easy categorization, Psalm 78 remains an ongoing enigma to biblical scholars. In this survey of a century and a half of literature on Psalm 78 (1870s to 2020s), one finds little to no scholarly consensus on the key aspects of the psalm (i.e., genre, *Sitz im Leben*, date, structure, and purpose). In detailing the historical trends in the study and interpretation of Psalm 78, this chapter situates the unique approach and emphases of the present study, namely, a literary and rhetorical analysis that considers the centrality of the wilderness frame (vv. 13–53) within the recital as a whole, as well as the psalmist's use of food language throughout the composition.[1]

TRACING THE HISTORICAL TRENDS IN THE STUDY OF PSALM 78 (1870S TO EARLY 2020S)

Scholarly interest in Psalm 78 has been sporadic at best, moving forward in fits and starts. This survey will document some of the major trends in engagement and interpretation of Psalm 78, beginning with the turn of the

1. Depending on their interests, readers may choose to move directly to chapter 3's discussion of Food Language and return to chapter 2 only if questions arise in later chapters about how this present study fits within the broader scholarship on Psalm 78.

twentieth century and continuing to the early 2020s. This survey not only offers context for the study of Psalm 78 but also highlights the major movements in biblical studies in general and the study of the Psalms in particular.

Commentaries with a Concern for Psalm 78's Literary Features (1870s to 1900)

Of the hundreds of commentaries written on the Psalms in the nineteenth century, two key commentators remain a steady part of the scholarly conversation, namely, Delitzsch[2] and Kirkpatrick.[3] Both commentators, writing at the close of the century, show sustained attention to Psalm 78's literary features. While consistent in their general approach to the psalm, these two scholars disagree on many of the central features of the text.

Delitzsch praises the psalm's literary richness. He muses: "As regards its style, the Psalm is lengthened out after the manner of an epic; at the same time, however, it is concise after the manner of the apophthegm. The individual historical statements have a gnome-like finish, and a gem-like elegance."[4] He proposes an "old Asaphic origin" for the psalm.[5] And while he notes the psalm's dependence "in matter and language" on the books of the Pentateuch (i.e., Exodus, Numbers, Deuteronomy), Delitzsch simply acknowledges that a decisive date for the psalm would be of great importance for the question of the Pentateuch.[6]

Kirkpatrick also notes the literary richness and intentional shaping of the psalm. He offers a thorough list of intra-textual links within the psalm and identifies possible textual connections to other biblical texts. Noting the didactic tone in the psalm, Kirkpatrick argues that its intention is "evidently positive, to draw warnings for the present and the future from the consideration of the past."[7] After surveying evidence for a vari-

2. Delitzsch, *Commentar über den Psalter* (ET, *Biblical Commentary on the Psalms*). Technically, Delitzsch's commentary falls slightly outside the date range being considered; however, his work is a significant contribution to the study of Psalm 78.

3. Kirkpatrick, *Psalms 42–89*.

4. Delitzsch, *Biblical Commentary on the Psalms*, 414.

5. Delitzsch, *Biblical Commentary on the Psalms*, 413–14.

6. Delitzsch, *Biblical Commentary on the Psalms*, 414.

7. Kirkpatrick, *Psalms 42–89*, 463. While he assumes that the psalmist's decision to conclude the psalm with the choice of Zion/David was purposeful, he also contends that the rebuke of Ephraim in v. 67 "is not the main purpose of the Psalm." The question of the role of the divine "rejection" of Israel/Ephraim in vv. 59 and 67 will drive much of future scholarship. Kirkpatrick's view will become a minority opinion.

ety of possible dates for composition, Kirkpatrick postulates a time near the fall of the Northern Kingdom.[8]

Even within this small sample of commentators, one finds the presence of both continuity and discontinuity of opinions about the basic features of Psalm 78. Both commentators emphasize the literary richness of the psalm and the presence of possible intertextual connections with other biblical texts. Both commentators—as fitting this genre of writing—present an even-handed concern with all events portrayed in the psalm, whether the events in Egypt, the wilderness, or the land. Yet even with a similar approach to the text, the commentators show disagreement on the date and purpose of the psalm. In fact, this diversity of opinion regarding date and purpose will continue into the present time.

The Unresolved Question of the Genre of Psalm 78 (1920s)

The rise of form criticism in the early twentieth century paved the way for the systematic classification and study of individual psalms within genre collections. Gunkel's focus on form and social setting moved the conversation away from the unique elements of individual psalms to a concern for common features across the Psalter. This move away from literary and rhetorical concerns to form-critical concerns will be seen for the next fifty years of research on Psalm 78.

For Gunkel, Psalm 78 poses a problem for genre classification. Instead of fitting neatly into one of his major genres (*Gattungen*) or minor groupings, Psalm 78 defies Gunkel's system of classification.[9] In his later work, Gunkel groups Psalms 78, 105, and 106 together in the category of Legends (*Legenden*), based on a use of existing historical texts within these psalms.[10] In light of Psalm 78's mixed genre and the assumed presence of textual borrowing, Gunkel dates Psalm 78 as a late postexilic composition.[11] Gunkel's classification conundrum regarding Psalm 78 can be seen even in current discussions of the psalm.

8. Kirkpatrick, *Psalms 42–89*, 463.

9. Gunkel, *Psalmen*, 342. In his later work, Gunkel continues to reference the psalm in discussions of hymns, royal psalms, wisdom psalms, and "the legend." Gunkel and Begrich, *Introduction to the Psalms*, 43, 56, 60, 100, 103, 120, 111, 247–49, 298–300.

10. Gunkel and Begrich, *Introduction to the Psalms*, 248.

11. Gunkel, *Psalmen*, 341–42. As will be noted later in the discussion of Mowinckel's proposal, this breakdown of established forms is assumed to be a late feature of psalmography when psalms no longer arose out of a cult setting.

Considerations of Possible Deuteronomic and Pentateuchal Influence in Psalm 78 (1950s)

Gunkel's assumptions about textual borrowing and a late date for Psalm 78 were challenged in the 1950s as scholars considered explanations for shared language that didn't depend on literary dependence. Psalm 78's didactic tone and its heavy use of historical traditions moved scholars to reconsider the psalms in the context of tradition circles with shared language. Two studies from the 1950s are noteworthy.

In the article "Die Entstehungszeit des Ps. 78 und des Deuteronomiums," Junker places Psalm 78 within the Deuteronomic circle associated with Hezekiah's reform. He observes that the psalm reflects a strong Deuteronomic influence.[12] Junker finds in v. 9 a reference to the defeat of the Northern Kingdom by the Assyrians, an event that he assumes would have been fresh on the mind of the psalmist who penned the composition.[13] When viewed in this eighth-century context, the psalm would have functioned as a means to urge the people of Judah to learn from the example of Ephraim and avoid repeating the sins of their fathers.[14]

Eissfeldt considers Psalm 78 together with Deuteronomy 32 because of their common features in form and content.[15] While he assigns a date between 1200 BCE–1020 BCE for Deuteronomy 32, Eissfeldt assumes a slightly later date for Psalm 78, a time prior to the North-South split of 930 BCE.[16] His proposal for Ps 78 is based primarily on the fact that the historical content of the psalm extends into the reign of David (and possibly into Solomon's reign; cf. v. 69's reference to the temple).[17] Eissfeldt assumes the Philistine presence in the eleventh century (1070–1020 BCE) as the background for reading the later events of the psalm[18] and insists that it cannot be demonstrated that the psalmist depended on the Pentateuch or any of its assumed sources.[19] Eissfeldt views the purpose of

12. Junker, "Entstehungszeit des Ps. 78 und des Deuteronomiums," 487.

13. Junker, "Entstehungszeit des Ps. 78 und des Deuteronomiums," 492.

14. Junker, "Entstehungszeit des Ps. 78 und des Deuteronomiums," 491.

15. Eissfeldt, *Lied Moses*.

16. Eissfeldt, *Lied Moses*, 37.

17. Particularly important to his proposed date is the fact that the psalm lacks any mention of the divided kingdom.

18. Eissfeldt, *Lied Moses*, 42.

19. Eissfeldt, *Lied Moses*, 34.

the psalm as an attempt to legitimate Jerusalem's claim to be the inheritor of the ark, which had traditionally resided at Shiloh.[20]

Thus while Junker finds a heavy deuteronomistic influence in the psalm, Eissfeldt finds none at all. While Eissfeldt assigns a date during the United Monarchy, Junker positions the psalm three centuries later during the reforms of Hezekiah. As will be seen in this survey, contradicting viewpoints on the date and purpose of the psalm will continue to mark the history of scholarship on Psalm 78.

Contested *Sitz im Leben* of Psalm 78 (1950 to 1960s)

The question of the *Sitz im Leben* of Psalm 78 gained particular attention in the 1950s and 1960s. During this time, proposals for both a cultic and non-cultic origin for the psalm were advanced.

Mowinckel considers Psalm 78 to be an example of non-cultic, late Israelite psalmography.[21] He identifies ten psalms as examples of psalmography associated with the circles of the "wise men" and "wisdom schools" of Israel.[22] He notes that two chief characteristics mark these psalms. First, they lack a consistent style or form: "As the poets would no longer compose poetry for a definite cultic occasion, the preservation of the modes of composition was no longer supported by their 'place in life,' as it used to be, and the different modes and motives were mixed up."[23] Second, these psalms tend to have a didactic tone: "This poetry is more or less influenced by the style and contents of the poetry of wisdom."[24] Mowinckel also observes that, in the case of Psalm 78, the psalm turns to questions of theodicy as it testifies "to the faithfulness of Yahweh and the breaking of the covenant by the people, proving the justice of punishment and disaster."[25] All these features of the psalm make Mowinckel conclude the psalm has a non-cultic origin.

Weiser imagines Psalm 78's reflection on history as being uttered by a priest as part of a cultic liturgy, possibly a Covenant Renewal

20. Eissfeldt, *Lied Moses*, 42.

21. In his list of non-cultic psalms, Mowinckel includes Psalms 1, 34, 37, 49, 78, 105, 106, 111, 112, and 127. Mowinckel, "Psalms and Wisdom," 213.

22. Mowinckel, "Psalms and Wisdom," 206.

23. Mowinckel, "Psalms and Wisdom," 206.

24. Mowinckel, "Psalms and Wisdom," 213.

25. Mowinckel, "Psalms and Wisdom," 214.

Festival.[26] From Weiser's perspective, this psalm would have directly followed a recital of the *Heilsgeschichte*.[27] He notes: "History is here reflected upon in a way which takes for granted that an account of this history has already been given to the cult community."[28] Weiser finds a possible correspondence in the liturgy used in the feast of the Renewal of the Covenant found in the "Manual of Discipline" (1QS i:16–ii:1).[29] He assumes a date for the psalm broadly between the fall of the Northern and Southern Kingdoms.[30]

In light of its extended didactic introduction that precedes the historical recital, Psalm 78 has presented a challenge to those who have sought to establish its specific *Sitz im Leben*. While scholars often agree on the didactic nature of the psalm, the question of the psalmist's identity—a priest, sage, Levite—remains a contested issue. Without a clear sense of *Sitz im Leben*, questions about the date and purpose of Psalm 78 continue to be debated.

An Investigation of Tradition History in Psalm 78 (1960s)

Within his larger study of the wilderness murmuring tradition, George Coats considers Psalm 78 through the lens of tradition history.[31] Coats posits that Psalm 78 displays a variety of traditions at work in its individual sections.[32] In light of this diversity, Coats concludes that the present

26. Weiser assumes that the psalm is "most easily understood if we think of it as being uttered by a priest (v. 1: *torah*) in connection with the tradition of the Covenant Festival." Weiser, *Psalms*, 539.

27. Anderson also associates the psalm with the covenant festival, though he suggests Ps 78 may be the song that recites the *Heilsgeschichte* rather than the song that follows the recital. Anderson, *Book of Psalms*, 561.

28. Weiser, *Psalms*, 538.

29. In this ceremony, YHWH's saving deeds are recounted by the priests and followed by an account of the "sins of Israel" by the Levites. The ceremony concludes with the congregation confessing their own sins and the sins of their forefathers and seeking God's mercy.

30. Weiser, *Psalms*, 540.

31. Coats, *Rebellion in the Wilderness*.

32. He notes: "Vss. 9–16 and 44–66 have roots in the positive tradition of Yahweh's aid to Israel in the wilderness and the negative element of Israel's idolatry in the land. . . . The unit in vss. 17–41 has its roots in the murmuring tradition as it is known in the Pentateuch, but reflects a peculiar interpretation of this tradition which can be attributed to the Deuteronomist. . . . The final unit, vss. 67–72, corresponds with the murmuring tradition as it appears in the Pentateuch and must be considered a part of that tradition, untouched by the Deuteronomist." Coats, *Rebellion in the Wilderness*, 223–24.

psalm points to a post-Deuteronomistic date, although he admits that a precise date cannot be determined with certainty.[33] Coats's particular interest in the wilderness murmuring tradition leads him to spend extended time on the wilderness events of Psalm 78. This scholarly interest in Psalm 78's wilderness material will be short-lived. As will be seen in the discussions that follow, the concluding section of the psalm (vv. 54–72) quickly becomes the central focus of scholarly study, with little attention shown to the material in the wilderness frame (vv. 13–53) in the coming years.

Positing a Political/Polemical Intent to Psalm 78 (1960 to 1970s)

The political intent of Psalm 78 is the central focus of two studies in the late sixties and early seventies. In his article "Psalm 77/78: ein 'politisch Lied,'" Hofbauer considers Psalm 78 as a "political song," a teaching composition made up of riddles. For Hofbauer, the riddle is found in vv. 67–72 with the replacement of Ephraim/Shiloh with Judah/Zion and the appointment of David to lead his people.[34] He argues that the psalmist presents the rejection of Ephraim/Shiloh as the logical result of a series of Israel's misdeeds (vv. 9–64). For Hofbauer, the psalmist's references to the sins of "Ephraim" (vv. 9–11) refer specifically to the northern tribes, a connection he finds within the psalm itself, as well as in prophetic writings.[35] Hofbauer posits a date for the psalm during the time of Solomon's reign.[36]

Robert Carroll's 1971 article "Psalm LXXVIII: Vestiges of a Tribal Polemic" draws upon his earlier work on election traditions in the

33. Coats, *Rebellion in the Wilderness*, 224. Regarding this post-Deuteronomic date, Coats observes: "But this conclusion does not resolve the problem, since the psalm draws on traditions that have a much longer history than this. It seems more adequate to suggest, then, that the psalm will not support one sweeping conclusion concerning its date of origin and dependency on pentateuchal sources. The present form may be late and reflect the whole of the Pentateuch. But we must allow the possibility that different traditions of different dates and different degrees of contact with the pentateuchal sources may compose this final form. Whether this is in fact the case must be determined by an examination of those traditions" (203).

34. Hofbauer, "Psalm 77/78," 41.

35. Hofbauer, "Psalm 77/78," 41.

36. Hofbauer, "Psalm 77/78," 42–43.

Prophets.[37] Like Hofbauer, Carroll's interest lies in Psalm 78's conclusion with its sudden shift in focus from Ephraim to Judah (v. 67). He is also struck by the psalmist's use of the lexeme בחר. He notes: "The term בחר is part of the election terminology of the Old Testament. . . . Its occurrence in a negative form in verse 67 suggests a polemical intent, especially as it is prefixed to an enumeration of the specific election tradition of the Judean kingdom."[38] Carroll argues that the exodus election tradition had a special meaning for the clans of the Ephraimite: "The divine election associated with the exodus was their charter for existence in the land and legitimated their claim to be the people of Yahweh."[39] On the other hand, Judah's claim for its existence was based "on the election of David to be his king and Zion to be his city."[40] He finds a polemical purpose for the psalm, assuming that "part of the function of Ps. lxxviii was to provide the election tradition of David and Zion with an Israelite pedigree."[41] Carroll is quick to note that the events described in vv. 59–66 could in fact reflect any of a variety of possible scenarios in Israel's history; he concludes that "a precise date for the psalm must be left open."[42]

Focusing primarily on the conclusion of the psalm (vv. 67–72), Hofbauer and Carroll emphasize the possible political intent of Psalm 78. Both proposals largely ignore the wilderness material (vv. 13–53), although this composes the majority of the psalmist's recital. This omission will be addressed in the decades to come.

Regarding Psalm 78 as a Historical Recital (1970 to 1980s)

In the seventies into the early eighties, several studies considered the role and function of the Psalter's historical recitals. In a chapter entitled "The 'Re-Presentation' of History in the Psalms," Claus Westermann argues for the vital role that "re-presenting"[43] history plays in the continuation of a

37. Carroll, "Significance of the Election Traditions."

38. Carroll, "Psalm LXXVIII," 136.

39. Carroll, "Psalm LXXVIII," 143–44.

40. Carroll, "Psalm LXXVIII," 144.

41. Carroll, "Psalm LXXVIII," 147.

42. Carroll, "Psalm LXXVIII," 146–47.

43. The translator notes that the German terms used here are difficult to capture in English. "The German terms, *Vergegenwärtigung* and *vergegenwärtigen*, are used by the author as technical terms and are translated here as 're-presentation' and 'to re-present,' following common practice. The German words carry both the notion of 'presenting

community in crisis. He contends: "The phenomenon of looking back at God's earlier acts of deliverance occurred because the sense of continuity experienced by Israel threatened to collapse under duress."[44] Regarding Psalm 78, he observes: "Praise for the acts of God in history occurred because the experience of God's acts evoked the kind of praise that had to continue and had to be passed on (Ps. 78). To cease praising God would be to forget his deeds, and forgetting would, of necessity, lead to the end of God's relationship with the people."[45] For Westermann, historical recital provided the lifeline that guaranteed a people's survival into the future.

In his dissertation entitled "The Context and Function of Historical Recitation in Ancient Israel: A Study of the Historical Psalms, 78, 105, and 106," Archie Lee explores the historical situations that would have called forth three of the Psalter's historical recitals. He asserts: "The psalmist did not compose the historical summaries to satisfy some individual or national nostalgic sentiment but incorporated into the historical survey a lesson and an admonition. He was governed in his liberty to select relevant historical traditions by the current theological streams and the people's immediate experience."[46] Lee considers Psalm 78 a work that reflects "the fall of the Northern Kingdom, the miraculous deliverance of Jerusalem and the contemporary theological tendencies of Hezekiah's reform."[47] His argument draws largely on how the psalmist presents the account of the Egyptian plagues with language reminiscent of Judah's experience of the Assyrian invasion.[48] For Lee, Psalm 78 functions as a pedagogical lesson, similar in tone and message to the theology of history found in the Prophets and Deuteronomy.

---

to the mind' and of 'actualizing or making relevant to the present,' for which no single English word is a happy translation." Westermann, "'Re-Presentation' of History in the Psalms," 214.

44. Westermann, "'Re-Presentation' of History in the Psalms," 246.

45. Westermann, "'Re-Presentation' of History in the Psalms," 246.

46. Lee, "Context and Function of Historical Recitation," 3.

47. Lee, "Context and Function of Historical Recitation," iii.

48. Lee, "Context and Function of Historical Recitation," 112–18. Lee summarized his argument regarding Psalm 78's plague account in his article "Context and Function of the Plagues Tradition," 83–89. Here he proposes that Ps 78:49–50 resembles the woe oracle against Assyria found in Isa 10:5–7 in both theme and verbal correspondences. He argues that this link provides an interpretive clue for determining the function of the plague tradition within the psalm. He finds that "the miraculous escape of Jerusalem from destruction by the Assyrian army (701 BCE) certainly strengthens the 'signs and wonders' of Yahweh and the belief in the inviolability of Zion and the Davidic house (Ps. 78.68–72)" (85).

In his book *Historical Motifs in the Psalms*, Erik Haglund considers the function of various historical traditions in the Psalms. Regarding Psalm 78's use of these traditions, Haglund notes: "In this psalm the history from the Egyptian plagues to the establishment of the kingdom is presented as a series of events where the people have been disbelieving and apostate and God punishing and gracious. All this is told as an explanation to the fall of the Northern Kingdom (cf. v. 9ff. 60–64, 67)."[49] The psalm, he argues, is marked by a "free manner of handling the traditions" and assumes that the psalm must have been written during a time when the source material "had not yet received the form known to us."[50] From this evidence, he concludes: "Thus we must consider a time of origin quite soon after the fall of the Northern Kingdom, such as the reign of Hezekiah."[51] Haglund finds no cultic function for Psalm 78, but instead sees it emerging from a learned tradition and classifies it as a "Psalm of Instruction."[52]

With this move to consider Psalm 78 as a "historical recital," Psalms scholarship begins to take a turn toward more holistic considerations of texts and their rhetorical potential.

Reconsidering Psalm 78's Literary Features (1970 to 1980s)

The 1970s and 1980s witnessed a renewed interest in the poetic features of biblical texts and how these features contribute to the meaning and purpose of a composition.[53] This move to consider the composition as a holistic unit undergirds two key essays on Psalm 78.

In a *CBQ* article entitled "Psalm 78: A Contribution to the Theology of Tenth Century Israel," Antony Campbell reasserts his view that Psalm 78 is a theologically driven tenth-century composition that documents a "new order" associated with Jerusalem in Judah over against Shiloh in

49. Haglund, *Historical Motifs in the Psalms*, 99.

50. Haglund, *Historical Motifs in the Psalms*, 100.

51. Haglund, *Historical Motifs in the Psalms*, 100–101.

52. Haglund, *Historical Motifs in the Psalms*, 88.

53. This interest is often attributed to the impact of James Muilenburg's famous work, "Form Criticism and Beyond."

Ephraim.[54] Campbell's approach rests in what he perceives as the psalm's "unity of structure and substantial integrity of composition."[55]

Campbell maintains that Psalm 78 unfolds as two recitals, a recital of rejection—Israel's rejection of YHWH (vv. 9–58),[56] followed by YHWH's rejection of Israel (vv. 59–64)—and a recital of election, namely, YHWH's election of Jerusalem/David (vv. 65–72). Campbell spends significant time developing this argument through an analysis of what he refers to as the psalm's "literary architecture."[57] In particular, he highlights the psalmist's use of balancing,[58] correspondences,[59] and "nesting" of events.[60] Campbell concludes that "the concern of the psalm is a tenth century concern: how to understand and interpret theologically the events from Shiloh to Jerusalem."[61] Campbell's argument for an early

54. Campbell, "Psalm 78," 61. This is a position first advanced in his 1975 work, *Ark Narrative*. Campbell's study of the Ark Narratives (1 Sam 4–6; 2 Sam 6) considers Psalm 78 as possible adaptation of the Ark tradition. He argues that the psalm reference in v. 59b ("and he utterly rejected Israel") is the same message expressed in narrative form by 1 Sam 4 and 5:2–4(5). He concludes that Psalm 78 offers a similar perspective to the Ark Narratives which view the events as a theological narrative of rejection and election, although he notes: "Ps 78 supplies what is totally lacking in the Ark Narrative, a reason and a justification for this rejection" (223).

55. Campbell spends over two-thirds of his article (pp. 51–75) substantiating this claim. Campbell, "Psalm 78," 51.

56. Campbell is one of few scholars who includes vv. 9–11 as part of the psalmist's recital of history.

57. Campbell, "Psalm 78," 59. Campbell provides a visual representation of the argument of the psalm on pp. 59–60.

58. For example, Campbell observes how the psalmist in vv. 12–20 balances depiction of YHWH's gracious provision and Israel's deceitful rebellion: "In harsh juxtaposition, the wonder of abundant water is acknowledged, to be followed not by gratitude but greed, not thanks but testing: 'Can he also give bread, or provide meat for his people?' (v 20b). Five lines of graceful wonder are balanced by five lines of ungrateful sin." Campbell, "Psalm 78," 55.

59. Unique to Campbell's work is his opinion that v. 9 plays a significant role in the psalm as a whole. Observing the lexical choices for the description of the sons of Ephraim in v. 9 and the reoccurrence of the same vocabulary in v. 57, Campbell proposes: "The reference to v 9 at this point is most apt; the recital has come full circle, the culminating point of rejection has been reached." Campbell, "Psalm 78," 57.

60. Campbell sees the episodes of rejection as "nested" recitals: "The recital of history is structured on a balancing and nesting of its parts. The recital of rejection is balanced by the recital of election. Nested within the recital of rejection, the rejection of Yahweh by Israel is balanced by the rejection of Israel by Yahweh; nested within the recital of Yahweh's rejection by Israel are the first and second recitations with their balancing emphases." Campbell, "Psalm 78," 60.

61. Campbell, "Psalm 78," 76. Campbell concludes his study by acknowledging that a psalm like Psalm 78 "could be especially valued" under the reforms of Hezekiah and Josiah (79).

date is based primarily on refuting traditional evidence put forward for the psalm's dependence on Pentateuchal traditions and possible Deuteronomic influence.[62] For Campbell, Psalm 78 is "a poetic presentation of a theological interpretation of history."[63]

In his article "In Zion and David a New Beginning: An Interpretation of Psalm 78," Richard Clifford asserts that past scholars have failed to acknowledge "the rhetoric of the work, i.e., how the psalm works as a piece of liturgical poetry."[64] He argues that insufficient attention has been given to the overall arrangement of the psalm, specifically its use of "repetition of key words and phrases, chiasm, paronomasia or word play, and especially in the parallel structure of the two historical recitals."[65] Clifford divides the psalm into an introduction (vv. 1–11) and two recitals of history (vv. 12–39; 40–72).[66] He identifies two parallel structures in the sequence

62. Against these so-called misconceptions, Campbell contends, "It is not a late psalm. It is not a specialized offshoot of the murmuring tradition. It is not a product of dtr circles, nor does it depend on the present pentateuchal text. It is not a liturgical expansion of the so-called historical credo. It is not without unity, both of structure and purpose." Campbell, "Psalm 78," 75.

63. Campbell, "Psalm 78," 77.

64. Clifford, "In Zion and David a New Beginning," 127.

65. Clifford, "In Zion and David a New Beginning," 127.

66. Clifford argues for the break in the first recital at v. 39. He notes that v. 40 "evidently begins the second recital of history because it repeats the site of the wilderness events, 'in the wilderness' and 'in the wasteland.'" Clifford, "In Zion and David a New Beginning," 128. Clifford later seems to change his mind regarding where these two recitals actually divide. In his 2003 commentary on the Psalms, he seems to adapt his position, now noting: "'In the wilderness,' 'in the desert' (v. 40) summarizes and concludes the first recital." Clifford, *Psalms 73–150*, 47. Clifford's failure to account for the language of Israel's rebellion (vv. 40–42) within his dual recital is a weakness of his proposal. McCann offers a helpful addendum to Clifford's proposal. He suggests viewing vv. 9–11 as the opening of the first recital. Seen this way, each recital would then begin (vv. 9–11 // vv. 40–42) "by noting the people's unfaithfulness before describing God's gracious activity." McCann, "Book of Psalms," 991. Clifford's structure—even with its weaknesses—remains the dominant proposal for Psalm 78. See Tate, *Psalms 51–100*, 287–88; Mays, *Psalms*, 255; Brueggemann and Bellinger, *Psalms*, 340; DeClaissé-Walford et al., *Book of Psalms*, 617.

of "miracle, sin, divine anger, and punishment" (vv. 12–32 // 40–64)[67] followed by divine response (vv. 33–39 // 65–72) in the two accounts.[68]

Clifford argues for a date during the time of the divided monarchy, most likely during the reign of Hezekiah or Josiah: "The Deuteronomic language and the concern of the psalm to unite all Israel under the Davidic monarchy in a single place of worship suggests a time during the Hezekian reform of the late eighth century (cf. 2 Chr 30:1–12) or the Josianic reform of the late seventh century."[69] He contends that in the end of the psalm, two major defeats in the Northern Kingdom converge: the destruction of Shiloh and the destruction of Samaria.[70]

Clifford's general argument mirrors Campbell's proposal in several respects. Both view the psalm as a presentation of two historical recitals, although they differ in their proposed structures. Both approach Psalm 78 as a largely unified literary composition. In addition, Clifford follows Campbell in identifying "the tent of Joseph, tribe of Ephraim" (v. 67) as the tribal territory and not the tribe itself.[71] However, their proposals also

67. Within this paradigm, Clifford categorizes the divine provision of manna and quail (vv. 21–32) as an example of "divine anger and punishment" in the first recital, while the Egyptian plagues (vv. 44–55) are categorized as a "miracle" or a gracious act of YHWH in the second recital. As will be argued in chapter 5, the psalmist's depiction of these related events shows striking similarities and are best viewed together, not as separate unrelated events. In addition, if in fact vv. 40–41 begin the second recital, God's gracious acts begin with the decidedly negative note of Israel's rebellious heart.

68. Campbell perceives the arrangement of the two recitals as a scheme of "provision-sin // sin-provision," an alternative that offers a better reading of vv. 40–41. Unlike Clifford, Campbell clearly articulates his reasons for the section breaks: "The first recitation is introduced by five verses concerned with these glorious deeds (vv 12–16). Then the major emphasis is on the rebellious behavior of Israel—so out of harmony with the gracious deliverance she had experienced. One function of the second recitation may be to emphasize this disharmony. This time it is the rebellious behavior that is relegated to the introductory verses (vv 40–43). The gracious deliverance from Egypt to the promised land is then depicted. And this is the second function of this recitation: to bring the story into the promised land where the rebellion continues." Campbell, "Psalm 78," 57.

69. Clifford, "In Zion and David a New Beginning," 138.

70. Clifford argues: "The liturgy combines into one divine action the rejection of Shiloh and later northern shrines." Clifford, "In Zion and David a New Beginning," 138.

71. Clifford notes: "In vv 21, 31, 33, 55, 59, 72, Jacob/Israel designates the whole people, not only the northern tribes. The poem's view that all Israel has sinned is important. To anticipate somewhat, the destruction of Shiloh, the national shrine before its destruction in the mid-eleventh century, is a punishment dealt to all Israel. The tribe of Ephraim/Joseph is no longer the site of the shrine. Judah is the new location. The northern tribes per se are not rejected." Clifford, "In Zion and David a New Beginning," 132.

radically differ in regard to proposed date, use of Pentateuchal sources, and Deuteronomic influence. While both Campbell and Clifford emphasize the general literary features of the psalm and posit a theological motivation behind its structure, they fail to explain the inclusion of specific events in the recital and never address the rhetorical purpose of the psalmist's depiction of these events.

Insights on Psalm 78 from Structural Analysis (1980 to 1990s)

In the midst of a growing interest in the literary nature of biblical texts, "structural analysis" arose as a method that seeks to "deal synchronically with the surface structure" of texts and study individual psalms as "coherent wholes."[72] This method is known for its consideration of the text from multiple levels, from small-scale features (e.g., the colon) to large structural features of a text (e.g., chiasm and inclusio). Three studies in the 1980s–90s examined Psalm 78 using this approach.

Korpel and de Moor use Psalm 78 as a concluding example in their discussion of principles related to the structure of early Northwest Semitic poetry, as well as the benefits of these principles for the exegesis of ancient poems.[73] They observe: "We modern readers are conditioned to read a text in a strictly linear way, from beginning to end. However, the skillful exploitation of the repetitive effect of external parallelism tends to lend a more or less concentric structure to the larger building-blocks of ancient North-West Semitic poetry."[74] Korpel and de Moor challenge the notion of finding key information at the conclusion of a literary composition, a trend that had come to dominate the study of Psalm 78 during the past several decades. They note: "We for our part are accustomed to look at the end of a composition for the general conclusions, a pithy recapitulation of the main points or the outcome of the captivating story. In the kind of poetry we try to describe here, however, we often find the

72. Howard, "Recent Trends in Psalms Study," 353–54. While lauding structural analysis's focus on textual coherence, Howard criticizes the method's failure to appreciate the work as poetry. "Many of these structural studies end up as catalogues of large-scale literary devices, of chiasms, inclusions, and the like, often spanning many verses. The structures of psalms are laid bare (although often no unanimity on a given psalm's structure is reached), with very elaborate diagrams, but too often little is said of a psalm's art or its meaning" (354).

73. Korpel and de Moor, "Fundamentals of Ugaritic and Hebrew Poetry," 1–61.

74. Korpel and de Moor, "Fundamentals of Ugaritic and Hebrew Poetry," 54.

heart of the matter right in the middle where it belongs as the kernel out of which everything grew in accordance with the laws of parallelistic expansion."[75] Regarding the structure of Psalm 78, they argue that vv. 32–39—a statement of "the enduring faithfulness and mercy of God"—sit at the heart of the psalm, framed by vv. 1–16 // 17–31 and vv. 40–55 // 56–72 which describe "the ever reoccurring unfaithfulness of Israel."[76] They argue that in order to highlight the importance of this theological declaration (vv. 32–39), the poet "deliberately re-arranged historical traditions that had long been fixed by the time he was writing for the sole purpose of a well-balanced concentric structure."[77] While Korpel and de Moor offer new categories to consider Psalm 78's structure and general purpose, they offer no proposal for the psalm's date or *Sitz im Leben*.

In his article "Psalm LXXXVIII [*sic*]: Der Rätsel Lösung?" Füglister follows Korpel and de Moor's concentric model of Psalm 78, but sees it organized in seven concentric strophes with vv. 32–39 also serving as the center-point.[78] Unlike Korpel and de Moor's purely linguistic study, Füglister considers the purpose and date of the psalm. He views Psalm 78 as a "history psalm" (similar to Pss 105, 106, 136) that depicts the negative events of Israel's history in order to highlight Davidic kingship as God's ultimate goal.[79] Since the psalm neither mentions nor presumes the exile, Füglister proposes a preexilic date for the psalm.[80]

In *Les psaumes redécouverts*, Marc Girard argues for the cohesive unity of Psalm 78 at both syntactic and structural levels.[81] Like Clifford and Campbell, he views the psalm as two historical recitals. Unlike the previous proposals for the psalm's structure, Girard divides the composition by Israel's locations: Egypt and the wilderness (vv. 12–53) and the promised land (vv. 54–72). He argues that both divisions employ a concentric structure, with slight variations. In the first recital, Girard finds

75. Korpel and de Moor, "Fundamentals of Ugaritic and Hebrew Poetry," 54.

76. Korpel and de Moor, "Fundamentals of Ugaritic and Hebrew Poetry," 57.

77. Korpel and de Moor, "Fundamentals of Ugaritic and Hebrew Poetry," 54–55. Koopmans offers an addendum to Korpel and de Moor's division of the "plague account" (their Canto D) that strengthens their general argument for chiastic patterning. Koopmans, "Psalm 78," 121–23.

78. Füglister, "Psalm LXXXVIII [*sic*]," 275. Füglister considers v. 9 as the exception to the psalm's literary coherence. He assumes that it is a gloss (270).

79. Füglister, "Psalm LXXXVIII [*sic*]," 267.

80. Füglister, "Psalm LXXXVIII [*sic*]," 270.

81. Girard, *Psaumes redécouverts*, 335.

a clear concentric structure, employing an ABCD // $D^1C^1B^1A^1$ formula where the relationships are based on reoccurring terms:

A two miracles of water (vv. 12–16)
B contention among the people (vv. 17–20)
C divine retaliation (vv. 21–22)
D a food miracle (vv. 23–25)
D^1 a food miracle (vv. 26–29)
C^1 divine retaliation (vv. 30–39)
B^1 contention among the people (vv. 40–42)
A^1 two miracles of water (vv. 43–53)[82]

Girard divides the second recital as follows:

A a miracle of establishment (vv. 54–55)
B contention among the people (vv. 56–58)
C divine retaliation (vv. 59–67)
A^1 a miracle of establishment (vv. 68–72)[83]

Girard compares Psalm 78 to "midrashic" literature which employs a free interpretation of history, where the psalmist's rearrangement of events is deliberate and purposeful.[84] He concludes that the psalm is a didactic lesson given by the psalmist to call his people back to an observance of the Law through a contemplation of God's wonders not only in the past, but also in the present.[85]

While all these studies in structural analysis consider God's gracious involvement as central to Psalm 78's historical recital, Girard uniquely considers the wilderness section (vv. 12–53) as a unified whole. Girard's alternative proposal for two recitals (vv. 12–53 // 54–72) offers a significant alternative for viewing the psalm's structure.[86]

The Rhetorical Force of Psalm 78 (Early 1990s)

Two scholars look beyond the literary features of Psalm 78 to consider the rhetorical force of the composition. Greenstein considers the psalmist's

82. Girard, *Psaumes redécouverts*, 358. My translation.

83. Girard, *Psaumes redécouverts*, 358. My translation.

84. Girard, *Psaumes redécouverts*, 355.

85. Girard, *Psaumes redécouverts*, 373.

86. Vesco follows Girard's proposal for the structure of Psalm 78. Vesco, *Psautier de David traduit et commenté I*, 695–718.

rhetorically motivated rearrangement of history, while Brueggemann explores the rhetorical force of historical reflection.

Greenstein's 1990 article "Mixing Memory and Design: Reading Psalm 78" constitutes the first truly rhetorical (i.e., suasory) study of Psalm 78.[87] Greenstein begins his article with a provocative statement: "How we choose to read matters. With regard to Psalm 78, it can make the difference between interpreting the psalm as a hopeless rejection of Israel for its 'deeply rooted' guilt, or as a hopeful prophetic effort to reform the people."[88] Greenstein reads the psalm as "an exercise in rhetoric, telling it like it is for the purpose of changing it."[89] He argues that beside the simple act of recounting history, the psalmist relies on two key rhetorical strategies. First, the psalmist "evokes the traditions of Israel in language they should recognize if not recall."[90] Second, "the psalmist takes special pains to recall the remoter past for them. He leads them on a journey of remembrance by taking them back before the exodus, to the plagues and the staggering wonders that God had wrought then."[91] For Greenstein, this backward movement of memory on the part of the psalmist is itself a rhetorical act as the psalmist "exemplifies his theme [the need to remember] through the rhetorical act of remembering."[92] Although Greenstein offers

87. Greenstein, "Mixing Memory and Design," 197–218. Greenstein begins by establishing the uniqueness of his own study with an annotated survey of past proposals for Psalm 78's purpose and structure. His argument totals thirteen pages; his endnotes engaging with alternative interpretations extend for another nine (and in a much smaller font!).

88. Greenstein, "Mixing Memory and Design," 197. Greenstein goes on to challenge the tendency among many scholars to read the psalm with a focus on Israel's rebellion and faithlessness. This reading troubles him because it seems to reinforce "classical Christian theological interests" as it leads to the view of Israel as the "failed covenant partner to be superseded by the Church" (199).

89. Greenstein, "Mixing Memory and Design," 197. Greenstein takes on the "structure"-based proposals of Campbell, Clifford, and Korpel and de Moor. He calls their approaches "flat readings" and "aerial readings" of the text that identify "an overall geometric design in the text at the expense of the twists and turns by which the text unfolds in the course of reading" (198). Greenstein critiques the ideological bias that often results from these "two-dimensional" readings of the psalm: "Rather than see any kind of movement, of dynamic relationship, these formalist critics depict static entities in polar opposition-bad Israel, good God" (199).

90. Greenstein, "Mixing Memory and Design," 208. Regarding this technique, Greenstein notes that the psalmist "repeatedly evokes the familiar language of the common tradition. In referring to events that are narrated in the Torah and in the Former Prophets, the psalm reverberates with the vocabulary and plot details of the primary narrative" (201).

91. Greenstein, "Mixing Memory and Design," 209.

92. Greenstein, "Mixing Memory and Design," 209. He concludes: "The psalm, as

a helpful rhetorical reading of Psalm 78 as a coherent composition, he fails to explore the specific rhetorical power of individual events in the text.

In his book *Abiding Astonishment*, Walter Brueggemann approaches the historical psalms (Pss 78, 105, 106, 136) as examples of self-conscious rhetoric.[93] Regarding the rhetorical intention of these accounts, Brueggemann observes two goals. First, "they seek to make available to subsequent generations the experience and power of the initial astonishment which abides with compelling authority."[94] Second, "by continuing and extending the recital beyond the originary events into monarchal history (as does Psalm 78), the recital affirms that this Yahwistic, 'astonished' way of discerning Israel's present, on-going life is as valid as was the initial astonished discernment of Yahweh in the past."[95] For Brueggemann, "Israel's historical recital is a stylized retelling of its past, and therefore an intentional shaping of the present and a passionate yearning for a specific future."[96]

Brueggemann argues that each of the historical psalms seeks to provoke a different response from the audience, e.g., obedience (Ps 105), petition (Ps 106), gratitude (Ps 136), and new political possibilities (Ps 78). Regarding the political intention of Psalm 78, he observes: "The God who has utterly rejected is the God who has chosen afresh; Israel is invited by Yahweh into a new political possibility."[97] Brueggemann's conclusion regarding Psalm 78 draws heavily on the final section of the psalm (vv. 59–72), with no consideration given to the material in the wilderness frame (vv. 13–53).

Both Greenstein and Brueggemann recognize Psalm 78's suasory power to impact the present audience through a recital of the past. Greenstein's critiques of those who read the psalm against a linear horizon and

I read it, is not about history; it deals in memory. It is not about something called memory; rather, through the rhetoric adopted by the psalmist for jogging the people's recollection, he exercises their memory by exercising his own."

93. Brueggemann, *Abiding Astonishment*. Although Brueggemann employs the terms "rhetoric"/"rhetorical" with great frequency, he never actually defines these terms. Instead, he relies on the dialogical contrast of "history" (i.e., "what happened") and "rhetoric" (i.e., "what is remembered" and "how it is said"). See his comments on pp. 13–14.

94. Brueggemann, *Abiding Astonishment*, 34. Brueggemann borrows the phrase "abiding astonishment" from Martin Buber, who used the expression to refer to the impact of "miracles" reported in the biblical text. Buber, *Moses*, 77. Cited in Brueggemann, *Abiding Astonishment*, 30–31.

95. Brueggemann, *Abiding Astonishment*, 34.

96. Brueggemann, *Abiding Astonishment*, 29.

97. Brueggemann, *Abiding Astonishment*, 29.

those who confine the psalm to a concentric configuration help to open the way for considering Psalm 78's nonchronological presentation of the wilderness events as a rhetorically driven choice on the part of the psalmist. In addition, Greenstein's consideration of vv. 12–55 brings a renewed focus on the wilderness food events and the Egyptian plagues. Although Brueggemann's study of Psalm 78 ignores the wilderness frame (vv. 13–53), his understanding of the rhetorical intention of recital—especially its ability to evoke the "power of the initial astonishment"—may help to explain the psalmist's particular interest in describing and presenting the wilderness events.

Extended Attention to Psalm 78 (1990s)

In the 1990s, two dissertations were written on Psalm 78. Paula Sharpe Hiebert's 1992 Harvard dissertation under the direction of Professor Frank Cross presents a tradition-historical and textual study of Psalm 78. After offering a translation of the text with extensive text-critical comments, she examines the plague tradition (vv. 44–51) and the wilderness tradition (vv. 14–31) as separate chapters.[98] In light of her research, she concludes that both accounts are independent and early traditions. Hiebert ends her study by considering the literary structure and setting for the psalm as a whole. She finds an essential unity to the psalm, observing three divisions in the psalm: vv. 1–8 // 9–64 // 65–72. She argues that the body of the psalm focuses on the history of Ephraim and their rebellious response to YHWH's care and saving power (vv. 9–64), while the psalm ends with an announcement of a new order that has been inaugurated with David's kingship (vv. 65–72).[99] In light of the prevalence of linguistic features of early Hebrew poetry, she concludes that the psalm was written during the United Monarchy.[100]

Charles McLain's 1996 Westminster Theological Seminary dissertation looks at Psalm 78 as an example of "political accession justification" for the Davidic dynasty. In contrast to those who identify Psalm 78 with the classifications of "history" or "wisdom literature," McLain claims

98. Hiebert's study of Psalm 78 includes a chapter on the Plague account (ch. 2) and a chapter on the wilderness account (ch. 3)—with no explicit rationale for this order of engagement. Her dissertation lacks an introductory chapter where one would expect an explanation of this choice.

99. Hiebert, "Psalm 78," 201–2.

100. Hiebert, "Psalm 78," 202–11.

that Psalm 78 includes sufficient similarities to ANE-biblical models of "political justification" that it should be included within this genre designation. McLain considers the psalmist's references to Ephraim as key markers within the structure of the composition. He contends that Psalm 78 employs the rhetorical categories of apology and polemic typical of propaganda and shows affinities to Judges–Ruth.[101] He concludes that the psalm is a "discourse in order to argue for a Davidic claim."[102] McLain offers a tentative proposal for an early date for the composition during the United Monarchy.[103]

The studies by Hiebert and McLain provide the first extended analyses of Psalm 78. Both scholars date Psalm 78 early: Hiebert on linguistic evidence, McLain on thematic considerations. Both scholars assume that the psalm has political implications. While Hiebert addresses the material found in the wilderness frame, her primary concern is with its lexical, not rhetorical, significance. While McLain's concerns are rhetorical in nature, the content of his study draws him primarily to the end of the psalmist's recital (vv. 42–72).

Contemplating Psalm 78 Within the Asaph Collection (1980 to 1990s)

In the late eighties to early nineties, the Asaph Collection (Pss 50, 73–83)—of which Psalm 78 holds a significant place—was the focus of two very different studies. Nasuti considered the collection on a linguistic level, while Goulder explored its liturgical function.

Nasuti approached the Asaph Collection with an interest in tradition history.[104] He set out to isolate the linguistic elements that the Asaph psalms share among themselves and those which they share with streams of tradition outside the Psalter. He identified a common tradition of an "Ephraimite" stream reflecting a northern Israelite perspective. Nasuti

101. McLain, "Investigation of Psalm 78," 260–74.

102. McLain, "Investigation of Psalm 78," 289.

103. McLain concludes: "The probable date of composition is during the United Monarchy for David or Solomon. The psalm was probably targeted at dissatisfied portions of society whether in the north or south. The psalm may have equally served to retain loyalties in the southern tribes and to reclaim loyalties in the northern tribes to Davidic rule. The extensive polemic of the psalm provides a stark warning against abandoning the rule of the Davidic dynasty for northern rule." McLain, "Investigation of Psalm 78," 288.

104. Nasuti, *Tradition History and the Psalms of Asaph.*

observed that Psalm 78 displays close linguistic ties to the rest of the Asaph psalms (as well as the larger Ephraimite tradition stream) and that these ties are dispersed throughout the psalm. He situates Psalm 78 in preexilic Judah, possibly at the time of Hezekiah or Josiah.[105]

Michael Goulder argues that the Asaph psalms function as a unified liturgical collection.[106] He observes a "pervasive sense of crisis" across the collection[107] and suggests a time frame during "the brief period between 732 and 722, when Israel was divided from Judah, but had lost its northern and eastern tribes to Assyria; when Tiglath-Pileser captured Gilead and Galilee, all the land of Naphtali (2 Kgs 15.29), but Samaria was not yet taken."[108] Goulder envisions the Asaph psalms as part of a New Year's Festival in Israel at the worship site of Bethel.[109] He reads Psalm 78 as an admonition by the king to his people.[110]

The studies by Nasuti and Goulder consider Psalm 78 not just as a composition, but now as part of a collection. Reading Psalm 78 within its larger collection (i.e., Book 3, Psalms of Asaph, Historical Psalms) is a trend that continues into present times.

Considering Psalm 78 Within the Psalter (1990 to 2000s)

While the interest in literary and canonical readings of the Bible had been gaining traction in biblical studies, it was the release of Gerald Wilson's

105. Nasuti notes: "The list of offenses in particular would seem to point beyond the time of the Philistine crisis, as would the presence of such a developed Ephraimite vocabulary. It is likely that the rejection of Ephraim here is symbolic of the more radical rejection of the Northern kingdom in 721, while the choice of Judah and David is symbolic of the continued existence of that tribe under a Davidic monarch. In view of the Ephraimite nature of the psalm, it is likely that this monarch is to be seen as either Hezekiah or Josiah, the two great reforming kings of post-721 Judah." Nasuti, *Tradition History and the Psalms of Asaph*, 92.

106. Goulder, *Psalms of Asaph and the Pentateuch*. He summarized the key aspects of his proposal in Goulder, "Asaph's History of Israel," 71–81.

107. Goulder, "Asaph's History of Israel," 74.

108. Goulder, "Asaph's History of Israel," 75.

109. After the fall of the Northern Kingdom in 722, he imagines that the psalms of Asaph were taken to Jerusalem, redacted for this new setting, and remained in use. Goulder, "Asaph's History of Israel," 75.

110. Goulder assumes that Psalm 78's exhortation to "my people" is in fact spoken by the king in the midst of the festival. Goulder, *Psalms of Asaph and the Pentateuch*, 108–9.

The Editing of the Hebrew Psalter[111] that opened the door for a variety of studies of the shape and shaping of the book of Psalms.

J. Clinton McCann's essay "Books I–III and the Editorial Purpose of the Hebrew Psalter," builds on Wilson's initial proposal that the purpose of the final form of the Psalter was to "address the apparent failure of the Davidic covenant in light of the exile, the diaspora and the oppression of Israel by the nations in the postexilic era."[112] By citing evidence that Wilson did not include in his initial study, McCann seeks to "add further depth and dimension to Wilson's conclusion."[113] McCann argues that by considering the psalms that begin Books I–III, "one discovers a pattern that serves to instruct the postexilic community not only to face the disorienting reality of exile but also to reach toward a reorientation beyond the traditional grounds for hope, that is, beyond the Davidic/Zion covenant theology."[114] McCann views Psalm 78 as a psalm of "hope," one of the psalms in Book 3 that "look to God as judge of all the earth and that rehearse God's past deeds on Israel's behalf despite Israel's faithlessness."[115] McCann contends that the shaping of the Psalter shows that the experience of exile and dispersion "was not only a time for lamenting but also a time for forging new expressions of hope in an attempt to enable the community to survive."[116]

While McCann's study focuses primarily on the thematic cohesion in Book 3, Robert Cole's study of Book 3 utilizes rhetorical criticism and canonical criticism to analyze its individual psalms, as well as consider the collection as a whole.[117] Cole establishes strong lexical and thematic ties between Psalm 77 and 78 and argues that Psalm 78 is a partial answer to Psalm 77's lament. He notes: "Psalm 78 has responded to 77's lament concerning continual divine anger by pointing out that Israel's rebellion was continual as well. Nonetheless, hope is kept alive by the promise in 78.65–72 that the Davidic covenant is not forgotten."[118] For Cole, Psalm 78 is viewed primarily as a chronicle of Israel's rebellion.

111. Wilson, *Editing of the Hebrew Psalter.*

112. McCann, "Books I–III and the Editorial Purpose," 93.

113. McCann, "Books I–III and the Editorial Purpose," 93.

114. McCann, "Books I–III and the Editorial Purpose," 95.

115. McCann, "Books I–III and the Editorial Purpose," 100.

116. McCann, "Books I–III and the Editorial Purpose," 98.

117. Cole, *Shape and Message of Book 3.*

118. Cole, *Shape and Message of Book 3*, 76. Cole offers a much more extensive study of Psalm 78's dialogue with Psalm 77 in his PhD thesis: Cole, "Rhetorics and

While much of the conversation during this period (1990–2000s) focused on the shaping of the Psalter as a whole, a growing movement to consider individual psalms together with their adjacent psalms also emerged.[119]

Psalm 78 and Historiography (2000 to 2010s)

During the 2000s into the 2010s, the question of historiography dominated discussions of the "historical psalms" and Psalm 78's place in this collection. One of the unique foci of these studies is the question of the identity-shaping function of historical recital. As will be seen in the survey that follows, these studies have a common concern for the hermeneutical function of the reuse of biblical texts and the significance of the compositional shape of the Psalter.

Adele Berlin situates Psalm 78, as well as Psalms 44, 69, and 137, as exilic compositions in light of "the importance of the theme of destruction and exile."[120] She finds that they all "address the problem of exile in stereotypical language and style, and they share certain theological assumptions; yet each has its own thesis, its own particular concern about an aspect of the exilic experience."[121] Contrary to the view of most scholars, Berlin contends that Psalm 78 "presents its interpretation of history as a proof that the Temple will be rebuilt and the Davidic line will continue."[122] She considers Ps 78:59–70 in light of the literary trope of "city laments," claiming that the psalm "has not been adequately interpreted, especially in regard to its use of Shiloh."[123] She argues that in vv. 59–70 the psalmist makes an explicit distinction between the destiny of Shiloh and the Jerusalem Temple. Unlike Jeremiah, who uses Shiloh as an example of what would happen to Jerusalem if the people continued to sin (7:12–14; 26:6, 9), here in vv. 59–70 the psalmist is reversing Jeremiah's use of Shiloh in order to argue that Shiloh was never intended to

Canonical Structure."

119. This interest is a hallmark of the commentary discussions in the Hermeneia commentary on the Psalms by Frank-Lothar Hossfeld and Erich Zenger, as well as the two-volume work on the Psalms by Jean-Luc Vesco. Hossfeld and Zenger, *Psalms 2*, 293–94, 300; Vesco, *Psautier de David traduit et commenté I*, 695–96.

120. Berlin, "Psalms and the Literature of Exile," 65.

121. Berlin, "Psalms and the Literature of Exile," 65.

122. Berlin, "Psalms and the Literature of Exile," 65.

123. Berlin, "Psalms and the Literature of Exile," 78.

be permanent and that Jerusalem is in fact God's permanent dwelling.[124] She finds that Psalm 78 fits well within an exilic time frame, noting: "The psalm knows the Deuteronomistic traditions, and, it seems to me, knows and is responding to Jeremiah 7.34. The psalm's silence about the events of 586 does not mean that it was written before they occurred. In fact, the best reading of the psalm takes those events as implied, as understood by the audience, and as the subtext against whose background the poet writes."[125] Regarding Psalm 78's purpose, she concludes: "It is a psalm of restoration—of comfort and hope in the belief that Judah, unlike Ephraim, will not be rejected forever."[126]

In his essay "From Exodus to David—History and Historiography in Psalm 78," Markus Witte views Psalm 78 as a unique example of historiography.[127] He bases this on the psalm's lengthy prologue, where the psalmist "outlines the form and function of his view on history in a programmatic way."[128] He notes that Psalm 78 "tends towards systematization, through which the events of history are qualified as miracles, and human reaction to them as either faith or sin."[129] He situates Psalm 78 in the Second Temple period and concludes that the purpose of the psalm is to present the audience with an opportunity to reflect on their present experience of life with God. In this light, the psalm presents a challenge to the audience and a call to intentionally respond with a "constant remembrance of God's deeds," a "trust in God being the Lord of history and being merciful," and a "loyalty to the God-given Torah."[130]

Judith Gärtner considers the historical psalms (Pss 78, 105, 106, 135, 136) through the lens of "collective memory" with an interest in the

124. Berlin, "Psalms and the Literature of Exile," 81. She continues: "Jeremiah wants to warn Judah that its destiny will be the same as that of Shiloh/the Northern Kingdom, while the psalmist wants to prove that the destinies of Shiloh/Israel and Jerusalem/Judah are diametrically opposed. Unlike the provisional tent-tabernacle at Shiloh, says the psalm, the Temple was constructed to be as permanent as the world itself."

125. Berlin, "Psalms and the Literature of Exile," 81–82.

126. Berlin, "Psalms and the Literature of Exile," 83.

127. Regarding the designation of historiography, Witte explains: "The way in which society reflects on its past, the way in which it shapes the inner space of its memory, the way in which it constructs its own history in a creative act, and the way it makes it enriching for its present, all reveal essential characteristics of a society's cultural profile, of the structure of meaning that determines it, and of its identity." Witte, "From Exodus to David," 21.

128. Witte, "From Exodus to David," 21.

129. Witte, "From Exodus to David," 22.

130. Witte, "From Exodus to David," 39.

different conceptions of history found in these psalms.[131] Gärtner draws on the work of Voegelin and Assmann who explore the role of "remembered history" in the formation of a community's collective self-understanding.[132] Gärtner argues that the historical psalms are more than just a retelling of the narratives of the Hebrew Bible, but instead "they are each based on a separate historical hermeneutic, according to which different events are selected from the narrative context of the Pentateuch and reinterpreted."[133] These compositions are "identity-forming and identity-reassuring" and form the basis for a collective identity "by which the recipients draw from the past in order to reinterpret their present in light of their past."[134] Gärtner also considers historical psalms as a hermeneutical lens for understanding the composition and redaction of the Psalter.[135]

Gärtner views Psalm 78 as "a deliberatively designed composition" divisible into three sections: the proem (vv. 1–11) and two historical recitals (vv. 12–39; 40–72).[136] She argues that the psalm is primarily "a story of divine mercy"[137] and was intentionally written as a "reflective text" for its present context (Pss 74–79).[138] In light of its positioning, Gärtner argues for a postexilic date for Psalm 78.[139]

In her habilitation followed by a summary article,[140] Anja Klein considers the historical psalms (Pss 78, 105, 106, 114, 135, 136, 137) in the context of reception history. Beginning with the Song of the Sea (Exod 15), continuing through the Psalter, and moving to the penitential prayer

131. Gärtner, *Geschichtspsalmen*. She summarizes the main points of her habilitation turned monograph in a later article, "Historical Psalms," 373–99.

132. Gärtner, *Geschichtspsalmen*, 9–29.

133. Gärtner, "Historical Psalms," 373.

134. Gärtner, "Historical Psalms," 374–75.

135. Gärtner, "Historical Psalms," 376–77.

136. Gärtner, "Historical Psalms," 377–78. In her article "From Generation to Generation," Gärtner focuses on the proem (vv. 1–11) of Psalm 78 as a means for considering the process of "remembering" and "forgetting" in the Second Temple period. She concludes that through the recollection of history in Psalm 78, "the worshipper becomes aware of the paradigmatic significance of these events for his or her own time, in order that the individual may be reaffirmed in belonging to the people of God" (277).

137. Gärtner, "Historical Psalms," 379.

138. Gärtner, "Historical Psalms," 380–82.

139. Gärtner notes: "Due to the exilic date of Psalm 74 and the background of Psalm 79 in written prophecy, one can reasonably assume that the beginning of the composition of the collection was in the post-exilic period." Gärtner, "Historical Psalms," 382.

140. Klein, *Geschichte und Gebet*. This work was summarized as an article entitled "Praying Biblical History," 400–26.

of Nehemiah 9, she traces the reformulation of Israel's history and seeks to explain this "poetic rereading" as "biblical Judaism's search for identity."[141] Regarding the place of the historical psalms within the Psalter, she argues that "by interpreting biblical history at redactional turning points, the book gradually turns from a collection of individual prayer texts into the prayer book of Israel. In this process, the increasing references to biblical history in the psalms serve to identify both the speakers and the addressees as part of YHWH's people."[142] This literary search for meaning is a tangible expression of the cultural memory of biblical Israel.[143]

Klein argues that Psalm 78 was composed as the centerpiece of the Asaph palms.[144] She proposes that this psalm originally contained a linear account of history "starting from the miracles of YHWH in front of the fathers in Egypt (78:12–16). It then deals with the events in the desert (78:17–29*), describes the entry into the land (78:40–55a) and, finally, the events thereafter (78:56–72)."[145] She finds significant dependence on Exodus 15 but observes that "while the biblical events are cause for praise in Exodus 15, Psalm 78 retells a history of recurring sin."[146] She posits that the hermeneutical key is in fact the dramatic shift that occurs in the preamble of Psalm 78 (vv. 1–11): "The reception of biblical history in Psalm 78 carries a paradigmatic notion, since the conduct of the preceding generations serves as a cautionary tale."[147] In addition, this introduction serves as an invitation to each succeeding generation to "take an active part in the intergenerational contract by committing themselves to passing on tradition."[148]

In the article "The Growth of the Scriptural Corpus by Successive Rewritings," Sophie Ramond explores the selection and interpretation of earlier biblical texts in the historical psalms (Pss 78, 81, 95, 105–106, 114, 135–136).[149] She gives attention "to the nature of their historical reconstruction, to their intention, and to the identity of the community

141. Klein, "Praying Biblical History," 401.

142. Klein, "Praying Biblical History," 420.

143. Klein, "Praying Biblical History," 421.

144. Klein, "Praying Biblical History," 404.

145. Klein, "Praying Biblical History," 404. This set of divisions reflects Klein's reconstruction of Psalm 78's original history recital. See also Klein, *Geschichte und Gebet*, 110–26.

146. Klein, "Praying Biblical History," 405.

147. Klein, "Praying Biblical History," 405.

148. Klein, "Praying Biblical History," 406.

149. Ramond, "Growth of the Scriptural Corpus," 427–49. This article is based on her research in the monograph *Les leçons et les enigmes du passé.*

in which or for which they were composed."[150] She considers the psalms through the successive categories of creation, patriarchal tradition, the exodus, Sinai tradition, theme of land, Former Prophets, and Later Prophets. While acknowledging that the various constructions of Israel's history "served different purposes in different contexts," all the historical psalms "confront the distressing question of the exile. They turn their attention to Israel's experience of salvation during the Exodus and to the gift of the land, in order to provide an answer to the situation generated by the Babylonian domination."[151] She closes the article with a consideration of the redaction and composition of the Pentateuch.[152]

Ramond draws extensively on Psalm 78 in her study. She considers Psalm 78 the latest of the historical psalms.[153] She notes the common vocabulary shared with Exodus and Numbers, as well as the Later Prophets (Isaiah, Hosea, Jeremiah).[154] Ramond asserts that Psalm 78 has a particular status because of its polemical and political tone. She views the psalm as "an attempt to define Israel's identity,"[155] but one that attempts to create a "dialogue" between groups, possibly Jerusalemites and Samaritans, at the end of the Persian or beginning of the Hellenistic periods.[156]

As seen in the studies above, there has been a paradigm shift in the dating of Psalm 78. When considered alongside the larger collection of "historical psalms," scholars consistently posit a late date for the psalm, considering it as an exilic to even a Hellenistic composition.

Revisiting Earlier Trends and Emerging Methodologies (2000 to early 2020s)

The last two decades of scholarship on Psalm 78 have witnessed a revisiting of earlier methods in the study of this psalm, as well as great diversity in new approaches. Many of these new works on Psalm 78 reflect the earlier trends of the 1960s and 1970s such as tradition historical

150. Ramond, "Growth of the Scriptural Corpus," 429.
151. Ramond, "Growth of the Scriptural Corpus," 438.
152. Ramond, "Growth of the Scriptural Corpus," 444–49.
153. Ramond, "Growth of the Scriptural Corpus," 440.
154. Ramond, "Growth of the Scriptural Corpus," 433–34, 436–37.
155. Ramond, "Growth of the Scriptural Corpus," 440.
156. Ramond, "Growth of the Scriptural Corpus," 441.

studies[157] and viewing Psalm 78 as propaganda.[158] The concerns of the 1970s and 1980s for exploring the literary features of the text continue to resurface.[159] There has also been a renewal of the concerns of the 1980s and 1990s for reading individual psalms within their canonical contexts and within associated collections. This trend is seen in recent considerations of Psalm 78 as part of a larger study of the Asaph Collection[160] and Book 3 of the Psalter.[161] The trend that emerged in the 2000s to view Psalm 78 through the lens of historiography, with a specific interest in memory studies and social identity theory, continues into the present.[162] In addition, scholars have returned to the opening (vv. 1–8)[163] and closing (vv. 59–72)[164] sections of the psalm.[165]

157. Two PhD dissertations have addressed Psalm 78's use of historical traditions. The first is Jeffrey Leonard's 2006 Brandeis dissertation, "Historical Traditions in Psalm 78." His dissertation was followed by an article that used Psalm 78 as an exercise in considering inner-biblical allusions. Leonard, "Identifying Inner-Biblical Allusions," 241–65. The second is David Emanuel's 2007 Hebrew University dissertation, "The Psalmists' Use of the Exodus Motif," a work that considered the use of the Exodus motif within a selection of Historical Psalms (Pss 78, 105, 106, 135, 136). David Ray's study of Psalm 78's use of the *hiphil* stem in contexts of possible inter-biblical allusions offers an extension of this approach, as well. Ray, "Who Did What to Whom?," 65–84.

158. Tammuz, "Psalm 78," 205–21.

159. Wagner, "Recounting חידות מני־קדם in Psalm 78," 1–21. Wagner's concern here is the psalmist's use of tricolons within the formation of the composition as a whole.

160. Jones, "Psalms of Asaph." See also a summary of her argument in "Message of the Asaph Collection," 71–85. Karl Jacobson considers the rhetorical function of Israel's remembered past ("mnemohistory") within the Asaph Collection, with an extended study of Psalm 78. Jacobson, *Memories of Asaph*.

161. Pavan, *He Remembered That They Were But Flesh*. Pavan's lexicographical study of Psalms 73–89 gives particular attention to instances within Psalm 78 where remembering and forgetting occupy a significant place in the composition.

162. Boyd, "Rhetoric of Memory," 7–30.

163. Estes, "Psalm 78:1–8 as a Musical Intertext," 297–314.

164. Psalm 78's final section (vv. 59–72) has received notable attention, with a dissertation and two articles addressing the psalmist's reference to Shiloh. In her dissertation, "Royal Lineages: A Study of Psalm 78:59–72 in the Light of the Narrative Traditions," Dalrymple counters the assumption that the references to Ephraim/Judah refer to the Northern/Southern Kingdoms. In the article, "Reference to Shiloh in Psalm 78," Mark Leuchter argues that Psalm 78's polemic against Shiloh best fits a Solomonic background. In his article, "Ephraim and Treachery, Loyalty and (the House of) David," Amos Frisch counters Zakovitch's explanation of the initial paired sections within his concentric structure (vv. 1–8 // 68–72) and argues against the conditional nature of this election (vv. 68–72) when seen against the people's obligation to remember the Lord's deeds and observe his precepts which opens the psalm (vv. 1–8). Frisch, "Ephraim and Treachery," 191. See also Zakovitch, "'He Chose the Tribe of Judah,'" 117–202.

165. Gili Kugler's argument about the omission of Moses within the historical

During the last two decades, scholarship on Psalm 78 has also witnessed a growth in methodological diversity reflecting many of the trends seen across the field of biblical studies. This diversity of perspectives has been exhibited in explorations of Psalm 78 through the lens of a Bakhtinian dialogic,[166] trauma theory,[167] multidimensional readings of the psalm focused on the communication process (text, author, reader),[168] and a hermeneutic of curiosity.[169] And most directly related to this present study is Gillmayr-Bucher's exploration of social relations and identity formation as seen in the depiction of the divine provision of food in the wilderness (Ps 78:15–33).[170]

CONCLUSION

As shown in this survey of more than a century and a half of scholarship on Psalm 78, little to no consensus has been reached on the psalm's major features (i.e., genre, *Sitz im Leben*, date, structure, and purpose). Psalm 78 presents itself as an "enigma" (v. 2) and continues to be an enigmatic

recital rests on the introduction of David in the psalm's epilogue (vv. 67–72), as well as the pedagogical intent established in the psalm's prologue (vv. 1–7). Kugler, "Not Moses, but David," 126–36.

166. Kungu, "Dialogical Study of Psalm 78 and Isaiah 1." Kungu proposes that Mikhail Bakhtin's dialogism supplements insights gained from form criticism, rhetorical criticism, and intertextuality. He contends: "Bakhtin treats texts as unique compositions with unique perspectives, therefore going beyond the limits of convention found in early form criticism. These texts are treated as units of speech communication thereby overcoming the limitations of early rhetorical criticism reduced to stylistic [*sic*]. Dialogism accommodates a hostile rhetorical context and is therefore more appropriate than classical rhetoric in analyzing biblical texts that evidence ideological conflict. As units of speech communication, biblical texts have speakers, audiences, and historical contexts. This attention to historical persons and contexts goes beyond mere intertextuality" (39).

167. Hays, "Trauma, Remembrance, and Healing," 183–204.

168. Kim and van Rooy, "Dimension of the Text," 285–98; Kim and van Rooy, "Authorial Dimension," 468–84; Kim and van Rooy, "Dimension of the Reader," 101–17.

169. Jones, "Lessons Learned," 173–83.

170. Gillmayr-Bucher, "How Does Food Shape History?," 75–95. Gillmayr-Bucher argues that the depiction of the events in vv. 15–33 primarily highlight Israel's failure to trust in YHWH. She contends: "The memory of food-related episodes in Ps 78 problematizes the people's relationship with God and shows how the fundamental trust in God's care is challenged" (94). As I will argue in chapters 4 and 5, it is the extravagance of YHWH's provisions, in spite of Israel's rebellion, that becomes the dominant theme in this account, a point made even clearer when this food event is seen within the larger wilderness frame (vv. 13–53).

composition that defies easy classification. Literary analysis has called for an increased awareness of the stylistic components of the text. However, besides Greenstein's 1990 article, there has been no study of the specifically rhetorical function of the depiction and arrangement of particular events within the psalm, in particular within the wilderness material (vv. 13–53). With the trend toward focusing on the opening preamble (vv. 1–11) or the closing material (vv. 67–72), the psalm's central sections have been largely overlooked by scholars.[171] And besides the article by Gillmayr-Bucher, scholars have rarely commented on the prevalence of food language within the psalm. As will be demonstrated in the chapters that follow, the psalmist's inclusion of food events and use of food language plays a major role in the overall rhetorical strategy of the psalm.

171. A notable exception to this omission has been the work of scholars engaged in structural analysis.

3

Food Language in the Hebrew Bible

Its Dimensions, Associations, and Rhetorical Potential

INTRODUCTION

ACROSS TIME AND CULTURES, the daily need to eat and drink has ordered human life. As Margaret Visser notes: "For most of human history we have spent a much longer portion of our lives worrying about food, and plotting, working, and fighting to obtain it, than we have in any other pursuit."[1] This preoccupation with food is also reflected in the biblical text. As one author aptly notes: "Food fills the Bible from beginning to end, just as it fills a human life day after day."[2] Scholars have shown a far-reaching and protracted interest in food and meals in the New Testament.[3] However, until quite recently, little interest has been paid to food

1. Visser, *Much Depends on Dinner*, 12.

2. "Food," in Ryken et al., *Dictionary of Biblical Imagery*, 297.

3. The topic of meals has been explored through a wide range of methods and concerns with studies that have considered texts across the whole corpus of the New Testament. Although nowhere near exhaustive, this listing has sought to show the broad scope of New Testament research on meals. The topic of meals has been central to discussions of the "historical Jesus." See Crossan, "Life of a Mediterranean Jewish Peasant,"

and meals in the Hebrew Bible.[4] Yet as Knierim observes, this corpus of

1194–200; Bolyki, *Jesu Tischgemeinschaften*; Kollman, *Ursprung und Gestalt*. For a counter position, see Blomberg, *Contagious Holiness*, 19–31; Blomberg, "Jesus, Sinners, and Table Fellowship," 35–62. In addition, scholars have explored the possibility that early Christian communal meals were an extension of the Hellenistic symposium tradition. See Smith, *From Symposium to Eucharist*; Klinghardt, *Gemeinschaftsmahl und Mahlgemeinschaft*. Other scholars have explored Jesus' meal practice from a social and cultural perspective, clarifying the significance of social expectations embedded in a meal. Two foundational essays in the discussion are Neyrey, "Meals, Food, and Table Fellowship," 159–82; Neyrey, "Ceremonies in Luke-Acts," 361–87. See also Bartchy, "Historical Jesus and Honor Reversal," 175–83. For an excellent study of gender and meals in the Gospels, see Corley, *Private Women, Public Meals*. Scholars have investigated the accounts of Jesus' meals in each of the four Gospels, although the Gospel of Luke has by far held the most scholarly interest. On the Gospel of Matthew, see Steffen, "Messianic Banquet as a Paradigm." On the Gospel of Mark, see Klosinski's Claremont PhD dissertation, "Meals in Mark." On the Gospel of John, see Webster, *Ingesting Jesus*. For dissertations approaching Luke's meals from a variety of angles, see McMahan, "Meals as Type-Scenes in Luke"; Steele, "Jesus' Table-Fellowship with Pharisees"; Leonard, "Luke's Account of the Lord's Supper." See also Stinson's MA thesis, "Dining in the Kingdom." In addition, there have been studies on meals recorded in the book of Acts. See the work of Finger, *Of Widows and Meals*. Other studies consider the meals of Luke-Acts together; see, for example, Heil, *Meal Scenes in Luke-Acts*; Davis, "Significance of the Shared Meal in Luke-Acts." There have been several studies on meals mentioned in the Epistles. On the meal scene in Galatians, see Dunn, "Incident at Antioch (Gal 2:11–18)," 3–57; Jewett, "Gospel and Commensality," 240–52. On food and idol worship in Corinth, see Cheung, *Idol Food in Corinth*. On hospitality in 3 John, Malina, "Received View," 171–94. For a consideration of meals in Revelation, see Smit, *Fellowship and Food*.

4. It was not that scholars had never considered food and meals in the Hebrew Bible before this. But for most of the twentieth century, scholarship on the topic of food in the Hebrew Bible focused almost exclusively on food texts that directly related to the Israelite cult—covenant meals, sacrifice, and food laws. Notable exceptions to these studies include Smend, "Essen und Trinken," 447–59; Schmitt, *Essen in der Bibel*. The past twenty years have witnessed a growing rise of research in the area of food in the Hebrew Bible. In 1999, *Semeia* released a theme issue on the topic of food—with more than half of its articles focused on the Hebrew Bible. Brenner and van Henten, *Semeia 86*. Several of the contributors had recently produced notable monographs on meals in the Hebrew Bible, including Judith McKinley and Diane Sharon. McKinlay, *Gendering Wisdom the Host*; Sharon, *Patterns of Destiny*. A notable contribution in the early 2000s was Claassens, *God Who Provides*. But almost a decade after the *Semeia* volume, Nathan MacDonald lamented the continued lack of extended scholarly engagement with the topic of food in the Hebrew Bible: "Despite the importance of food to the Old Testament authors, the subject has received surprisingly little attention from modern biblical scholars." MacDonald, *Not Bread Alone*, 2. His response to this lacuna was two monographs which have become foundational to current studies of food in the Hebrew Bible: *Not Bread Alone* and *What Did the Ancient Israelites Eat?* A year later, Ellen F. Davis broadened the conversation on food with a monograph entitled *Scripture, Culture, and Agriculture*. That same year a *Festschrift* honoring Rainer Kessler employed the topic of biblical meals as its unifying theme. Geiger et al., *Essen und Trinken in der Bibel*. This past decade has witnessed a burst of academic interest in the topic of food in the Hebrew Bible. Scholarship has often drawn on two converging trajectories, archaeology

texts shows an even greater concern with food.[5]

Although eating and drinking is a commonplace and universal aspect of human life, the significance of these acts when they appear in the biblical text can often elude the contemporary reader. Writing on the role of food in Genesis 2–4, Carol Meyers critiques the modern tendency to "interpret ancient texts as if the world was the same in essential ways for the ancients as for us."[6] She cautions the reader: "Food is not the same kind of issue for us in the developed world as it was for the ancient Israelites. We have too much. . . . [T]hey often had too little. And few of us have a direct connection with our food sources."[7] Meyers highlights the need for readers to develop not only an awareness of food in the biblical text, but an *informed awareness* of food's significance when it is used by the

---

and biblical studies. Three monographs reflect this convergence: Shafer-Elliott, *Food in Ancient Judah*; Greer, *Dinner at Dan*; Welton, *"He Is a Drunkard."* For a linguistic angle on the subject, see Peters, *Hebrew Lexical Semantics and Daily Life*. In addition, see the following collection of essays: Altmann and Fu, *Feasting in the Archaeology and Texts*. For an annotated bibliography that lists many of the shorter-length studies on food in the OT and NT, see Altmann, "Food and Food Production." In addition, *The T&T Clark Handbook of Food in the Hebrew Bible and Ancient Israel* provides an excellent sampling of short articles on various topics related to the economic, cultural, social, and practical aspects of food in ancient Israel, as well as articles surveying food references across the HB. Some recent monographs have sought to address the topic of food in individual books of the Hebrew Bible, most notably Deuteronomy and Isaiah. For Deuteronomy, see Altmann, *Festive Meals in Ancient Israel*. For Isaiah, see Abernethy, *Eating in Isaiah*; Stulac, *History and Hope*. While food plays a significant role in the Psalms, there have been no published monographs on the topic. However, there is an unpublished PhD thesis on the topic (Reed, "Food in the Psalms") and a growing number of essays: MacDonald, "'Eyes of All Look to You,'" 1–14; McCann, "Bread for the World," 303–10; Gillmayr-Bucher, "How Does Food Shape History?," 85–95; Stinson, "Sourdough and Bitter Tears," 177–84; Stinson, "Turning Tables in Israel's History," 588–98. While nowhere near exhaustive, this survey of major works published during the past two decades on the topic of food in the Hebrew Bible has sought to highlight, as MacDonald noted above, the need for further research in this area.

5. According to Knierim's cursory calculations, "On every three pages of the NRSV, the people mentioned in the Old Testament eat or drink four times, whereas those in the New Testament eat or drink twice." Based on these approximates, he concludes: "The Old Testament evidently pays a great deal of attention to human food consumption, and it does so rather evenly in all its parts." Knierim, "Food, Land, and Justice," 229.

6. Meyers, "Food in the First Family," 138.

7. Meyers, "Food in the First Family," 137–38. Wendell Berry makes a similar observation about contemporary consumers: "Most urban shoppers would tell you that food is produced on farms. But most of them do not know what farms, or what kinds of farms, or where the farms are, or what knowledge of skills are involved in farming. For them, then, food is pretty much an abstract idea—something they do not know or imagine—until it appears on the grocery shelf or on the table." Berry, "Pleasures of Eating," 145–46.

author. This chapter seeks to raise the reader's awareness of food events/ language in the Hebrew Bible, as well as provide categories for articulating the rhetorical power of food.[8]

As a means of identifying the significance of food uses in the biblical text, this chapter explores food through its basic dimensions.[9] Five primary dimensions of food will be discussed here—the physical dimension, the sensory dimension, the social dimension, the locational dimension, as well as the patterned dimension (i.e., its ability to picture an ordered reality).[10] In order to better appreciate the significant breadth with which the biblical writers employ food language, each of these dimensions will be considered along with examples drawn from Israel's history (narrative texts) and the Psalter (poetic texts).[11] The chapter will conclude by addressing the question: Why might the biblical authors be drawn to use the language of food?

DIMENSIONS OF FOOD: ASSOCIATIONS AND ILLUSTRATIONS

Margaret Visser observes: "Food is never just something to eat."[12] In order to understand the significance of a food reference, modern readers must first enter the world of the text. This process of understanding can be more difficult when talking about something as *seemingly* familiar and ordinary as food. Philippe Guillaume chides the naïve reader: "As a body of literature written by scribes who grew most of the food they ate, the Hebrew Bible assumes a world that is beyond the immediate reach of

8. While an ancient audience would have instinctively been more attuned to the role of food and food language in the biblical text, many modern Western readers have lost the vital connection to the realities of agrarian life. A concern for a renewed understanding and awareness of the centrality of food cultivation and production in the Hebrew Bible undergirds Ellen F. Davis's monograph, *Scripture, Culture, and Agriculture*. See also Stinson, "Summer and Winter, Seedtime and Harvest," 55–65.

9. To my knowledge, no one has set out to create categories for considering food language's rhetorical potential. Although these categories are basic, the identification of specific dimensions of food is forging new ground for considering food's rhetorical force.

10. This is not an exhaustive list; it simply limits the categories to the most basic dimensions of food.

11. Psalm 78 is in some sense a "hybrid" of two genres—historiography and poetry. In light of this convergence, it will be useful to illustrate the rhetorical power of food language by drawing from examples in both genres.

12. Visser, *Much Depends on Dinner*, 12.

academics who live in affluent post-industrial urban settings where hunger is absent and the relation between work and food is entirely mediated through money."[13] The growing divide that separates food consumers from food producers requires that if one wants to appreciate the rhetorical force of a food-related passage, one must stop and consider the reality of food in all its various dimensions. Five specific dimensions of food—the physical, sensory, social, locational, and patterned dimensions—will be addressed below with particular attention given to their associations for an ancient Israelite audience. For each dimension of food, examples from both narratives from the Hebrew Bible and individual psalms where this dimension of food is being employed for rhetorical effect will be explored.

The Physical Dimension: Food as Nourishment

The first dimension of food to be considered is its physical dimension and its association with life and death. Food—defined as both solid and liquid nourishment—allows for the preservation and strengthening of life. Without food, humans can live little more than a month; without water, one will die within the week. And as a contemporary writer and mother of two reminds us, "we are born hungry," entering the world dependent on others to meet our basic needs.[14]

According to the creation account in Genesis, this continuous need for food was part of the original "very good" design for humanity and the creaturely world (Gen 1:29–31). Here, the Creator's provision for the physical needs of humans and animals occurs concurrently with their creation. Carol Meyers observes: "It is no accident that the food sources for humanity are announced in Gen 1 as soon as human beings are created (Gen 1:29) and that food-producing plants are mentioned in Gen 2 before the creation of humankind is described (Gen 2:5–7)."[15] The order of the creation account in Genesis 1–2 highlights the central fact that

13. Guillaume, *Land, Credit, and Crisis*, 1. Davis offers a similar reminder: "Throughout the Iron Age and into the Persian Period at least, the vast majority of Israelites—eighty-five percent or more—were farmers. So, even if many or most of the biblical writers and editors were urbanites holding 'desk jobs,' they had grown up and still lived in close quarters with agriculturalists. Also, most urban residents in ancient Israel engaged in tilling the fields within walking distance of the city." Davis, "Propriety and Trespass," 74.

14. Warren, *Liturgy of the Ordinary*, 71.

15. Meyers, "Food in the First Family," 137.

without a source for food, creaturely existence is impossible. And it is through the daily divine provision of this physical need for food that humanity and animals experience the sovereign care of the Creator.

Since this physical need for food is a foundational reality of life, this dimension of food can easily be exploited for rhetorical effect. As will be seen in the texts below, the experience of a lack of food—whether actual or perceived—can quickly provoke anxiety and fear as the awareness of the possibility of imminent death begins to surface.

Physical Dimension of Food in Narratives from Israel's History (Exod 16:3; 17:3; Num 20:4; 21:5)

Israel's time in the wilderness put them in a context where the reality of death by starvation or dehydration was an ever-present possibility. Without divine intervention, the nation would have quickly perished within this desolate environment. We see Israel's food fears expressed at various times in the narrative. The narrator gives voice to these concerns both at the start and concluding years of Israel's journey. The Israelites' fear of starvation begins to surface as they enter the wilderness (Exod 16:3): "If only we had died by the hand of YHWH in the land of Egypt, when we sat by pots of meat and ate our fill of bread; for you have brought us out into this wilderness to kill (מות) this whole assembly with hunger (רעב)." The Israelite's fear of death by dehydration follows later in Exod 17:3b: "Why did you bring us out of Egypt, to kill (מות) us and our children and livestock with thirst (צמא)?" By including their children and cattle in the complaint, the Israelites draw their circle of concern even wider, thus intensifying their accusation against Moses.

Israel's discontent later in their desert journey echoes these earlier complaints, although their fear of starvation has now been replaced by their dissatisfaction with the current provision of manna. Their concern for death by dehydration, however, remains as the Israelites quarrel with Moses: "Why have you brought the assembly of YHWH into this wilderness for us and our livestock to die (מות) here?" (Num 20:4). Israel's frustration with their wilderness food experience escalates in their complaint in Num 21:5: "Why have you brought us up out of Egypt to die (מות) in the wilderness? For there is no food (לחם) and no water (מים), and we loathe this miserable food (לחם הקלקל)." The reality of death by dehydration—with an undercurrent of dissatisfaction with manna—fuels both these wilderness complaints in Numbers.

As witnessed in YHWH's continuous provision of food and water on their wilderness journey, the Israelites' complaints are in fact unfounded. However, the rhetorical force of their argument gains its persuasive strength from the physical dimension of food and the reality of death by starvation and dehydration if left alone in this wilderness environment.

Physical Dimension of Food in the Psalms (Ps 102)

In the Psalter, the physical dimension of food is often drawn upon in laments to express the desperation of the petitioner. In Psalm 102, the psalmist acknowledges the extent of their physical distress focusing on a lack of appetite (v. 5): "I have forgotten to eat my food" (שכחתי מאכל לחמי).[16] Later in v. 10, the psalmist draws from the language of food to express desperation, this time by describing their fast with language of eating and drinking: "For I eat ashes for food and mix tears with my drink" (כי אפר כלחם אכלתי ושקוי בבכי מסכתי). Here the desperation of the psalmist is emphasized as the nearness of death brought on by illness or some other physical distress is a looming reality. In both complaints, the physical dimension of food language is used to magnify the psalmist's anguish.

The Sensory Dimension: Perception, Taste, and Experience

A second significant aspect of food is its sensory dimension. Food is experienced primarily through the sense of taste, although sight and smell are often involved as well.[17] Possibly as a result of the various ways food is experienced, there are also a variety of associations connected to the sensory dimension of food. A primary association is the connection of taste with perception. Avrahami notes: "The sense of taste is a critical sense with which we learn about and analyze the world."[18] In Job 12:11 (cf. 34:3), the ideas of taste and perception are drawn closely together when

16. Smend observes that for the psalmist the boundaries between physiology and psychology are fluid. Smend, "Essen und Trinken," 448.

17. In her book *The Senses of Scripture: Sensory Perception in the Hebrew Bible*, Yael Avrahami explores synaesthetic links in biblical texts where multiple senses are engaged or referenced by the author.

18. Avrahami, *Senses of Scripture*, 95.

Job queries his friend Zophar: "Does not the ear test words as the palate tastes food?" (הלא אזן מלין תבחן וחך אכל יטעם לו). Avrahami notes that the metaphorical use of adjectives that apply to taste (e.g., sweet and bitter) can signify "a concrete assessment of food, and an abstract assessment of anything else in reality (such as speech, human behavior, and more)."[19] The sensory dimension of food can also be used to describe physical and spiritual experiences,[20] employing verbs such as "to be hungry" (רעב), "to be satisfied" (שבע), "to desire" (אוה), and "to be filled" (מלא). Taste also has an aesthetic aspect. As Kass observes: "Tastes and flavors are both recognized and appreciated for themselves, quite apart from the quenching of hunger or the subsequent usefulness of the food."[21] He goes on to remark that the sheer delight in experience "stirs the soul beyond concern for the merely necessary, transcending the preoccupation with survival, indeed, in the very activity whose main purpose is to promote survival."[22] As will be seen in the examples below, the sensory dimension of food provides the biblical authors with a palate rich with associations.

Sensory Dimension of Food in Narratives from Israel's History (Josh 9:3–15)

Joshua 9:3–15 describes a ruse involving food where the Gibeonites trick Israel into making a covenant of peace.[23] The narrator notes that the Gibeonites act their part with cunning (ערמה),[24] donning worn-out clothes and sandals, carrying patched wineskins and provisions of dry and crumbly bread. This final element of their disguise—their virtually inedible food—becomes the central evidence for the Gibeonites' claim of authenticity. In v. 13, the Gibeonites exclaim: "Here is our bread; it

19. Avrahami, *Senses of Scripture*, 95.

20. Considering the theological aspect of taste, Episcopal priest and writer Robert Capon muses: "To be sure, food keeps us alive, but that is only its smallest and most temporary work. Its *eternal* purpose is to furnish our sensibilities against the day when we shall sit down at the heavenly banquet and see how gracious the Lord is. Nourishment is necessary only for a while; what we shall need forever is *taste*." Capon, *Supper of the Lamb*, 40.

21. Kass, *Hungry Soul*, 89.

22. Kass, *Hungry Soul*, 89–90.

23. L. Daniel Hawk comments on the literary and rhetorical play across the whole episode. Hawk, *Joshua*, 138–44.

24. The adjective ערום is used to describe the serpent in Gen 3:1, another occasion involving food and deception.

was hot when we took it from our houses as provisions, on the day we set out to come to you, but now, see, it is dry and it is crumbling." Here the sensory dimension of food proves to be the crux of the encounter (v. 14), as "the men sampled their provisions" (ויקחו האנשים מצידם) as the means of truth-seeking.[25] The rhetorical power of this episode lies in Israel's choice to trust their own "taste-test" instead of seeking guidance from "the mouth of YHWH" (פי יהוה).[26]

Sensory Dimension of Food in the Psalms (Ps 34)

Psalm 34's acrostic structure makes it a difficult psalm to classify. Its tone is didactic, although it possesses the elements of an individual thanksgiving psalm.[27] The psalmist draws on the language of food twice in the psalm (vv. 9, 11). Verse 9 emphasizes the sensory dimension of food: "Taste and see that YHWH is good" (טעמו וראו כי טוב יהוה). Mays construes the verb "to taste" in a general sense, as to "find out by experience."[28] Jacobson reads the text literally as the psalmist's experience of a sacrificial meal accompanying a thanksgiving ritual, noting: "Here the poetry of the psalm invites people to experience God's goodness sensually—by tasting, smelling, and consuming the gifts of creation."[29] This literal sense of eating food gains added weight from the second reference to food in v. 11. Here the psalmist draws again from the sensory dimension of food, contrasting the hunger (רעב) of young lions with the satisfaction of those who seek YHWH. Unlike the lions, those who seek YHWH will not lack (לא חסר; cf. Ps 23:1) any good thing—the assumed referent here being "food." (v. 11).[30] Here in Psalm 34, food's sensory dimension becomes the invitation to experience YHWH's goodness in tangible form.

25. Both the subject and action are ambiguous here. Woudstra notes three possible options for the scenario: the Gibeonites are exhibiting their provisions, Israel is sampling the provisions, or this is a communal eating of bread as a covenantal ritual. Scholars almost universally assume the second option. Woudstra, *Book of Joshua*, 159.

26. Robert Hubbard notes: "Their actions naively trust the matter to their human senses rather than to divine guidance." Hubbard, *Joshua*, 286.

27. Mays, *Psalms*, 151.

28. Mays, *Psalms*, 153.

29. DeClaissé-Walford et al., *Book of Psalms*, 326.

30. Craigie observes: "The young lions thus symbolize the essence of self-sufficiency in the provision of physical needs. In contrast, those who fear the Lord are not self-sufficient; they depend on another, God, for the provision of their basic needs. And yet, as the psalmist demonstrates, it is the self-sufficient predators of this world who

The Social Dimension: Food as an Expression of Social Cohesion

In addition to its physical and sensory dimensions, food consumption often has a social dimension as well. In many instances, food consumption and social bonding begin simultaneously when a newborn infant feeds at its mother's breast. Within the context of family life, the daily sharing of food provides a cohesive center for maintaining and strengthening relational ties. Within the larger sphere of community life, formal meals often seek to enact a symbolic sense of familial cohesion among strangers.

For sociologists and anthropologists, the study of meal practices provides a window into cultures and ethnic communities.[31] As anthropologist Veronika Grimm aptly notes: "Food habits are a language through which a society expresses itself."[32] Patterns of food consumption define social grouping, often serving symbolic functions. Food choices can define communities through taste and ingredients,[33] as well as by the manner in which one eats.[34] These details of food consumption often symbolically express cultural and community priorities. For much of the world, the act of eating out of a common pot or plate becomes a daily symbolic act that reinforces the centrality of family and community. Thus, one finds that social groups are defined and differentiated, as anthropologist Gillian Feeley-Harnik notably quips, "by who eats what with whom."[35]

Social status can also be symbolically expressed in mealtime gatherings. Communal consumption provides an avenue for people

---

would lack, while the God-fearing would have all their needs met." Craigie and Tate, *Psalms 1–50*, 280.

31. For an introduction to the conversation on food in the social sciences, see Mintz and Du Bois, "Anthropology of Food and Eating," 99–119; Beardsworth and Keil, *Sociology on the Menu*. Two classic works that provide theoretical categories for the discussion are Goody, *Cooking, Cuisine, and Class*; Harris, *Good to Eat*. For a survey of the vast array of intersections between food and culture, see Solomon H. Katz's three-volume compendium *Encyclopedia of Food and Culture*.

32. Grimm, *From Feasting to Fasting*, 3.

33. For a discussion of the relationship between food preference and social identity, see Arnott's edited collection of essays in *Gastronomy*; MacBeth, *Food Preferences and Taste*.

34. For a lively discussion of eating utensils and their significance, see Visser, *Rituals of Dinner*, 167–96.

35. Feeley-Harnik, *Lord's Table*, 11. In regard to contemporary American culture, she notes: "It is not irrelevant that the lunch counter was an important focus of the civil rights movement of the 1960s" (13).

to demonstrate the nature and extent of relationships. In this regard, anthropologist Mary Douglas argues that individual meals possess a language of their own.[36] To illustrate this point, she "codes" a full day of ordinary meals within her own household using an elaborate system of classifications for the types of food eaten during the day. She observed that meals—as seen through the patterns of social relations being expressed at the table—encode a message about "different degrees of hierarchy, inclusion and exclusion, boundaries and transactions across boundaries."[37] In her study, Douglas identified a set of patterns that mark the extent of relational intimacy among those who share certain foods. She observed that drinks were typically shared with strangers, acquaintances, and co-workers; meals, on the other hand, were enjoyed together by family, close friends, and honored guests. She concludes that it is the structured context of the meal that both provides and maintains social boundaries.[38] A significant social threshold is therefore crossed when a guest is invited to share a meal.

Social Dimension of Food in Narratives from Israel's History (2 Sam 9)

While there are a variety of texts that could illustrate the social dimension of food, an example from the life of David—a key figure from Psalm 78—seems apropos. After David's kingdom has been established in Jerusalem, David seeks to honor the memory of Jonathan by inquiring if anyone remains of the house of Saul (2 Sam 9:1). Mephibosheth, a son of Jonathan crippled from childhood, receives the king's generous attention and is invited to sit at the king's table. While there are political and pragmatic implications to David's hospitality, Brueggemann contends that here "the accent is on generosity and the honoring of Mephibosheth."[39]

36. Douglas, "Deciphering a Meal," 249–75.

37. Douglas, "Deciphering a Meal," 249.

38. Douglas, "Deciphering a Meal," 256. Douglas concluded: "The grand operator of the system is the line between intimacy and distance. Those we know at meals we also know at drinks. The meal expresses close friendship. Those we only know at drinks we know less intimately. So long as this boundary matters to us (and there is no reason to suppose it will always matter) the boundary between drinks and meals has meaning."

39. Brueggemann, *First and Second Samuel*, 262. Brueggemann is countering the argument that eating at the king's table provided David a way to keep an eye on an heir of Saul.

Not only does this gesture designate a rise in social status,[40] but the narrator also construes this act with symbolic social significance. The narrator concludes the episode (2 Sam 9:11b) by commenting that Mephibosheth ate at David's table "as one of the king's sons" (כאחד מבני המלך). David's inclusion of Mephibosheth in continuous meal fellowship draws on the symbolic link between communal eating and family solidarity. With this invitation of table fellowship, David provides a tangible expression of welcome into his family. As Alter observes: "Mephibosheth's condition is ostensibly that of an unofficially adopted son."[41] Through this food event, social cohesion finds symbolic expression.

Social Dimension of Food in the Psalms (Ps 41)

In contrast, Psalm 41 draws on the social dimension of meals to highlight the pain of broken relationship. Here the psalmist struggles against the antagonism of his enemies while still expressing praise for YHWH's deliverance and sustaining power. One of the images used in the psalm's lament is the experience of broken meal fellowship. Verse 10 (ET 9) notes: "Even my close friend in whom I trusted, who ate my bread, has lifted up his heel against me." The offender is described by three phrases that reflect relational intimacy—my close friend (איש שלומי), my trusted one (בטחתי בו), and "the one who ate my bread" (אוכל לחמי).[42] Here it is not only the act of violence that leads the psalmist to cry out, but also the social disruption underlying this act. For here, the solidarity created by meal fellowship has been abandoned and spurned.

The Locational Dimension: Food as a Regionally Determined Reality

An often-overlooked dimension of food in the modern world is its locational nature. With the reality of globalization in the modern economy, a morning meal can be composed of products grown and produced across

40. As seen in other Hebrew Bible texts (1 Kgs 2:7; 18:19; 2 Kgs 25:27–29; cf. Jer 52:31–33), an invitation to the king's table represents an expression of "royal personage and special favor." McCarter, *II Samuel*, 261.

41. Alter, *David Story*, 243.

42. A fitting modern translation of this phrase would be the term "companion" (lit. "one who shares bread"; from the Latin *com*: "with" + *panis*: "bread").

the world (e.g., coffee sourced from Ethiopia, berries picked in California, bananas shipped in from Honduras). For most of history, however, diet has been determined by location, not by personal preference.

The food potential of Egypt, the wilderness of Sinai, and the land of Canaan are of particular concern within the biblical text.[43] Throughout history, Egypt has been known for the stable food supplies available along the Nile River. While Egypt experienced occasional famines (e.g., Gen 41:54–57), more often than not it became a refuge for the neighboring regions in times of agricultural crisis. The Israelites' experience of food in Egypt is only known through two food-related recollections during their journey in the wilderness.[44] Each depiction emphasizes the abundance and variety of foods remembered in this locale. In Exod 16:3b, the Israelites remember their time in Egypt as a time "when we sat by pots of meat and ate our fill of bread."[45] In Num 11:4b–5, the Israelites recall: "If only we had meat to eat! We remember the fish we used to eat in Egypt for nothing, the cucumbers, the melons, the leeks, the onions, and the garlic" (Num 11:4b–5). In both cases, Israel's grumbling over their imagined abundance in Egypt is a verbal attack, an attempt to persuade God to provide them with these same kinds of provisions in their current reality.

In the biblical account of Israel's wilderness wanderings, the limitation of the desert landscape to provide nourishment is noted with great frequency (i.e., Exod 16:3; 17:3b; Num 20:4; 21:5). Although there are references to naturally occurring water sources (Exod 15:27; cf. 15:23), the reality of the Sinai wilderness offered little in the way of sustenance. Thus, starvation and dehydration were a constant fear.

It is in the midst of the wilderness that the fecundity of Canaan becomes a central point of attention. References to Canaan as the land that flows with "milk and honey" (חלב ודבש) appear in a variety of contexts

43. As noted in chapter 1, the definition given for "food" includes examples of not just solid nourishment but liquid nourishment. The availability of potable water drives not just the wilderness narratives but other biblical accounts as well (e.g., Hagar in Gen 21:15–19).

44. In Joseph's entertaining of his brothers at table (Gen 43:32–34), no food elements are actually described. The social dimension is the central focus of the account—both exclusion (Egyptian and the Hebrews served separately, v. 32) and social honor (Benjamin given a significantly greater portion at the meal, v. 34).

45. Regarding this nostalgia for Egypt, Ellen Davis notes: "It is telling that they long for the food of Egypt—at least, the food that they imagine they might have enjoyed in Egypt." She goes on to note: "Meat, however, was eaten chiefly by the wealthy. So the Israelites speak more accurately than they may themselves realize when they recall sitting beside the fleshpots, eating bread." Davis, *Scripture, Culture, and Agriculture*, 70.

and serve as a striking commentary on the land's agricultural potential (Exod 3:8, 17; 13:5; 33:3; Lev 20:24; Num 13:27; 14:8; 16:13–14; Deut 6:3; 11:9; 26:9, 15; 27:3; 31:20). These comments about an abundant promised future (i.e., "milk and honey" in Canaan) have significant rhetorical value within the narrative storyline.[46] For God's promise of abundant food in a future land often served as the means of motivation for Israel to pursue and then continue on their journey through the wilderness.

Deuteronomy's depiction of Canaan's agricultural plenty has been used for various reconstructions of an ancient Israelite diet. However, one needs to give pause before assuming too much from this encyclopedic description of agricultural bounty:

> For YHWH your God is bringing you into a good land, a land with flowing streams, with springs and underground waters welling up in valleys and hills, a land of wheat and barley, of vines and fig trees and pomegranates, a land of olive trees and honey, a land where you may eat bread without scarcity, where you will lack nothing, a land whose stones are iron and from whose hills you may mine copper. You shall eat your fill and bless YHWH your God for the good land that he has given you. (Deut 8:7–10)

Most scholars acknowledge that the foodstuffs mentioned on this list could all be *grown* in the land of Israel. However, the point needs to be raised whether they were all, in fact, *eaten* by the average Israelite. Factors such as historical time period, geographic location, socioeconomic status, and even gender would influence the kinds of foods available to a specific population within Israel.[47] In a rain-reliant agricultural system, the frequent realities of drought and resulting famine also would affect food supplies. Thus, there is a need to distinguish between the fullest possible listing of foods available in ancient Israel and the likely components of the common diet.

Three crops dominated agricultural life in Israel—grains, grapes, and olives. These three agricultural crops—and their derivative food products—have come to be known as "the Mediterranean triad" and

46. Welton offers an intriguing argument that the expression "milk and honey" is a hendiadys to express "all food" from the ordinary—in this case milk—to the exceptional or rare, here depicted as honey. Welton, "Ethnographic and Biblical Studies," 18–19.

47. This concern for an accurate portrayal of the diet of ancient Israelites is the driving concern of Nathan MacDonald's study of the topic in *What Did the Ancient Israelites Eat?*

would have been foundational components of the average diet of an ancient Israelite.

Grains were the most important of the triad in terms of their contribution to diet. Magen Broshi estimates that bread or other grain-based foods would have contributed more than half the calorific intake of most inhabitants.[48] Both wheat and barley grew in Canaan, although wheat was the preferred crop for human consumption.[49] By far the most common way to consume grains was in the form of bread,[50] although grains could also be made into porridges or pan-roasted.[51]

A second member of the agricultural triad is the grapevine and its derivative product of wine. Unlike the regions of Egypt and Mesopotamia, the climate and soil of Palestine allow for grapevines to grow and thrive.[52] As Broshi notes: "Wine-growing in Palestine had hardly any geographical limits—vine was cultivated on almost any arable land, from the ridges of the Galilean Heights to the Negev. This is attested by thousands of winepresses found in all parts of the country."[53] Similar to contemporary practices, wine is often classified not only by age, but also by its geographic origin. As Broshi notes: "No other agricultural product

48. Broshi observes that these percentages have remained relatively constant even to the present time: "This is the case even today among the Arab population in Judea and Samaria, who consume 1330 calories from cereals, out of an average consumption of 2776 calories (i.e. 48 per cent)." Broshi, "Diet of Palestine," 123. Broshi's calculations for ancient Israelite diet are based upon the description of a "food basket" found in a Talmudic ruling that addresses the expected food ration that a husband must provide for his estranged wife (*m. Ket.* 5.8–9).

49. MacDonald, *What Did the Ancient Israelites Eat?*, 20–21.

50. This reliance on grains, and even more specifically bread, underlies the fact that the Hebrew word לחם is used not only for bread specifically but can also refer to food in a general sense. It also should be noted that wheat and barley are also core ingredients in making beer. Although there is debate about the referent for the Hebrew term שכר (often translated "strong drink"), Ebeling argues for the likelihood that this term refers to beer. She points to the simple fact that most nonbrewers overlook, namely that "the ingredients for making beer are the same required to make a basic loaf of leavened bread: cereal grains, water, and yeast." Ebeling, "Grains, Beer, and Bread," 109.

51. As Borowski notes: "In season, grain could be eaten fresh (whole or mashed) and when dry it could be parched or roasted for immediate consumption. Whole or cracked (Arabic *bulghur*, Turkish *burghul*) grain could be used in gruel (Gen 25:29, 34) and stew." Borowski, "Eat, Drink, and Be Merry," 99.

52. It is not that grapevines were utterly absent from the lands of Egypt and Mesopotamia. Walsh notes that royal vineyards would still have been cultivated, although the production of these vines would have been greatly affected by adverse growing conditions. Walsh, *Fruit of the Vine*, 21–27.

53. Broshi, "Wine in Ancient Palestine," 147.

depends as much on its geographical origin as wine, since the area of cultivation determines its quality and taste. Consequently, great importance is attached to the indication of place of origin—country, province, adjacent settlement, and even the particular vineyard."[54] The locational restrictions (e.g., soil and climate) for cultivating grapevines made wine a highly sought-after commodity among Israel's neighbors.[55] In particular, Egypt generally lacked the requisite temperature differentials needed for the fruiting and maturing of grapevines.[56] In addition to being used for wine, grapes also served as a supplement to the diet during the summer/autumn when they could be picked off the vines or sun-dried into raisins.

The third member of the triad is the olive/olive oil. Olive trees thrive in a Mediterranean climate and in the rocky, shallow soil of the highlands and foothills of Canaan.[57] Because of Canaan's excellent growing conditions, olive oil production became a major industry with surpluses exported to surrounding regions.[58] Olives provided a basic food product for ancient Israelites, primarily through the pressing of the fruit for oil.[59]

While grains would have provided the majority of one's daily calories, legumes (e.g., chickpeas, lentils, fava beans) may have been responsible for providing the needed dietary protein.[60] Legumes, however, are rarely mentioned in the Hebrew Bible.[61] Seasonal fruits and vegetables could be grown in parts of Canaan, but to what extent they were a part of a typical diet cannot be determined with certainty.[62]

54. Broshi, "Wine in Ancient Palestine," 149. For a full account of winemaking in ancient Israel, see Walsh, *Fruit of the Vine*, 87–193.

55. MacDonald, *What Did the Ancient Israelites Eat?*, 23. See also Stager, "First Fruits of Civilization," 172–87.

56. MacDonald notes that "temperatures need to be above 20°C during fruiting and below 10°C for some of the winter." MacDonald, *What Did the Ancient Israelites Eat?*, 22.

57. Borowski, *Agriculture in Iron Age Israel*, 118.

58. King and Stager, *Life in Biblical Israel*, 96. For a helpful study documenting olive oil production in ancient Israel, see Frankel, *Wine and Oil Production*.

59. Borowski contends that the raw fruit of the olive was not eaten as a foodstuff until salting and pickling methods were introduced in the Hellenistic or Roman periods. Borowski, *Agriculture in Iron Age Israel*, 123.

60. Regarding the place of legumes in an Israelite diet, Broshi notes: "They contain considerable amounts of protein but require cereal proteins to complement them for optimum value." Broshi, "Diet of Palestine," 126.

61. MacDonald finds only six references—four references to lentils, two references to flat beans. MacDonald, *What Did Ancient Israelites Eat?*, 26.

62. MacDonald notes: "Breads and porridges were probably supplemented ordinarily by vegetables, pulses and fruit. To what extent is unclear as these foodstuffs rarely leave a trace in the archaeological record." MacDonald, *Not Bread Alone*, 61.

The prevalence of meat consumption in ancient Israel is an issue that has drawn much discussion.[63] When household meat consumption is noted in the biblical texts, these instances typically occur in the context of royal banqueting (e.g., 1 Kgs 4:22–23) or hospitality offered to important guests (e.g., Gen 18:7–8; Judg 13:15).[64] While flocks and herds were regularly kept, their primary benefit would have been as living animals. Sheep and goats were kept for their milk, as well as for their wool/hair for textiles. Cattle served mainly as draft animals for farming. When meat was consumed,[65] there were clear restrictions on how it was to be processed (e.g., Lev 7:26–27; Deut 12:23–25) and what animals were restricted from Israel's diet (e.g., Lev 11; Deut 14:3–20).[66]

The survey above has provided a basic understanding of what would have been considered common and ordinary ingredients in an Israelite diet, as well as identifying what kinds of foodstuffs were regionally determined (e.g., wine), those that would have been counted as luxuries (e.g., meat) and those items excluded from an Israelite table (e.g., unclean animals). In addition, this discussion has sought to raise the awareness of the realities of food scarcities and deficiencies for an ancient Israelite diet.[67]

63. The growing field of archaeozoology—the scientific examination of animal bones recovered from archaeological excavations—has expanded our understanding of the place of meat in the diet of ancient Israelites. See discussion in MacDonald, *Not Bread Alone*, 62–65. Most scholars hold the view that meat would have been consumed only on rare occasions. See MacDonald, *What Did the Ancient Israelites Eat?*, 61–76; Meyers, "Food in the First Family," 143–44; King and Stager, *Life in Ancient Israel*, 68. These discussions of meat consumption focus primarily on domesticated animals. Ancient Israelites would also have consumed fish and birds, and to some degree wild game, as potential sources of meat. Fulton and Hesse, "Underrepresented Taxa," 171–82.

64. Meat was of course consumed within religious context as well. Milgrom observes: "The main function of all the well-being offerings is to provide meat for the table." Milgrom, *Leviticus*, 28.

65. The practice of culling flocks and herds would have also contributed meat for household use. For a discussion of this practice, see Boer, *Sacred Economy of Ancient Israel*, 62–64.

66. For a discussion of the basic issues involved in Israel's food laws, see Levine, *Leviticus*, 343–48; Milgrom, *Leviticus 1–16*, 704–42.

67. MacDonald notes: "A diet may contribute sufficient calories for survival, but be deficient in vitamins and minerals with serious consequences for human health. Indeed, as we shall see, a diet consisting of grain, legumes and olive oil has significant deficiencies." MacDonald, *Not Bread Alone*, 55–56.

Locational Dimension of Food in Narratives from Israel's History (Gen 18:1–8)

In Gen 18:1–8, Abraham welcomes three guests and provides them with a meal. The rhetorical irony of the event is heightened when close attention is paid to the description of the ingredients of this meal. After an invitation to his guests to come rest from their journey, Abraham proposes that "a little bread" (פת לחם) be brought to his guests (v. 5). A meal of "bread"—the mainstay of the diet in ancient Israel—would have been a typical offer to a guest. However, the modifier פת ("a small morsel")[68] strikes the reader as incongruous in a context of hospitality. Abraham's understatement may in fact be a statement of self-deprecation (cf. Gen 18:27). For as will be seen as the meal unfolds, the author's concern with the amount and quality of ingredients will be of central importance throughout. Following the guests' acceptance of Abraham's invitation, this small meal of bread quickly grows into a lavish feast composed of three different food groups: bread, meat, and dairy. This variety informs the reader that Abraham's meal was hardly a meager snack.

Abraham's preparations commence with a request for his wife Sarah to begin the process of making bread for his guests. The assigning of a woman in the household to the task of bread-making would have been typical in the division of household labor.[69] However, the quality of the ingredients and their quantity are noteworthy. Abraham insists that these cakes be made from "choice flour" (קמח סלת), an ingredient that was reserved for sacrificial offerings and fine breads.[70] The "three measures" (שלש סאים) of flour that Abraham requests is the equivalent to eight gallons/twenty-four liters of flour.[71] This second hyperbolic statement, immediately following the earlier reference to the smallness of the meal, serves to highlight the extravagance of Abraham's hospitality.

Abraham involves himself in preparations by selecting a calf and then requests that the servant hasten to prepare it (v. 7). Because of the economic liability of losing an animal in the herd, the inclusion of meat on this menu is unusual, especially Abraham's choice of a young calf (בן

68. This term appears only 14x in the MT—all referring to a small and insignificant amount.

69. For the role of women in bread-making, see Meyers, "From Field Crops to Food," 67–84.

70. King and Stager, *Life in Biblical Israel*, 358; Wenham, *Genesis 16–50*, 47.

71. Shafer-Elliot, *Food in Ancient Judah*, 144.

בקר). As Shafer-Elliot notes: "The hospitality meal Abraham ordered to be prepared was not standard. Most would have butchered a goat or sheep, which would have been more than generous."[72] Abraham specifically chooses this animal from the herd because it will be "tender and good" (רך וטוב), highlighting the fact that the host is calculating the sensory impact of this meal for his guests. Similar to the commands about bread preparation, here too Abraham focuses on the quality and the quantity of the extravagant provision for his guests.

When the meal is set before Abraham's guests, a third component is added to this meal, "curds and milk" (חמאה וחלב).[73] The narrative opens (18:1) with a reference to the time of day that this scene unfolds—during "the heat of the day" (חם היום). By focusing on the ingredients of this meal, one finds that Abraham drew from the ingredients readily available to him as a pastoralist. This meal of hospitality combined the ordinary (e.g., bread as a basic ingredient) and the extraordinary (e.g., meat). Through the use of hyperbole, the narrator heightens Abraham's stature as a host as this meal moves from "a small morsel of bread" to a lavish and tasty feast.

Locational Dimension of Food in the Psalms (Ps 104 and Pss 14/53)

The Psalter often draws on food language to depict God's gracious provision. In Psalm 104's hymn of God's providence in creation, the ingredients of the Mediterranean triad appear as a celebration of God's beneficent care of Israel: "You cause the grass to grow for the cattle, and plants for people to use, to bring forth food (לחם) from the earth, and *wine* (יין) to gladden the human heart, *oil* (שמן) to make the face shine, and *bread* (לחם) to strengthen the human heart" (vv. 14–15, italics mine). By referencing these three basic ingredients of daily life, the psalm presents a succinct argument for the holistic nature of God's care for humanity.

The components of the Mediterranean triad used in Psalm 104—bread (לחם), wine (יין), and oil (שמן)—occur with some regularity within

72. Shafer-Elliot, *Food in Ancient Judah*, 145.

73. While the consumption of dairy products is rarely mentioned in the biblical text, Welton argues that its inclusion here in Genesis 18 hints toward its more widespread enjoyment in daily life. She notes: "It therefore appears that non-household members, i.e. guests, are provided with dairy products as an explicit act of hospitality which the text points out in order to mark the offered fare as a generous diversion of food from the pastoral household's supply. Other household meals are not described as containing dairy, likely because dairy was available to household members throughout the day." Welton, "Ethnographic and Biblical Studies," 11.

the Psalter.[74] Of these three, the language of bread/food (לחם) appears the most often within the Psalter. The majority of occurrences of the term appear in contexts that celebrate God's general sustaining provision of food for humans and animals (i.e., Pss 37:25; 104:14–15; 132:15; 136:25; 146:7; 147:9) or in God's provision of food for Israel in the wilderness (i.e., Pss 78:20, 25; 105:40).

In addition to examples of divine provision, the regular place of bread in Israel's daily diet is employed with rhetorical nuance.[75] In Psalm 14 and Psalm 53,[76] the language of bread is used to describe the habitual nature of social injustice. Psalm 14:4 laments: "Have they no knowledge, all the evildoers who eat up my people as they eat bread, and do not call upon YHWH?" While the expression "to eat, devour" (אכל) is a stock expression for death or destruction, the additional phrase "as they eat bread" (אכלו לחם) draws on an image of life at table (cf. Ps 53:5).[77] Gunkel, commenting on this behavior, assumes that they devour God's people "as callously and indifferently as one eats bread."[78] Yet in light of the centrality of bread in the ancient Israelite diet, the habitual nature of this injustice seems more likely in view. As Hossfeld observes: "they do this day after day and regard it as 'perfectly normal.'"[79] By recognizing the centrality of bread in an ancient Israelite diet, the routine brutality of this injustice comes into sharp focus.

74. The word "bread, food" (לחם) occurs 19x (Pss 14:4; 37:25; 41:10; 42:4; 53:5; 78:20, 25; 80:6; 102:10; 104:14–15; 105:16, 40; 127:2; 132:15; 136:25; 146:7; 147:9). The word "wine" (יין) only 4x (60:5 [ET 3]; 75:9 [ET 8]; 78:65; 104:15). The word "oil" (שמן) occurs 10x (23:5; 45:8 [ET 7]; 55:22 [ET 21]; 89:21 [ET 20]; 92:11 [ET 10]; 104:15; 109:18, 24; 133:2; 141:5). Each of these three food groups—bread, wine, oil—have a variety of related words that could also be considered.

75. For a variety of rhetorical uses of "bread" language, see 14:4; 37:25; 41:10; 42:4; 53:5; 80:6; 102:10; 105:16; 127:2.

76. With the exception of differences in the use of the divine name (YHWH versus Elohim), Psalm 14 and Psalm 53 are largely identical in wording. For a discussion of the slight differences, see Hossfeld and Zenger, *Psalms 2*, 36–39.

77. Micah presents injustice in a much more provocative kitchen scene: "And I said: Listen, you heads of Jacob and rulers of the house of Israel! Should you not know justice?—you who hate the good and love the evil, who tear the skin off my people, and the flesh off their bones; who eat the flesh of my people, flay their skin off them, break their bones in pieces, and chop them up like meat in a kettle, like flesh in a caldron" (3:1–3 NRSV).

78. Quoted in Kraus, *Psalms 1–59*, 222.

79. Hossfeld and Zenger, *Psalms 2*, 43.

The Patterned Dimension: Showing a World in/out of Order

Food language—through its connection to patterned events—has the ability to present a picture of both an ordered and a disordered reality. This "world-ordering" aspect occurs through the logical progression or patterning of events that offer a picture of a stable and ordered world. In addition, this order can be destabilized when the patterning is intentionally broken. In this section, two arenas that relate specifically to food—agricultural process (i.e., food production) and hospitality (i.e., food consumption)—will be considered.

Food Production: Agricultural Process as a Patterned Activity

Agricultural patterning as a reflection of cosmic ordering is emphasized in God's promise found in Genesis 8 following the devastation of the flood:

> As long as the earth endures,
> seedtime and harvest, cold and heat,
> summer and winter, day and night,
> shall not cease. (v. 22)

This promise highlights the renewal of agricultural cycles, an order essential for growing food for the maintenance of physical life. While disruptions of agricultural cycles in the biblical texts are not always linked to divine judgment, they do always lead to social and economic disruption.

The Gezer Calendar provides a unique window into the rhythms of the farming year in ancient Israel.[80] It groups the twelve months of the farmer's year into eight consecutive seasons based on the required farming activities. It starts with the ingathering of autumn fruits:

> His two months are (olive) harvest,
> his two months are planting (grain),
> his two months are late planting;
> his month is hoeing up of flax,
> his month is harvest of barley,
> his month is harvest and feasting;
> his two months are vine-tending,
> his month is summer fruit.[81]

80. This Hebrew inscription was discovered during excavations at Gezer in 1908 and dates to the tenth century BCE. Scholars speculate about its purpose, some arguing that it could have been a young scribe's exercise. King and Stager, *Life in Biblical Israel*, 88.

81. Pritchard, *Ancient Near Eastern Texts Relating to the Old Testament*, 320.

Here an ordered account of the year is depicted through the lens of planting and harvesting.

Rolf Knierim contends that agricultural rhythms and seasons have a vital role in the biblical text to depict cosmic order.[82] Thomas Mann refers to this ordered reality as "food time."[83] He contends: "In addition to the sacred time of historical events (*Heilsgeschichte*), there is an 'uneventful' sacred time of creation (*Heilszeit*) that is seasonal and cyclical—when the rain comes, the crops grow, and the harvest is made, or when the 'fatted calf' is roasted."[84] In light of its patterned activity, agricultural production provides the biblical authors with a familiar image for depicting a world in order. Isaiah 28's "parable of the farmer" (vv. 23–29) draws on agricultural sequencing to paint a poignant picture of divine ordering in human events:

> Listen and hear my voice; Pay attention and hear my speech. Do those who plow for sowing plow continually? Do they continually open and harrow their ground? When they have leveled its surface, do they not scatter dill, sow cummin, and plant wheat in rows and barley in its proper place, and spelt as the border? For they are well instructed; their God teaches them. (vv. 23–26 NRSV)

Talmon calls attention to the detailed nature of this agricultural parable: "The author concretizes the abstract concept of a logical and consistent flow of history by presenting in persuasive detail a vignette-like portrayal of a farmer's equally logical and consistent procedures in raising his diverse crops."[85] The description of the ordered work of a farmer continues with the processing of agricultural products:

> Dill is not threshed with a threshing sledge, nor is a cartwheel rolled over cummin; but dill is beaten out with a stick, and cummin with a rod. Grain is crushed for bread, but one does not thresh it forever; one drives the cartwheel and horses over it but does not pulverize it. This also comes from the LORD of hosts; he is wonderful in counsel, and excellent in wisdom. (vv. 27–29 NRSV)

82. Knierim argues that God's preservation of this natural order is even more fundamental to Israel's understanding of their relationship to God as God's historical acts. Knierim, "Cosmos and History in Israel's Theology," 197. See also Stinson, "Summer and Winter, Seedtime and Harvest," 55–59.

83. Mann, "Not by Word Alone, 358.

84. Mann, "Not by Word Alone," 358.

85. Talmon, "Prophetic Rhetoric and Agricultural Metaphora," 271.

As Knierim observes: "The parable of the farmer in Isa 28:23–28 is paradigmatic for the Old Testament's own theological awareness of the fundamentality of the seasonal rhythm in which the farmer's activities of plowing and threshing are meaningful."[86] Here this agricultural rhythm is used rhetorically to instill trust in YHWH's hand in human affairs.[87]

While the agricultural cycle can depict a rightly ordered world, a departure from these patterns can also be used to show a world out of order. Drought, plagues, and warfare can all disrupt agricultural processes and drastically affect food supplies. If this disruption lasts long enough, it becomes a threat to human and animal existence. As Patricia Tull observes: "At one time it could simply have been assumed that prophecies about disrupted harvests would strike fear in any hearer's heart. They continue to resonate in regions of the world where food remains scarce."[88] Even simple deviations from the customary or expected agricultural pattern can be rhetorically significant. This can be seen in Mic 7:1: "Woe is me! For I have become like one who, after the summer fruit has been gathered, after the vintage has been gleaned, finds no cluster to eat; there is no first-ripe fig for which I hunger." Here disorder is pictured as Israel's vain search for summer figs long after the autumn grape harvest.[89] Talmon speculates that the author may be signifying "the people's contrariness through the reversal of the natural succession of the seasons."[90] Thus not only can agriculture's inherent patterns depict a world rightly ordered, but it can also provide a language for depicting a world in disarray.

86. Knierim, "Cosmos and History in Israel's Theology," 197.

87. As I have argued elsewhere: "For Judah, in the midst of impending invasion by the Assyrians, this parable may have held words of unexpected hope. Could it be that the inevitable judgment, like ploughing, would not last forever? And like the parable's sensible farmer, might God also know what tool to use in order to achieve a purposeful goal without destroying the nation? Might the pain of Judah's present moment belong, as Childs remarks, 'to a larger agricultural plan'?" Stinson, "Parable of the Sensible Farmer," 11.

88. Tull, "Persistent Vegetative States," 22. She acknowledges that this reality is easily missed by those who read the text from a situation of abundance: "The peril of famine no longer appears compelling or even particularly relevant in American locales where grocery shelves miraculously refill every night and health is compromised more often by too much food than too little."

89. Proverbs 26:10 picks up this same theme related to weather patterns and agriculture: "Like snow in summer and rain in harvest, so honor is not fitting to a fool."

90. Talmon, "Prophetic Rhetoric and Agricultural Metaphora," 277.

Patterned Dimension (Agriculture) in Narratives from Israel's History (Ruth)

The book of Ruth has an agricultural foundation that undergirds its narrative plotline. A famine in Canaan drives Elimelech and his family from Bethlehem to the land of Moab (1:1);[91] and it is news that YHWH has "visited his people in giving them food" that leads to Naomi and Ruth's return to Canaan (1:6). YHWH is here directly linked with the renewal of the natural order. It is this renewed ordering of creation that provides the temporal structure for the rest of the unfolding narrative. Naomi and Ruth return to Bethlehem "at the beginning of the barley harvest" (1:22b). Ruth's tenure working in Boaz's fields continued "until the end of the barley harvest and the wheat harvests" (2:23b). Here in the book of Ruth, it is agricultural "time"—told in the language of wheat and barley—that moves the story forward.

Patterned Dimension (Agriculture) in the Psalms (Ps 1)

The Psalter begins with an image of the world "in order," drawn from the realm of agriculture. Psalm 1:3 presents a picture of the life of the righteous: "That person is like a tree planted by streams of water that yields its fruit in its season, and its leaf does not wither. All they do prospers." In this psalm, the righteous one is depicted as a tree strategically planted by a water source and who "yields its fruit in its season" (פריו יתן בעתו)—an image reflecting the natural ordering of agricultural harvests. As Eidevall observes: "This is an image of the ideal condition: being at the same time both nourished and nourishing, both protected and productive."[92] In the Psalter, the expression "in its season/time" (בעתו) is used exclusively for God's provision of food through the regularity of seasonal growth of plants (Pss 1:3; 104:27; 145:15).[93] The fate of the wicked is also described

91. The locational dimension of food is also at work in this account. As Ellen Davis observes: "Bethlehem—'House of Bread'—is so named because in ancient times it served as the 'bread-basket' for nearby Jerusalem. . . . To this day it remains the most suitable place for growing grain in the vicinity of the capital city. The story begins with an ironic reversal of expectations, for it seems that now the pagan land of Moab (in modern Jordan) is more fertile than the promised land of Israel, with its House-of-Bread." Davis, *Who Are You, My Daughter?*, 5.

92. Eidevall, "Metaphorical Landscapes in the Psalms," 14.

93. Of its other nine uses in the MT, four instances relate to rain in its season (Deut

in the language of agriculture. Psalm 1:4 reads: "The wicked are not so, but are like chaff that the wind drives away." Here the psalmist is drawing upon an image from the processing of grain and the discarding of the chaff.[94] In the psalmist's picture of a rightly ordered world, one finds both blessing and judgment expressed in the natural ordering of agricultural processing. Here the righteous enjoy the fruitfulness of their actions and the wicked experience the result of their destructive actions, in this case being cast aside and forgotten like a useless and inedible by-product of food production (cf. Ps 35:5). Thus, we find that judgment, as well as blessing, is a part of God's ordering in the world.

Food Consumption: Hospitality as Patterned Experience Ruled by Expectations and Roles

Hospitality—as expressed in the provision of food to a guest, as well as shelter and protection—also has inherent patterns to its practice. Yet the patterns that undergird expressions of hospitality in the ancient world are often misread by modern readers. T. R. Hobbs challenges what he observes as the "teleological fallacy" found in biblical research on meal texts. He argues: "While there are a number of superficial similarities, conventions of hospitality presupposed by the First Testament writers are not to be confused with modern conventions of hospitality and the entertaining of guests. Both might involve the offer of food and shelter, but the two are really worlds apart."[95]

In the ancient world, hospitality involved social scripts with a set of rules and expectations for both host and guest. Scholars have put forth a variety of models to explain the social dynamics of hospitality, specifically as it was practiced in the ancient world. Julian Pitt-Rivers's 1968 article

---

11:14; 28:12; Jer 5:24; Ezek 34:26), two instances relate to the yearly agricultural production and processing of grain/wine (Job 5:26; Hos 2:9), and one instance refers to the regularity of constellations in their movement across the sky (Job 38:32). Two other instances in the Wisdom literature provide a variation of the other uses. Proverbs 15:23 refers to a "word in season" as a comparison to "an apt answer." And the expression in Eccl 3:11 follows the Teacher's juxtaposed polarities of appointed times/events, concluding: "He has made everything suitable for its time; moreover he has put a sense of past and future into their minds, yet they cannot find out what God has done from the beginning to the end."

94. The process of winnowing extracts edible kernels of grain from their outer husks called "chaff" through relying on wind to blow the lighter shell of the kernel away. King and Stager, *Life in Biblical Israel*, 89.

95. Hobbs, "Hospitality in the First Testament," 28.

"The Stranger, the Guest, and the Hostile Host: Introduction to the Study of the Laws of Hospitality" undergirds much of the conversation about hospitality in the biblical texts.[96] Pitt-Rivers argues that universal laws of hospitality (versus cultural codes of conduct) govern the interactions between host and guest.[97]

These laws of hospitality are most plainly seen when either the host or the guest violates the laws. Pitt-Rivers observes the following "laws" at work in the expectations established for hospitality's roles of guest and host. A guest infringes the "law" of hospitality:[98]

1. If he insults his host or shows any hostility or rivalry.
2. If he usurps the role of his host.
3. If, on the other hand, he refuses what is offered, he infringes the role of guest. Food and drink always have ritual value, for the ingestion together of a common substance creates a bond.

A host may infringe upon the "law" of hospitality in the follow reciprocal ways:[99]

1. If he insults his guest or shows any hostility or rivalry.
2. If he fails to protect his guest or the honor of this guest.
3. If he fails to attend to his guests, to grant them the precedence which is their due, to show concern for their needs and wishes, or in general to earn the gratitude which guests should show.

Mutual agreement on roles and duties guide the interactions of the two parties who often have no common history or prior relationship. For the duration of the interaction under the roof of the host, the guest's conduct

96. Pitt-Rivers, "Stranger," 13–30. A similar protocol for biblical hospitality has been proposed by Old Testament scholar Victor Matthews and New Testament scholar Bruce Malina. See Matthews, "Hospitality and Hostility," 3–11, and "Hospitality and Hostility in Judges 4," 13–21. See also Malina, "Received View," 171–94.

97. Pitt-Rivers notes that while expressions of hospitality are as varied as the cultures in which they are found: "Yet a certain general sense informs them all, entitling us to talk about the law of hospitality in the abstract in contrast to the specific codes of hospitality exemplified by different cultures. There is, so to speak, a 'natural law' of hospitality deriving not from divine revelation like so many particular codes of law, but from sociological necessity." Pitt-Rivers, "Stranger," 27.

98. Pitt-Rivers, "Stranger," 27–28. The following two lists are an abbreviated version of the originals that appear in the text.

99. Pitt-Rivers, "Stranger," 28.

is restricted in certain ways, and the guest is required to respond appropriately for the occasion.

The sharing of food at a meal binds guest and host together in a common experience. In a meal of hospitality, the host initiates the relationship between the two parties with an invitation to dine. The location of the meal establishes the spatial territory for the host's authority, for "a host is a host only on the territory over which on a particular occasion he claims authority. Outside it he cannot maintain the role."[100] This bounded aspect to responsibilities prompts the courtesy of showing a guest to the door or the gate at the end of the meal, an action that exhibits the host's concern for the guest's welfare, as well as establishing the boundary point at which the host is free from responsibility.

The nature of the relationship of host and guest requires that each respect the complementarity of their roles. Regarding this mutual agreement, Margaret Visser notes: "Both sides accept, for the sake of peace, order, and the benefit of the whole community, to be constrained by intricate sets of obligations."[101] However, once an infringement of the laws of hospitality occurs, the structure of the roles is destroyed. Within this new reality, "failure to return honour or avoid disrespect entitles the person slighted in this way to relinquish his role and revert to the hostility which it suppressed."[102] Failure to abide by the expectations of hospitality leads to disruption of the symbolic social structure. As Pitt-Rivers notes, "once they are no longer host and guest they are enemies, not strangers."[103]

Patterned Dimension (Hospitality) in Narratives from Israel's History (Judg 4:17–22)

The patterned dimension of hospitality is overturned in the meal in Judg 4:17–22, one of many scenes in the book that relies on situational reversal.[104] In this passage, the unexpected arrival of the man Sisera, the leader of the enemy army, at the tent of Jael, a Kenite woman, produces a scene that begins in hospitality and ends in hostility. This meal of hospitality contains numerous breaches of etiquette related to the roles of host and

100. Pitt-Rivers, "Stranger," 26.

101. Visser, *Rituals of Dinner*, 91.

102. Pitt-Rivers, "Stranger," 29.

103. Pitt-Rivers, "Stranger," 29.

104. For a discussion of ironic reversals in the book of Judges as a whole, see Klein, *Triumph of Irony in Judges*; Wenham, *Story as Torah*, 45–72.

guest. Here it is Jael, a woman, who offers hospitality to this foreign man. While this practice is not unknown, traditionally it is the man of the house who issues an invitation of hospitality.[105] A violation in etiquette occurs when Sisera usurps the role of host by directly requesting drink and protection (v. 19).[106] As noted above, once the laws of hospitality are violated, the relationship between host and guest dissolves. When these roles are disbanded, this meal of welcome becomes a context for violence.

Patterned Dimension (Hospitality) in the Psalms (Ps 23)

Psalm 23—a psalm of trust—provides a striking image of divine provision and protection in the Psalter. This psalm breaks into two sections: a picture of pastoral care of a shepherd and sheep (vv. 1–4) and the formal hospitality of a host and guest (vv. 5–6).

In Psalm 23, the patterned reality of hospitality undergirds the psalmist's two images of confident trust. Verses 1–4 present a pastoral scene of shepherd and sheep. Here the shepherd's provision of food is both appropriate and abundant. Eidevall aptly observes: "The metaphorical landscape evoked by the opening lines features two things: pasture and water (vv. 1–2). Nothing more is mentioned. . . . Now, what does a sheep need to survive, besides a good shepherd, for guidance and protection? Grass and water."[107] And in this instance, the food is in abundant supply. Goldingay observes: "Causing the flock to lie down there rather than simply feed suggests ample provision. It implies that they have eaten, are satisfied, and have no need to move on to look for further grass: this pasture will provide the next meal, too."[108] While this scene also acknowledges the reality of danger, the shepherd's presence is a tangible source of security (v. 4). In the second section of the psalm (vv. 5–6), the scene moves to one of host and human guest. Here, too, the food provision is appropriate to the guest and abundant. Instead of pastures and flowing streams (v. 2), the host "sets a table" (תערך . . . שלחן) and

105. As noted by Matthews, "Hospitality and Hostility in Judges 4," 15–16.

106. Surprisingly, Gudme's excellent article on hospitality and violence in the Hebrew Bible never addresses this particular infringement of the law of hospitality in Judges 4. Gudme, "Invitation to Murder," 101–3.

107. Eidevall, "Metaphorical Landscapes in the Psalms," 16.

108. Goldingay, *Psalms*, 1:349.

offers an "overflowing cup" (כוסי רויה) for his human guest (v. 5).[109] Here, too, the reality of danger and the host's protective presence is emphasized (vv. 5–6). As Kraus notes: "Yahweh makes his appearance as the beneficent host who visibly sets the table for one who is persecuted and in this way takes him into the sphere of his protection."[110] These two food images find their rhetorical force in the ordered reality of hospitality—a context of protection from both hunger and harm.

RHETORICAL POTENTIAL OF FOOD LANGUAGE IN THE HEBREW BIBLE

As seen in both narrative and poetic texts, the biblical authors employ various dimensions of food for rhetorical effect. Yet the question remains: Why might the biblical authors be drawn to use the language of food? The remainder of this chapter argues that food language provides a rhetorically rich medium because of its familiarity, its literary flexibility, and its multidimensionality.[111]

Based on his study of the metaphorical use of agriculture in biblical prophetic speech, Shemaryahu Talmon observes a tendency for the biblical authors to draw from "motifs, patterns and parables which are derived from experiences in which they and their audience share."[112] There is a growing consensus that familiarity with land care and farming was a fundamental reality shared by both biblical writers and their audience.[113] Whether in the daily rhythms of food consumption or the yearly cycles of food production, these ordinary experiences of life provided a common language for communication. Thus, the simple factor of familiarity in the form of a basic shared reality can partially explain the prevalence of food references within the biblical text.

As seen in this small sampling of texts, food language has great literary flexibility. The biblical authors draw on literal and metaphorical depictions of food production, distribution, preparation, and consumption.

109. Kirkpatrick observes: "He provides for the joys as well as the necessities of life." Kirkpatrick, *Psalms 1–41*, 127.

110. Kraus, *Psalms 1–59*, 308.

111. Contra Reed who argues for a solely theological basis for the Psalms' use of food language. Reed, "Food in the Psalms," 503.

112. Talmon, "Prophetic Rhetoric and Agricultural Metaphora," 267.

113. In particular, see the work of Ellen F. Davis who has championed this view, most notably in *Scripture, Culture, and Agriculture*.

Food events provide both the context and the content of discussion in examples from the narratives of Genesis, Exodus, Numbers, Deuteronomy, Joshua, Judges, Ruth, and Samuel. Uncertain food supplies bring about fear (Exodus/Numbers) and restored production brings hope (Ruth). Food consumption is associated with deception (Joshua), welcome (Genesis, 2 Samuel), and death (Judges). Food language's literary flexibility allows for metaphorical usage as seen in Psalms 1, 14/53, 23, 34, 41, 102, and 104. Food language is used to describe an ordered world (Ps 1), human injustice (Ps 14; cf. Ps 53), social disruption (Ps 41), and the experience of distress (Ps 102). In the Psalms, food language depicts YHWH's gracious provision as a host (Ps 23) and Sustainer of creation (Ps 104), as well as a celebration of divine-human relationship (Ps 34). Thus, one finds that food language's literary flexibility contributes to its rhetorical power as it is used both literarily and figuratively across various genres and contexts.

Finally, food language's multidimensionality allows the biblical authors to draw on a constellation of food dimensions at any one time, exploiting the complex web of associations. This can be the physical dimension of food's life-sustaining quality or the sensory dimension of food's pleasurableness. With the emotional and social realities of community life, food language can be used to speak of community cohesion and disruption. Because of food's locational dimension, food language can evoke the ordinariness and extraordinariness of a situation. The patterned dimension of food allows an author to use food language to depict order and chaos, hospitality and hostility. Each dimension has a powerful rhetorical potential. Yet when multiple dimensions of food are referenced, a compounded rhetorical effect is created. In these cases, the audience is confronted with an image or scenario with increasing conceptual complexity—engaging the audience on multiple levels of experience (e.g., emotional, visceral, intellectual). There is a synergy as multiple dimensions collide in one food reference. In addition, because of food language's primarily positive associations (e.g., life, pleasure, community, order), when it is used to depict judgment or distress, there is a profound sense of disorder and shock that arises from this reversal.

CONCLUSION

This chapter has provided a primer on the various dimensions of food in the Hebrew Bible. While these dimensions would have been familiar to an ancient Israelite, modern readers tend to overlook or misinterpret the significance of food references in the text. Differentiating these five foundational dimensions of food—the physical, sensory, social, locational, and patterned dimensions—allows the rhetorical uses of specific associations related to each dimension to be seen more clearly. This chapter has also demonstrated through both narratives and poetic texts how each of these dimensions of food is present across the Hebrew Bible. In the chapters that follow, these categories will be used to explain the rhetorical force of food in Psalm 78, especially as these five dimensions and their associations converge in a single psalm. As will be seen, it is this convergence that adds to the rhetorical power of food in Psalm 78. For it is food's multidimensionality that provides the psalmist with rhetorically rich soil to grow and nourish confident trust in the hearts of a postexilic people.

4

Provision of Food in the Wilderness (Psalm 78:13–31)

INTRODUCTION

PSALM 78 EXPLICITLY MENTIONS two central food events in its historical recital—the provision of food in the wilderness and the destruction of food supplies in the plagues on Egypt. This chapter and the following one—chapter 5—will focus on these two food accounts, while the remaining instances of food language within Psalm 78 will be considered in chapter 6.

The psalmist showcases the wilderness food account in two key ways. First, the psalmist allots almost a quarter of the historical recital to its description.[1] And second, the psalmist positions this food account at the start of the recital, placing it even before the Egyptian plagues (vv. 44–51) which served to propel Israel into the wilderness.[2] Although other wilderness events are briefly mentioned in the surrounding

1. Extending for seventeen verses or forty cola, this food account (vv. 15–31) is the most developed scene in the psalmist's historical recital. This distribution of cola is based on Fokkelman, who finds a total of 165 cola in the psalm. Fokkelman, *Psalms in Form*, 85–87.

2. As will be seen in the following chapters, the psalmist departs from a purely chronological presentation of the wilderness events and relies instead on various structural devices to organize the recital.

material,[3] the extended recollection of YHWH's "table in the wilderness" (vv. 15–31; cf. v. 19) becomes the primary avenue for the psalmist's consideration of the foundational years of YHWH's relationship with Israel.[4]

Three food elements are described in the psalmist's recital of God's wilderness provision—water from a rock (vv. 15–16), bread/manna (vv. 23–25), and meat/winged birds (vv. 26–28).[5] Each of these food elements will be addressed within its own section and discussed in a similar manner: a consideration of other depictions of this food event within the Hebrew Bible,[6] Psalm 78's literary distinctives, how the psalmist frames the event within Psalm 78,[7] and how specific dimensions of food are em-

3. The specific wilderness "events" are limited to the opening and closing of the Red/Reed Sea (vv. 13, 53), guidance by cloud/fire (v. 14), and divine "shepherding" (vv. 52–53a). The remainder of the wilderness report consists of the narrator's evaluation of Israel's rebellious response and a reflection on God's compassion (vv. 32–43). The survey of trends in the study of Psalm 78 shows significant variation in proposals for the psalm's structure. In this study, I will use the designation "wilderness frame" to refer to the frame created by the opening (v. 13) and closing (v. 53) of the Red/Reed Sea. I am not alone in identifying this feature as a key structural device within the psalm. See Girard and Vesco, although they both include v. 12 as part of the frame. Girard, *Psaumes redécouverts*, 358–64; Vesco, *Psautier de David traduit et commenté I*, 706–12. Even Clifford acknowledges that v. 12 is "transitional," linking back to v. 11b and forward to v. 43. Clifford, "In Zion and David a New Beginning," 128.

4. Reflections on Israel's wilderness journey are also found in Deut 1:19—3:29 (cf. 8:2–5, 15–16; 9:22–24; 10:6–7; 29:5–8), in several Psalms (105; 106; cf. 81:7; 95:8–11; 114:8; 135:10–12; 136:16–22), and in prophetic literature (Jer 2:2–6; Ezek 20:10–26; Hos 2:14–15; 13:4–5; Amos 2:10; 5:25). Davies, "Wilderness Wanderings," 912.

5. Psalm 78 does not use the term "quail" (שלו) in its description, relying instead on the designations "meat" (שאר) and "winged bird" (עוף כנף). Because the word "quail" (שלו) appears in a majority of the other accounts in the Hebrew Bible, I will employ "quail" as a generic term when referring to this food event.

6. I will look at other biblical texts that mention the event, starting with the "wilderness narratives," then turning to the Psalms and other texts in the Hebrew Bible. A primary concern in this section is to identify any vocabulary Psalm 78 shares with these depictions. In order to distinguish between the recounting of these events in Exodus/Numbers and the later representations of the events in Deuteronomy, I will use the term "wilderness narratives" when referring to the events recorded in Exodus–Numbers. The central wilderness narratives are found in Exod 13:17—18:27; 32:1—34:35; Num 10:33—25:18; 31:1—33:49.

7. In Psalm 78, the narrator plays a vital role in determining how the audience interprets the wilderness food account. This interpretive assistance is required since each of the food events (water from a rock, manna, quail) occurs on at least two separate occasions within the wilderness narratives with differing prompts and results. In Psalm 78, the accounts of the provision of manna and provision of quail are presented back to back with no intervening commentary. In light of this close association, the discussion of the framing of the manna/quail account will be postponed until after both events have been analyzed.

phasized in the recounting of this event for rhetorical effect. The chart below offers a visual summary for how these food events are laid out within this section of the psalm:

<table>
<tr><th>Description of Divine Actions</th><th>Narrator's Evaluation</th><th>Israel's Response</th><th>YHWH's Response</th><th>Narrator's Evaluation</th><th>Description of Divine Actions</th><th>Israel's Response</th><th>YHWH's Response</th><th>Narrator's Evaluation</th></tr>
<tr><td>Opening of Red/ Reed Sea (v. 13)</td><td rowspan="2">Israel's Response = Sin/ Rebellion (v. 17)</td><td rowspan="3">Demand for Food (vv. 19–20)</td><td rowspan="3">Divine Anger (v. 21)</td><td rowspan="3">Israel Lacks Faith (v. 22)</td><td rowspan="2">Provision of Manna (vv. 23–25)</td><td rowspan="3">They Ate and Were Satisfied (vv. 29–30)</td><td rowspan="3">Divine Anger; Killed Fattest (v. 31)</td><td rowspan="3">Israel's Sin and Failure to Believe in Wonders (v. 32)</td></tr>
<tr><td>Guidance by Cloud/ Fire (v. 14)</td></tr>
<tr><td>Provision of Water from Rock (vv. 15–16)</td><td>Israel's Motivation = To Test God (v. 18)</td><td>Provision of Quail (vv. 26–28)</td></tr>
</table>

The chapter will close by considering the rhetorical implications of the psalmist's depiction of the wilderness food account as a whole (vv. 13–32).

PROVISION OF WATER FROM A ROCK (PS 78:15–16)

יבקע צרים במדבר וישק כתהמות רבה:
ויוצא נוזלים מסלע ויורד כנהרות מים:

> He split rocks open in the wilderness and gave them[8] drink abundantly as from the deeps.
> He made streams come out of the crag and caused waters to flow down like rivers.[9]

8. MT lacks an object, something that Tate notes is a common tendency of the psalmist: "Note the omission of object suffixes with verbs in vv 6, 21, and 38." Tate, *Psalms 51–100*, 281.

9. Most commentators consider these verses original to the composition. Jacquet, however, assumes that the ordering of the text is defective. He repositions v. 15b to follow v. 16, creating a description of the water's abundance that more closely resembles

Parallel References to the Provision of Water from a Rock

References to God's provision of water in the wilderness occur across the Hebrew Bible, appearing in the Torah (Exod 17:1–17; Num 20:1–13; Deut 6:16; 8:15b; 9:22; 33:8), Prophets (Isa 48:21), and Writings (Pss 78:15–16, 20; 81:8 [ET 7]; 95:8; 105:4; 106:32; 114:8). As will be seen in this study, Psalm 78 offers a unique lens for viewing this event; for here, divine provision for Israel's physical need is celebrated as an example of YHWH's generous and abundant provision.

Water Provision in the Wilderness Narratives (Exodus–Numbers)

Divine intervention to provide water is explicitly mentioned on three occasions during Israel's wilderness journey (Exod 15:22–27; 17:1–7; Num 20:1–13). In the first instance (Exod 15:22–27), the Israelites had been traveling through the wilderness for three days without water. Here at Marah, God gives Moses instructions for making a naturally occurring water source potable.[10] In the remaining two accounts (Exod 17:1–7; Num 20:1–13), the source of the water—as in Psalm 78—is a "rock" (צור/סלע) in the wilderness.

Provision of Water at Rephidim (Exod 17:1–7)

This account of divine provision of water from a rock occurs directly following the provision of quail and manna in the wilderness of Sin (Exod 16). Here at Rephidim, the narrator notes that there is "no water for the people to drink" (אין מים לשתת העם, 17:1). The people "quarreled" (ריב) with Moses voicing their concern: "Give us water so that we may drink" (תנו לנו מים ונשתה, v. 2a). Moses' evaluation of their request is strongly negative as he equates their "quarrel" (ריב) with a "test" (נסה) of YHWH (v. 2b). The people then accuse Moses of bringing not only the adults, but their children and cattle, into the wilderness only to die of thirst (v. 3b).[11] Out of fear for his own life, Moses brings this concern

Israel's description of the event in v. 20. Jacquet, *Psaumes et le coeur*, 515.

10. Israel's first stop on their wilderness journey is at Elim, a site that included a naturally occurring water source (Exod 15:27). By including this account, the narrator introduces the possibility that Israel could have encountered other such naturally occurring water sources on their journey.

11. As noted in chapter 3, here the physical dimension of food is being exploited

to YHWH, who instructs him to strike (נכה) the rock (צור) in order to provide water (v. 6a).[12] The narrator offers no description of the water's appearance, only a statement of Moses' obedience in following through with the command (v. 6b). The account ends by explaining the names given to the location (Meribah and Massah)—because the Israelites "quarreled" (ריב) and "tested" (נסה) YHWH.

Since there is no actual description of water in Exodus 17, YHWH's command to Moses (v. 6) provides the only opportunity for finding lexical links with Psalm 78. Comparing the depiction of this event in Exod 17 and Psalm 78,[13] one finds parallels in the words used for "rock" (צור), the verb used for the issue of the water that "goes out" (יצא), and the general mention of "water" (מום):[14]

והכית בצור ויצאו ממנו מים ושתה העם

> Exod 17:6b: Strike[15] the <u>rock</u>, and <u>water</u> will <u>come out</u> of it, so that the people may drink.

Although these are common lexemes in the MT, their combination is much more limited: "water" (מים) from a "rock" (צור) occurs only 6x in the MT (Exod 17:6; Deut 8:15; Isa 48:21; Pss 78:20; 105:41; 114:8);

---

for rhetorical effect.

12. Moses is commanded to use the rod with which he struck the Nile. Sarna notes the subtle link to the first of the Egyptian plagues. "Whereas on the earlier occasion, striking with the rod had deprived the Egyptians of drinking water, the same action now serves to satisfy Israel's need for water." Sarna, *Exodus*, 94.

13. In this study, I will underline terms when they also appear in Psalm 78's recounting of the same event.

14. All these terms are used with a high degree of frequency in the MT. The word "rock" (צור) has the most limited use, occurring 76x in the MT (4x in Exodus; 24x in Psalms). Its use in Exodus occurs only here in 17:6 (2x) and in Moses' encounter with YHWH while hidden in a "rock" (צור) in Exod 33:21–22 (2x). The verb "to go or come out" (יצא) occurs 1075x (94x in Exodus; 34x in Psalms). The word "water" (מים) appears 585x in the MT (44x in Exodus; 53x in Psalms).

15. The verb "to strike" (נכה) does not occur in Psalm 78's initial description of water from a rock (vv. 15–16). However, the verb does appear later in Israel's description of the water event (v. 20):

הן הכה צור ויזובו מים ונחלים ישטפו

> Even though he <u>struck</u> the <u>rock</u> so that <u>water</u> gushed out and torrents overflowed.

Besides this occurrence in v. 20, the psalmist uses the verb נכה to describe the death of Egypt's firstborn (v. 51) and in v. 66 with Israel's enemies (צרר)—which may be an example of intentional wordplay with the word "rock" (צור).

"water" (מים) which "comes out" (יצא) occurs 12x in the MT (1x in Exodus, 17:6; 1x in Psalms, 78:16).

This account of water from the rock at Rephidim is memorialized not as a gracious act of divine provision, but as an example of Israel's wilderness rebellion.[16] Since this encounter follows on the tail of the miraculous provision of quail and manna (Exod 16),[17] Israel's lack of faith in Moses/YHWH to provide for their physical need for water takes on an ironic tone.

Provision of Water at Kadesh (Num 20:1–13)

In Num 20:1–13, Israel is camped at Kadesh, where the narrator notes: "there was no water for the congregation" (לא־היה מים לעדה, v. 2). Here the people "quarreled" (ריב) with Moses (v. 3; cf. Exod 17:2),[18] and voice their lack of faith in Moses' ability to lead them successfully through the wilderness (v. 4; cf. Exod 17:3): "Would that we had died when our kindred died before YHWH! Why have you brought the assembly of YHWH into this wilderness for us and our livestock to die here? Why have you brought us up out of Egypt, to bring us to this wretched place? It is no place for grain, or figs, or vines, or pomegranates; and there is no water to drink" (Num 20:3–5).[19] YHWH tells Moses and Aaron to speak to the crag (סלע), and it will bring forth water (v. 8). Moses responds in anger toward the people and disobeys the divine command (vv. 10–11a); yet, God still provides water for the people. The account ends by naming the location the "waters of Meribah" (מי מריבה) where the sons of Israel "quarreled" (ריב) with YHWH (v. 13).

There are various lexical parallels between the description of the water event in Numbers 20 and Psalm 78. Both the divine command (Num

16. As will be seen in the Hebrew Bible, the names Massah and Meribah become synonymous with Israel's testing of YHWH and their quarreling in the wilderness. For references to Massah, see Exod 17:7; Deut 6:16; 9:22; 33:8; Ps 95:8. For references to Meribah, see Exod 17:7; Num 20:13, 24; 27:14; Deut 33:8; Ps 81:8 [ET 7]; 95:8; 106:32.

17. Unlike the ordering in Exodus 16–17 (quail, manna, water from a rock), Psalm 78 reverses the order of these events. In Ps 78:20, it is the provision of water that fails to persuade Israel of God's ability to provide bread and meat.

18. The narrator notes that the people assembled against Moses and against Aaron (v. 2), although their quarrel was directed at Moses.

19. Kok observes that the "figs, vines, and pomegranates" that the Israelites long for here are the very items that the spies brought back to the Israelites camped at Kadesh-Barnea to testify of the land's bounty (Num 13:23). Kok, *Sin of Moses*, 78.

20:8) and the description of the event (20:11) contain parallel vocabulary to Psalm 78 including the word for "crag" (סלע), the verbs "to go out" (יצא) and "to drink" (שקה), the modifier "great, many" (רב), as well as the word "water" (מים).[20]

ודברתם אל הסלע לעיניהם ונתן מימיו
והוצאת להם מים מן הסלע והשקית

> Num 20:8b: You shall speak to the crag before their eyes to yield its water. Thus you shall bring out water from the crag for them; thus you shall provide drink.

וירם משה את ידו ויך את הסלע במטהו
פעמים ויצאו מים רבים ותשת העדה ובעירם

> Num 20:11: Then Moses lifted up his hand and struck the crag twice with his staff; abundant water came out, and the congregation and their livestock drank.

The expression "abundant water" (מים + רב) occurs 28x in the MT (2x in Numbers; 7x in Psalms). References to "water" (מים) from a "crag" (סלע) occur only 5x (Num 20:8, 10, 11; Ps 78:16; Neh 9:15)—all referring to the wilderness water miracle. Water (מים) which "comes out" (יצא) occurs 12x in the MT (3x in Numbers—Num 20:8, 10, 11; 1x in the Psalms—78:16).

This account of "water from a rock" in Numbers exhibits a similar progression in events when compared to the account found in Exodus.[21] In each, the narrator begins by acknowledging Israel's physical need for water (Num 20:2; cf. Exod 17:1). And in both cases, this reality leads directly to the people "quarreling" (ריב) with Moses (Num 20:3; Exod 17:2).[22] In Exod 17:7, the location is named because Israel "quarrels" (ריב)

20. In the MT, the term "crag" (סלע) occurs 63x (6x in Numbers; 9x in Psalms). In the Numbers references, all but one use of סלע appears in Numbers 20 (vv. 8, 10, 11; cf. 24:21). The verb "to come or go out" (יצא) occurs 1075x in the MT (70x in Numbers; 34x in Psalms), and the verb "to drink" (שקה) occurs 62x (4x in Numbers; 7x in Psalms). The modifier "great, many" (רב) appears 422x in the MT (17x in Numbers; 57x in Psalms). The word "water" (מים) appears 585x in the MT (45x in Numbers; 53x in Psalms).

21. The striking difference in the two accounts is that instead of a focus on Israel's rebellion, here in Numbers 20, Moses' own lack of trust is highlighted. Instead of "speaking" to the rock, Moses strikes the rock after a verbal outburst against the people (v. 10–11). As a result of this lack of trust, Moses is no longer permitted to bring the Israelites into the land (v. 12).

22. As will be seen in later discussions, the theme of "quarreling" (ריב) is surprisingly

and "tests" (נסה) YHWH; in Num 20:13, the name assigned only reflects Israel "quarreling" (ריב) with YHWH.[23]

Both wilderness water narratives focus on Israel's initial response to the lack of water. In each account, the narrator shows little or no concern for describing the water itself or the effect of the miracle on Israel. Exodus 17:6 simply mentions Moses' completion of YHWH's command; Num 20:11b provides only a short description of the event. In these narrative texts, the key identifying features of the water accounts are the name given to the location (Meribah/Massah) and the water's surprising source ("a rock," צור/סלע).

References to Water from a Rock in the Psalms

While the theme of divine provision of water appears in various psalms (e.g., Pss 23:2; 65:11–12; 104:10–13; 107:35), references to divine provision of water in the wilderness occur in only six psalms (Pss 78:15–16, 20; 81:8 [ET 7]; 95:8; 105:41; 106:32; 114:8). Three of these psalms recall the event by simply mentioning its location and offer no description of the provision of water (i.e., Meribah in Ps 81:8 [ET 7]; 106:32; Meribah/

absent in Psalm 78. This omission may derive from the fact that Moses—who is never mentioned in Psalm 78—is the primary human target for the people's "quarreling" in the "wilderness narratives." Instead, the language used for Israel's disobedience in Psalm 78 is "rebellion" (מרה, vv. 8, 17, 40, 56) often paired with language of "testing" (נסה, vv. 18, 41, 56). For a discussion of this omission of Moses in Psalm 78, see Kugler, "Not Moses, but David," 126–28.

23. Scholars have observed a sharp contrast in YHWH's response to Israel's pre-Sinai and post-Sinai rebellions (see discussion in following section on the quail). However, these water accounts do not follow this pattern. Childs offers an alternative description for the patterns of response seen here. "Pattern I is found in its clearest form in Ex. 15.22f.; 17.1ff.; and Num. 20.1–13. Accordingly, there is an initial need (15.22, 23; 17.1; Num. 20.2) which is followed by a complaint (15.24; 17.2; Num. 20.3), then by an intercession on the part of Moses (15.25; 17.4; Num. 20.6), which issues in the need being met by God's miraculous intervention (15.25; 17.6ff.; Num. 20.11). In contrast to this, Pattern II is found in its clearest form in Num. 11.1–3; 17.6–15 (EVV 16.41–50); 21.4–10. Accordingly, there is an initial complaint (11.1; 17.6; 21.5), which is followed by God's anger and punishment (11.1; 17.10; 21.6), then an intercession from Moses (11.2; 17.45; 21.7), and finally a reprieve of the punishment (11.2; 17.50; 21.9)." Childs, *Book of Exodus*, 258. Childs goes on to note: "In Pattern I, there is always a genuine need—whether of food or water—which is made specific and calls forth the complaint, whereas in Pattern II the complaint is introduced without a basis in a genuine need, and it is usually explicitly characterized as an illegitimate murmuring: 'the rabble had a strong craving' (Num. 11.4), or 'the people became impatient, and called the manna 'this worthless food' (21.4)."

Massah in Ps 95:8). The remaining three psalms (Pss 78:15–16, 20; 105:41; 114:8) contain an explicit mention of "water from a rock."

In the psalms where the water event is identified by name (i.e., Meribah/Massah), there is often an additional reference to the negative association of the location. Psalm 95:8 notes that here Israel "hardened their hearts" (קשה לבב); Ps 106:32 notes that here Israel "angered" (קצף) God.[24] Simply speaking these place names gives voice to the rebellion that occurred there—Meribah ("to quarrel") and Massah ("to test"). The inclusion of a secondary descriptor—hardened hearts, anger—serves to intensify the conflict associated with these locations.

In the psalms that provide a description of the water event (Pss 78, 105, 114), all three use an identical term for "rock" (צור), as well as a reference to "water" (מים):

יבקע צרים במדבר וישק כתהמות רבה
ויוצא נוזלים מסלע ויורד כנהרות מים

> Ps 78:15–16: He split rocks open in the wilderness and gave them drink abundantly as from the deeps. He made streams come out of the crag and caused waters to flow down like rivers.

פתח צור ויזובו מים הלכו בציות נהר

> Ps 105:41: He opened the rock, and water gushed out; it flowed through the dry land[25] like a river.

ההפכי הצור אגם מים חלמיש למעינו מים

> Ps 114:8: Who turns the rock into a pool of water, the flint into a spring of water.

As noted earlier, the term "rock" (צור) also appears in the account found in Exod 17:1–7. In Psalm 105's depiction of the events, "water from a rock" (v. 41) follows the provision of quail and manna (v. 40)—mirroring the order of the food account found in Exodus 16–17 (quail, manna, water from a rock). In Ps 114:8, "water from a rock" appears in the last verse

24. In the case of Ps 81:8 [ET 7], Meribah is an occasion where God "tested" (בחן) Israel—not the reverse.

25. The term for "dry land" (ציה) used in Ps 105:41 also appears in Ps 78:17 in the narrator's evaluation of Israel's response to God's provision of water from a rock. This link is a substantial one in light of the fact that the word "dry land" (ציה) appears only 18x in the MT. Its only other occurrence with an explicit reference to Israel's wilderness wanderings occurs in Jer 2:6.

of the psalm with no reference to food provisions. In addition to these similarities, all three psalms present the water event in a positive light as evidence of God's gracious provision.

Additional References to Water from a Rock in the Hebrew Bible

There are three other occasions in the Hebrew Bible where references to wilderness water events occur: Deuteronomy, Isaiah, and Nehemiah. The references in Deuteronomy contain several allusions to the water events through their location names, Massah (Deut 6:16; 9:22) and Massah/Meribah (Deut 33:8). Deuteronomy 8:15b provides an explicit link through the mention of bringing water from a "rock."

המוציא לך מים מצור החלמיש

Deut 8:15b: He made water come out for you from flint rock.[26]

The provision of water from a rock here in Deut 8:15b is mentioned before the provision of manna (v. 16), similar to the order in Psalm 78.

Deutero-Isaiah is filled with various references to divine provision of water in the wilderness (e.g., Isa 41:18; 43:20; 44:3; cf. 35:6); however, Isa 48:21 contains the only explicit reference to provision of water from a rock:

ולא צמאו בחרבות הוליכם מים מצור הזיל למו
ויבקע צור ויזבו מים

They did not thirst when he led them through the deserts; he made water flow for them from the rock;
he split open the rock and the water gushed out.[27]

26. In Deut 32:13b, divine food provisions are said to come from a "rock" (סלע / צור), utilizing both terms found in Ps 78:15–16. Here, the substances extracted from the rock are "honey" (דבש) and "oil" (שמן):

וינקהו דבש מסלע ושמן מחלמיש צור

Deut 32:13b: He nursed him with honey from the crags, with oil from flinty rock.

27. The verb "to flow" (זוב) used here in Isa 48:21 also appears in Israel's description of the water event in Ps 78:20a:

הן הכה צור ויזובו מים ונחלים ישטפו

Even though he struck the rock so that water gushed out and torrents overflowed.

This reference in Isa 48:21 provides a striking lexical parallel to the language used in Ps 78:15–16.[28] In addition to the reference to "splitting the rock" (בקע צור), both texts use derivatives of the root "to stream" (נזל), a rare term in the MT.[29]

In Nehemiah 9, this wilderness water event is remembered in a prayer which takes the form of a historical recital moving from creation (v. 6) through to the exiles' return to the land of Canaan (vv. 36–37). Verse 15a notes:

ומים מסלע הוצאת להם לצמאם

and you brought water for them out of the rock for their thirst.

A more general reference to the provision of water in the wilderness occurs later in this prayer in v. 20b: "you did not withhold your manna from their mouths and gave them water (מים) for their thirst (צמא)." Because this mention of water directly follows God's provision of manna, this water reference likely refers back to the provision of water from a rock in v. 15—although here the source of the water is not included.

Of these three occurrences that mention water from a rock, Isa 48:21 provides the closest parallel to Psalm 78 with the use of the verb "to split, cleave" (בקע) and the reference to "streams" (נזל) and "water" (מים). Deuteronomy 8:15 and Neh 9:15 pick up the language of "water" (מים) that "comes/goes out" (יצא) from a rock (cf. Exod 17:6; Num 20:8; Ps 78:16).[30] Deuteronomy 8:15 and Isa 48:21 are similar to Exod 17:6 with its use of the term צור (cf. Ps 78:15); Neh 9:15's use of the term סלע is similar to Numbers 20 (cf. Ps 78:16).

Summary of Parallel References to Water from a Rock

As seen in the survey of texts above, recollections of God's provision of water from a wilderness rock occur in a variety of texts across the Hebrew Bible. The term צור is used most often for the source of water (Exod 17:6;

28. While noting the common language, Füglister observes that the emphasis in Deutero-Isaiah is eschatological. Füglister, "Psalm LXXXVIII [*sic*]," 283.

29. The root "to stream" (נזל) occurs only 16x in the MT, with two occurrences in Psalm 78. Besides its use in 78:15 to describe the waters flowing from a rock, this word appears in the description of the first of the Egyptian plagues (v. 44) where the waters turn to blood so that the people could not drink of "their streams" (נזליהם).

30. As noted in the discussion in the above section "Provision of Water at Rephidim," the combination of "water" (מים) that "comes/goes out" (יצא) only occurs 12x in the MT.

Pss 105:41; 114:8; Deut 8:15; Isa 48:21; Ps 78:15), although the term סלע also appears (Num 20:8, 10, 11; Ps 78:16; Neh 9:15). Whenever there is an explicit reference to the location of the event (Meribah/Massah), these recollections generally focus on Israel's rebellion—a theme found in Exodus 17 and Numbers 20. However, whenever the reference mentions the actual provision of water from "a rock" (צור/סלע), the associations are generally positive (Pss 78:15–16, 20; 105:41; 114:8; Deut 8:15; Isa 48:21; Neh 9:15).

Literary Analysis of Psalm 78's Depiction of Water from a Rock (vv. 15–16)

Psalm 78's recounting of this wilderness event is striking in its lexical choices to describe the source of the water, the water's abundance, and YHWH's direct involvement. Two features of the psalmist's description of the water's source are noteworthy: the presence of dual words for "rock"—צור (v. 15) and סלע (v. 16)—and the use of the plural "rocks" (צרים) in v. 15. As seen in the discussion above, these two words for "rock" mirror the water sources in Exod 17:6 (צור) and Num 20:8, 10, 11 (סלע).[31] While the term צור is a common word for "rock" across the MT (76x in MT; 14x in Pentateuch; 4x in Exodus; 24x in Psalms),[32] the term סלע has a slightly more restricted use in the Pentateuch and Psalms (63x in MT; 7x in Pentateuch; 6x in Numbers; 9x in Psalms). In the MT, the first occurrence of each term is in the wilderness water accounts (i.e., Exod 17:6; Num 20:8). Considering the variety of words for "rock" available to the psalmist,[33] it seems plausible that the psalmist is explicitly calling to

31. The LXX loses this lexical distinction between the two water events by using the term πετρα in both the Exodus account and Numbers account. In all the other parallel passages which mention water from a "rock," the LXX also uses the term πετρα.

32. The word "rock" (צור) is used 3x in Psalm 78. Twice it refers explicitly to the source of water in the wilderness (78:15, 20). A third use occurs in 78:35 where Israel remembers that God was their "rock" (צור) and "redeemer" (גאל). The motif of God as rock may simply signify that God was their place of safety (cf. Deut 32:4, 37; Ps 18:2, 31); however, in the context of Psalm 78, this use of the term may also call to mind God's specific actions of providing water in the wilderness. Fernandes contends: "In this context, where 'remembering' is the key to understanding the poem, one finds it impossible to consider the use of the word צור to refer to God in this verse as entirely distinct from the uses of the word צור in speaking of the site and nature of God's mighty demonstrations of power in vv. 15 and 20." Fernandes, *God as Rock in the Psalter*, 259.

33. While צור and סלע—in addition to אבן (284x in MT)—are the more common terms, Andrew Hill notes that "the OT uses more than a dozen Heb. words meaning rock, stone, pebble, boulder, etc." Hill, "אבן," 249.

mind the two separate water events through the choice of the two terms for "rock." The positioning of these two terms (צור in v. 15; סלע in v. 16) follows the order of the wilderness narratives—water from a "rock" (צור) in Exodus 17 and water from a "rock" (סלע) in Numbers 20. Thus with this choice of lexemes, the psalmist is able to call to mind forty years of divine provision with just these two verses.[34]

Another point to note regarding the water's source is the psalmist's use of the plural form "rocks" (צרים)[35] in v. 15. In Ps 78:20a, Israel recounts the water event but uses the term צור in the singular: "Even though he struck the rock (צור) so that water gushed out and torrents overflowed." In order to remedy this discrepancy in number between vv. 15 and 20, the Septuagint translates the plural "rocks" with the singular *πετρα*.[36] However, by retaining the plural צרים v. 15, the multiple occurrences of divine water provision during Israel's wilderness journey are emphasized.[37]

While the wilderness narratives offer little or no description of the water or its effect on Israel, Psalm 78 offers an expansive commentary on this divine provision. First, the psalmist employs a great variety of words for water in the description of the event (vv. 15–16):

יבקע צרים במדבר וישק כתהמות רבה:
ויוצא נוזלים מסלע ויורד כנהרות מים:

> He split rocks open in the wilderness and gave them drink abundantly as from the deeps.
> He made streams come out of the rock and caused waters to flow down like rivers.

The term מים is a common word for "water" in the MT (585x) and is used three times in Psalm 78 with reference to the Red/Reed Sea (v. 13) and the wilderness provision (vv. 16, 20). The term "river" (נהר) in v. 16 is also a common term across the Hebrew Bible (137x in MT), although its use in the Psalms is limited (15x). The remaining two words occur even fewer

34. The terms צור and סלע appear together only twice in the MT as a poetic word pair (Deut 32:13; Isa 2:21). The infrequent use of these terms in parallel strengthens the argument for the author's rhetorical intent.

35. The plural term "rocks" (צרים) occurs eight other times in the MT and is used either to describe a barren environment (Num 23:9; 1 Sam 24:2; Isa 2:19, 21; Hab 1:6; Job 28:10) or "flinty knives" (Josh 5:2, 3).

36. The LXX brings added continuity to the account by using the same singular form of the word *πετρα* for all three "rock" references (v. 15 צרים; v. 16 סלע; v. 20 צור).

37. A point made by Vesco, *Psautier de David traduit et commenté I*, 707.

times in the MT. The word translated "the deep" (תהום) occurs 36x in the MT (12x in the Psalms); the word translated "stream" (נזל) occurs only 5x in the MT (Exod 15:8; Isa 44:3; Ps 78:16, 44; Prov 5:15).

Secondly, the psalmist explicitly emphasizes the abundance of the water provision. In v. 15, the term "great, many" (רב) is used as an adverbial modifier of the verb "to drink" (שקה), accentuating the magnitude of provision: "he gave them to drink abundantly."[38] This abundance of provision is also highlighted by the use of the term "deeps" (תהמות). In Exodus, this term is used to describe the powerful waters of the Red/Reed Sea that drown the Egyptians (Exod 15:5, 8); here in the hand of the psalmist, the water of the "deeps" (תהמות) now becomes a source of bounteous provision and physical blessing to Israel.

Throughout this account there is a focus on YHWH's initiative and active involvement in meeting Israel's needs.[39] YHWH is pictured as a host helping to quench Israel's thirst (ישק). YHWH is shown bringing forth (יוצא) streams and causing waters to flow (יורד). Here the focus is on YHWH's sovereign power as nature responds to his bidding.

In Psalm 78, the psalmist provides a unique lens for viewing the wilderness water events. Here, the psalm calls to mind both wilderness water provisions through the dual references to a "rock" (צור and סלע). And contrary to the wilderness narratives, the depiction of the water miracles in Psalm 78 focuses on God's gracious and abundant provision of Israel's need for water.

Framing of the Water from a Rock Event (Ps 78:13–17)

This water event takes on added rhetorical significance when viewed within the narrator's framing of this event. The account opens with three divine actions listed in succession: the parting of the Red/Reed Sea (v. 13), guidance by cloud/fire (v. 14), and provision of water from a rock

38. A similar intensification using the modifier מאד occurs in v. 29, here in the context of food: "And they ate and were very satisfied" (ויאכלו וישבעו מאד). In v. 15, the focus on the extravagant gift of drinking water would be in keeping with the lavish provision of food later in the psalm (v. 29). This extravagance is also seen in God's guidance in the wilderness in v. 14. Hossfeld observes: "Especially striking are the circumstances of the guidance: it is a matter of being led continually, around the clock, with the cloud by day and the light of fire by night." Hossfeld and Zenger, *Psalms 2*, 296.

39. David Ray offers an insightful analysis of Psalm 78's employment of the *hiphil* verb form to emphasize divine causation of these wilderness events. Ray, "Who Did What to Whom?," 72–74.

(vv. 15–16). The psalmist links the divine provision of water from a rock (v. 15) back to the previous water miracle at the Red/Reed Sea (v. 13). This is done through the repetition of the verb "to split/cleave" (בקע).[40] While in v. 13 YHWH "splits the sea" (בקע ים), here in v. 15 YHWH "splits rocks in the wilderness" (יבקע צרים במדבר). In addition, the continuity of aquatic vocabulary draws these texts together: "sea" (ים, v. 13), "water" (מים, vv. 13, 16), "the deeps" (תהמות, v. 15), "streams" (נזלים, v. 16), and "rivers" (נהרות, v. 16).[41] By connecting these two water events, the psalmist presents the provision of water from a rock in a positive light. As Clifford notes: "There is no indication in vv 12–16 of the murmuring of the people recorded in Exod 17:1–7 and Num 20:2–13."[42] In addition, the parallel water events (vv. 13, 15–16) are presented as a diptych of God's power over the natural world. As Goldingay notes: "God can split waters and make them like a cliff or split a cliff and make it produce waters; it is all the same to God."[43] Within the context of vv. 13–16, the psalmist presents this wilderness wonder of water from a rock as a display of sovereign power and divine grace.

The psalmist closes this frame (v. 17) with the first of a series of evaluations of Israel's inner motivations:[44]

> ויוסיפו עוד לחטא לו למרות עליון בציה
>
> Yet they sinned still more against him, rebelling against the Most High in the land of drought.

The fact that this negative evaluation appears after the recounting of three acts of divine grace magnifies the irony of Israel's response of sin (חטא) and rebellion (מרה). Instead of using the stereotypical verb from the wilderness narratives for Israel's disobedience—"quarreling" (ריב)—the psalmist employs the term "rebellion" (מרה), the preferred word in the psalm for Israel's disobedience (v. 17; cf. 78:8, 40, 56). The phrase "they

40. The Exodus account uses this verb in YHWH's command to Moses to "divide" (בקע) the sea (Exod 14:16), as well as the narrator's description of the completed action (v. 21). The verb בקע is also associated with the parting the waters of the Red/Reed Sea in Isa 63:12 and Neh 9:11. Uses of the word "split, cleave" (בקע) to describe God's wilderness provision of water from a rock is rare. The only other occurrence is Isa 48:21: "he split open (בקע) the rock and the water gushed out."

41. Tate, *Psalms 51–100*, 290.

42. Clifford, "In Zion and David a New Beginning," 132.

43. Goldingay, *Psalms*, 2:491.

44. I follow Seybold who views v. 17 as the concluding remark within this unit (vv. 12–17). Seybold, *Psalmen*, 310.

sinned still more against him" reminds the audience that Israel's rebellion was not a new development but had been an undercurrent even through these past experiences. When seen within this larger frame (vv. 13–17), both the immensity of YHWH's provision and the magnitude of Israel's sinful response are intensified.

Conclusion: Psalm 78's Depiction of the Wilderness Water Event (vv. 15–16)

Psalm 78's account of the provision of water in the wilderness (vv. 15–16) presents this event as God's gracious care for Israel. Seen in relation to parallel accounts of this event, Psalm 78 offers the most elaborate retelling of the event with a focus on the abundance of the provision. Although there are lexical parallels with the wilderness narratives, the psalmist departs from these basic narratives to present this event as a celebration focused on the unexpected gift of abundant waters. It is not until the conclusion of this litany of divine provision that the audience hears of Israel's rebellious response.

PROVISION OF MANNA (PS 78:23–25)

ויצו שחקים ממעל ודלתי שמים פתח:
וימטר עליהם מן לאכל ודגן שמים נתן למו:
לחם אבירים אכל איש צידה שלח להם לשבע:

> Yet he commanded the skies above, and opened the doors of heaven;
> He rained down on them manna to eat and gave them the grain of heaven.
> Each ate of the bread of the mighty;[45] he sent them provisions in abundance.

45. The LXX (as well as Vulgate and Syriac) translate the term אבירים as "angels" instead of the more literal translation "mighty ones." These lexical options will be discussed in the literary analysis of the passage.

Parallel References to the Provision of Manna

References to God's provision of manna[46] are less frequent in the Hebrew Bible than references to the wonder of water from a rock. The importance of water in a wilderness environment—even over the need for food—may explain this difference. Yet, one still finds references to manna across the Hebrew Bible appearing in the Torah (Exod 16:1–36; Num 11:4–9; Deut 8:3, 16), Prophets (Hos 13:5–6),[47] and Writings (Neh 9:15, 20; Pss 78:23–25; 105:40). In these texts, the provision of manna often appears concurrently with the provision of quail (Exod 16:1–36; Num 11:1–35; Ps 78:18–32; 105:40).[48] As will be seen in this study, Psalm 78 both incorporates and innovates with the manna tradition as it highlights the immensity of and divine involvement in this gift of food.

Manna Provision in the Wilderness Narratives (Exodus–Numbers)

Divine provision of manna is noted on three occasions in the wilderness narratives—Exod 16:1–36, Num 11:4–9, and Num 21:5. In this final reference, the Israelites complain to YHWH/Moses about their wilderness diet: "Why have you brought us up out of Egypt to die in the wilderness (מדבר)? For there is no food (לחם) and no water, and we detest this miserable food (לחם הקלקל)" (Num 21:5).[49] Although not specifically named, manna is the likely referent for this "miserable food" (לחם הקלקל). The remaining two accounts (Exod 16; Num 11) explicitly describe the provision of both manna and quail; yet in each passage, a different food element is emphasized. In Exodus 16, manna is showcased as a gracious act of provision and a context of divine testing, with only a short mention

46. As will be seen, there is great variety in terminology used to describe the wilderness food that God provides from heaven. In this section, I use the term "manna" both as a general reference and the specific lexeme for this food.

47. Joshua 5:12 refers only to the cessation of manna as Israel enters Canaan and can eat the produce of the land.

48. In Psalm 78, these events appear back-to-back with no intervening commentary. In addition, strong lexical links draw these accounts together, particularly through the verb "to rain" (מטר). In light of the close connection of these events in Psalm 78, I will delay the discussion of the framing of these events until after an investigation of parallel texts and a literary analysis of the depiction of each individual event (manna/quail).

49. The term "miserable, worthless" (קלקל) occurs only here in the MT. The *hiphil* of קלל means "to treat with contempt" in 2 Sam 19:44; Isa 23:9; Ezek 22:7. *HALOT* notes: "The exact meaning disputed; possible interpretations: according to the context and versions, wretched food." Koehler and Baumgartner, "קלקל," 1106.

of the arrival of the quail (v. 13). In Numbers 11, the focus is on the quail, with the monotonous diet of manna in the wilderness serving as the initial flash point for Israel's gastronomical discontent (v. 6). Each of these events will be discussed with particular attention given to their description of the manna.[50]

Provision of Manna at Wilderness of Sin (Exod 16:1–36)

After the respite at Elim (Exod 15:27) where Israel enjoyed naturally occurring "springs of water" (עינת מים) and "date palms" (תמרים), they travel to the wilderness of Sin (16:1). Unlike the water accounts that began with an explicit acknowledgment of Israel's physical need for water (i.e., Exod 15:22; 17:1), Exodus 16 includes only an implicit reference to their lengthy duration in the wilderness, a total of six weeks (v. 1).[51] The people "complain" (לון) to both Moses and Aaron about their hunger (רעב, v. 2) and recall their experience in Egypt (v. 3) where they sat by "pots of meat" (סיר הבשר) and ate their "fill of bread" (לחם לשבע).[52] In response to this perceived crisis of food,[53] YHWH tells Moses: "I am going to rain (מטר) bread (לחם) from heaven (מן־השמים) for you, and each day the people shall go out and gather enough for that day" (v. 4). This provision is described as a test (נסה) of their obedience to follow God's instructions (v. 5). Moses and Aaron inform the people that YHWH has "heard" (שמע) their complaining (Exod 16:7, 8, 9)[54] and will respond. In v. 12, YHWH speaks of his plan to meet this need for food: "I have heard (שמע) the

50. These texts (Exod 16; Num 11) will be considered again in the following section with a particular emphasis on the provision of quail.

51. Exodus 16:1 notes that it is "the fifteenth day of the second month after their departure from the land of Egypt."

52. The language of this Egyptian recollection of their "fill of bread" (לחם לשבע) is later picked up in Moses' speech in v. 8 as he notes that YHWH will give you your "fill of bread" (לחם . . . לשבע) in the morning. In v. 12, YHWH tells Moses to tell the people that "you shall have your fill of bread" (תשבעו־לחם). With the repetition of the phrase "fill of bread," Moses and YHWH's responses seem to bear a sarcastic edge as they answer the Israelites' request by mimicking their own words.

53. Childs notes: "Israel is not presented as starving to death and crying out for bread. Instead the people long for the 'fleshpots of Egypt' and for 'bread aplenty.'" Childs, *Book of Exodus*, 284.

54. In Ps 78:21, the psalmist uses the same expression YHWH "heard" (שמע) in regard to Israel's complaint about food (cf. v. 59 where the divine "hearing" occurs in the context of idol worship).

complaining of the Israelites; say to them, 'At twilight you shall eat (אכל) meat (בשר), and in the morning you shall have your fill (שבע) of bread (לחם); then you shall know that I am YHWH your God.'"[55] The narrator briefly describes the arrival of the quail in the evening (v. 13a) and manna the following morning (v. 13b–14). The Israelites are confused when the manna appears (v. 15), asking: "What is it?" (מן הוא). Moses offers a brief explanation: "It is the bread (לחם) that YHWH has given (נתן) you to eat (אכל)."

The remainder of this food account in the wilderness of Sin (vv. 16–36) focuses on instructions on the daily gathering of portions (v. 16) and Israel's general failure to follow instructions (vv. 17–22), followed by further instructions for Sabbath provisions (v. 23–26) and Israel's failure to keep these instructions (v. 27–30). The narrative continues with commands for keeping a memorial portion of the manna (vv. 32–34), a note on the duration of this wilderness food supply (v. 35) and a clarifying note on weights/measures (v. 36).

Specific descriptions of the manna occur in vv. 14, 23, and 31. Verse 14 describes its initial appearance on the ground—"a fine flaky substance, as fine as frost" (דק מחספס דק ככפר). Verse 23 provides information on the preparation of the manna: "Bake what you want to bake, boil what you want to boil." Verse 31 notes the name given to it (מן, "manna") and comments on its appearance—"like coriander seed, [but] white" (כזרע גד לבן)[56]—and taste—"like wafers with honey" (כצפיחת בדבש).[57]

Several lexical parallels exist between the description of the manna event in Exodus 16 and Psalm 78. These are mostly found in the two divine speeches (Exod 16:4, 12), as well as Moses' explanation of the manna (v. 15). In the divine speeches, lexical parallels occur in the verb "to rain"

55. Regarding the repetition of information in the text, Childs notes that "the point of the speech is not to provide new information, but rather to confirm what Moses has already promised. If in v. 4, it did not seem that God had heard the complaint, now he makes clear that he has. Moses' point has been confirmed: God is the one being accused and God is the one who will make himself known by his supplying Israel's need." Childs, *Book of Exodus*, 288.

56. Sarna notes that this reference to coriander seed "relates only to its shape and size, not its color, which is dark." Sarna, *Exodus*, 91.

57. Houtman notes that צפיחת is "a hapax legomena, usually derived from צפה and, going by Arabic and Ethiopian terminology and in light of the context, taken to mean 'flat cake,' 'wafer.'" Houtman, *Exodus*, 352.

(מטר), the root "to satisfy" (שבע), the noun "bread" (לחם), as well as the source of the food being "heaven" (שמים).[58]

ממטיר לכם לחם מן השמים

Exod 16:4a: I am going to rain bread from heaven for you.

ובבקר תשבעו לחם

Exod 16:12c: in the morning you shall be satisfied with bread.

Additional shared lexemes occur in Moses' response to the Israelites (Exod 16:15), in particular the verbs "to eat" (אכל) and "to give" (נתן), and the noun "bread" (לחם).[59]

ויאמר משה אלהם הוא הלחם אשר נתן יהוה לכם לאכלה

Exod 16:15: Moses said to them, "It is the bread that YHWH has given you to eat."

While many of these terms—such as "eat" (אכל), "satisfied" (שבע), "bread, food" (לחם)—are common lexemes associated with food consumption, the clustering of terms becomes significant. As seen in Exodus 16, manna is primarily associated with the verb "to satisfy" (שבע). The verb "to satisfy" (שבע) appears in vv. 8, 12 in regard to manna, while the verb "to eat" (אכל) is used to refer to YHWH's provision of "meat"/quail (vv. 8, 12). The expression "to satisfy with bread/food" occurs various times in the MT as an expression of contentment (i.e., Jer 44:17; Ps 132:15; Prov 12:11; 20:13; 28:19; 30:22; cf. Job 27:14).[60] The language of "bread, food" (לחם) that rains down (מטר) occurs only in Exod 16:4. However, Exod

58. The verb "to rain" (מטר) is the most notable of the words, occurring just 17x in the MT (3x in Exodus; 3x in Psalms—2x in Ps 78). The root שבע occurs 123x in MT, with the verbal form "to satisfy" (שבע) occurring 97x and the noun form "abundance" (שבע) occurring 8x. Its use in Exodus is confined to the manna account, occurring only 2x as a verb (Exod 16:8, 12) and 1x as a noun (16:3). In the Psalms, the root שבע appears 23x as a verb and 2x as a noun. The noun "bread, food" (לחם) occurs with great regularity, 341x in MT (21x in Exodus; 19x in Psalms), as does the word "heaven" (שמים), which appears 421x in MT (14x in Exodus; 74x in Psalms).

59. The verb "to eat" (אצל) occurs 814x in MT (52x in Exodus; 30x in Psalms). The verb "to give" (נתן) occurs 2014x in MT (115x in Exodus; 95x in Psalms). As noted above, the noun "bread, food" (לחם) also occurs with great regularity, 341x in MT (21x in Exodus; 19x in Psalms).

60. It is interesting that in Isa 55:2, the prophet seems to use the terms לחם/שבעה as parallel expressions: "Why do you spend your money for that which is not bread, and your labor for that which does not satisfy?" (למה תשקלו כסף בלוא לחם ויגיעכם בלוא לשבעה).

16:4a and Ps 78:24 both refer to bread/manna that "rains" (מטר) from "heaven" (שמים).[61] In light of the infrequent use of the term "to rain," 17x in MT (3x in Exodus; 3x in Psalms), this verbal choice holds considerable weight.[62]

Provision of Manna at Taberah (Num 11:4–9)

In Numbers 11 manna is simply mentioned as the motivating cause for the Israelites' complaint about their monotonous diet: "our strength is dried up, and there is nothing at all but this manna (מן) to look at" (v. 6). According to the narrative itinerary, the Israelites would have been eating manna for over a year at this point (cf. Num 9:1).

In this account in Num 11:4–9, manna is described based on appearance,[63] taste, and preparation possibilities. In v. 7, the narrator describes the manna's appearance with the same expression found in Exod 16:31—"like coriander seed" (כזרע־גד)—and adds that it is like "bdellium, gum resin" (בדלח).[64] Here in Num 11:8, manna's taste is likened to "cakes with oil" (לשד השמן) compared with the Exodus account's "wafers with honey" (כצפיחת בדבש).[65] In addition, the narrator provides an extensive description of cooking techniques used for its preparation: "they ground it in mills or beat it in mortars, then boiled it in pots and made cakes of it" (v. 8). There are no substantial lexical parallels that exist between the

61. There is only one additional example where these lexemes are directly associated. In Gen 19:24, YHWH rained sulfur/fire from heaven on Sodom and Gomorrah (cf. Exod 9:23 where the link between heaven and the "raining" hail is less specific).

62. Observing this lexical connection, Fishbane notes: "the explicit reference in Ps. 78:24 to the manna raining from heaven, and the description of the manna in Ps. 78:24–5 as a heavenly good, strongly suggest that its composer was in some manner dependent upon the formulation preserved in Exod. 16." Fishbane, *Biblical Interpretation in Ancient Israel*, 327.

63. This emphasis on manna's appearance strikes an ironic note in light of the Israelites' complaint in v. 6: "there is nothing at all but this manna to look at" (אין כל בלתי אל המן עינינו).

64. These comparisons offer little help to the modern reader. The word גד occurs only in Exod 16:31 and Num 11:4, while the only other occurrence of the term בדלח is in Gen 2:12, here in the context of gold and onyx stone.

65. Wisdom of Solomon 16:20–21 seems to resolve this taste discrepancy by noting the variability of manna's taste: "Instead of these things you gave your people food of angels, and without their toil you supplied them from heaven with bread ready to eat, providing every pleasure and suited to every taste. For your sustenance manifested your sweetness toward your children; and the bread, ministering to the desire of the one who took it, was changed to suit everyone's liking" (NRSV).

description of the manna event in Numbers 11 and Psalm 78, besides the recurrent term "manna" (מן) found in Num 11:6, 7, 9 (cf. Ps 78:24).

In the wilderness narratives, manna is presented as both a blessing (Exod 16) and a bane (Num 11) for Israel. Both accounts focus on the appearance and taste of manna, as well as cooking instructions. Exodus 16 provides a detailed description of the manna's arrival in the wilderness, while Numbers 11 simply assumes its presence.

The account in Exodus provides the most lexical links with Psalm 78. The term "manna" (מן) first appears in Exod 16:31 (cf. Ps 78:24) and is linked to "being satisfied" (16:8, 12; cf. Ps 78:25, 29). It is also described as "bread from heaven" (לחם מן־השמים, Exod 16:4a; cf. Ps 78:25, "bread of the mighty" לחם אבירים) that will "rain" (מטר) down on them (Exod 16:4a; cf. Ps 78:24). In the Exodus account, the provision of manna is presented as a "test" (נסה) of Israel's obedience (cf. Ps 78:18 where Israel "tests" God).

References to Manna in the Psalms

The theme of divine provision of food appears numerous times in the Psalter (e.g., Pss 104:14–15; 132:15; 136:25; 146:7). It is striking, however, that the divine provision of bread/manna (לחם/מן) in the wilderness is mentioned only twice in the Psalter (Pss 78:23–25; 105:40).[66]

> ויצו שחקים ממעל ודלתי שמים פתח:
> וימטר עליהם מן לאכל ודגן שמים נתן למו:
> לחם אבירים אכל איש צידה שלח להם לשבע:
>
> Ps 78:23–25: Yet he commanded the skies above, and opened the doors of heaven;
> He rained down on them manna to eat and gave them the grain of heaven.
> Each ate of the bread of the mighty; he sent them provisions in abundance.

66. Psalm 81:11c [ET 10c] may provide an allusion to the wilderness provision of food, although the lexical links are tenuous:

> אנכי יהוה אלהיך המעלך מארץ מצרים הרחב פיך ואמלאה
>
> I am YHWH your God, who brought you up out of the land of Egypt. Open your mouth wide and I will fill it.

שאל ויבא שלו ולחם שמים ישביעם

Ps 105:40: They asked, and he brought quails and bread of heaven in abundance.

Psalm 105 offers only a passing comment on YHWH's provision of food in the wilderness compared with Psalm 78's extended description. Psalm 105:40's description of the manna event echoes Exodus 16's references to "bread from heaven" (לחם מן־השמים, 16:4a) and "to be satisfied with bread" (תשבעו־לחם, 16:12c). Psalm 105's descriptions show parallels to Psalm 78 in the source (שמים, "heaven"), substance (לחם, "bread"), and abundance of provisions (שבע, "to satisfy").

Additional References to Manna in the Hebrew Bible

There are three other contexts in the Hebrew Bible where references to the provision of manna in the wilderness occur: Deuteronomy, Hosea, and Nehemiah.

In Deut 8:3 and 8:16, manna references appear in the context of a didactic lesson that recalls God's past provision in the wilderness as motivation for future obedience in the land.[67] In Deut 8:3, Moses highlights the pedagogical function of manna:

ויענך וירעבך ויאכלך את המן אשר לא ידעת ולא ידעון אבתיך
למען הודעך כי לא על הלחם לבדו יחיה האדם
כי על כל מוצא פי יהוה יחיה האדם:

He humbled you by letting you hunger,[68] then by feeding you with manna, with which neither you nor your ancestors knew, in order to make you know that one does not live by bread alone, but by all that comes from the mouth of YHWH.

Deuteronomy 8:3 and Psalm 78 share the words "manna" (מן) and "bread" (לחם), and the verb "to eat" (אכל). In light of the instances in Exodus 16

67. This theme of remembering/forgetting runs through Deuteronomy 8 (זכר "remembering" vv. 2, 18; שכח "forgetting" vv. 11, 14, 19), as it does in Psalm 78 (זכר "remembering" vv. 35, 39, 42; שכח "forgetting" vv. 7, 11). For a helpful discussion of food and memory in Deuteronomy, see MacDonald's chapter "Chewing the Cud" in *Not Bread Alone*, 70–99, esp. 83–85.

68. The language of "hunger" (רעב) occurs only once in the wilderness narratives (Exod 16:3) in Israel's complaint that YHWH brought them into the wilderness to kill them with "hunger" (רעב). Israel's cravings (תאוה)—not their hunger—drive the discussion in Psalm 78.

where "bread" in the wilderness serves as a synonym for "manna" (vv. 15, 32), it may be possible that the terms "manna" (מן) and "bread" (לחם) are being used interchangeably here as well.[69] Deuteronomy 8:16 also references manna in the wilderness:

> המאכלך מן במדבר אשר לא ידעון אבתיך למען
> ענתך ולמען נסתך להיטבך באחריתך:
>
> He fed you in the wilderness with manna that your ancestors did not know, to humble you and to test you,[70] and in the end to do you good.

Psalm 78 shares only the lexemes "manna" (מן) and "to eat" (אכל). In these texts in Deuteronomy, neither the "heavenly" source of the food nor its abundant supply is emphasized; instead, the focus is on the trustworthiness of YHWH who "fed" (אכל) Israel in the wilderness.

The reference to divine provision of food in Hos 13:5–6 is often overlooked in discussions of manna.[71] Yet, the wilderness context and word choice add significant weight to this association:

> אני ידעתיך במדבר בארץ תלאבות:
> כמרעיתם וישבעו שבעו וירם לבם על כן שכחוני:
>
> It was I who knew you in the wilderness, in the land of drought. As soon as they ate, they were satisfied; they were satisfied, and their heart was proud; therefore they forgot me.

There is only one direct lexical parallel with Psalm 78's manna event, and this is through the repeated reference to the verbal root "to satisfy" (שבע).[72]

69. Acknowledging the tendency among preachers and scholars to view these two food references as a contrast between spiritual and material realities, Nelson counters this view and presents a moderating position: "The manna is not used to contrast miraculous providence with ordinary bread, but highlights the similarity of Yahweh's nurturing gifts in both wilderness and land." Nelson, *Deuteronomy*, 112.

70. Similar to Exod 16:4, manna is associated with divine testing of Israel (contra Ps 78:18 where Israel tests God).

71. The *Dictionary of the Old Testament: Pentateuch* article on "Manna" contains no mention of Hos 13. Strawn, "Manna," 560–62.

72. Here, McConville sees a variety of links to Deuteronomy 8's description of the wilderness, particularly the food events: "The thought in Hos. 13:4–8 is similar, with surprisingly close echoes of Deut. 8, extending even to vocabulary, mainly in Hos. 13:4–6: 'from Egypt' (Deut. 8:14; Hos. 13:4), 'satisfied' (*saba*, Deut. 8:12; Hos. 13:6), 'hearts lifted up' (Deut. 8:14; Hos. 13:6), 'forgetting' (Deut. 8:11, 14, 19; Hos. 13:6). Other elements are also present, for example 'feeding', though the terms used differ (Deut. 8:3; Hos. 13:6)." McConville, *Deuteronomy*, 167.

In Nehemiah 9, references to divine provision of manna occur twice in this historical recital. The first instance mentions "bread from heaven" (v. 15) and the second refers to "manna" (v. 20):

ולחם משמים נתתה להם לרעבם

For their hunger you gave them bread from heaven. (v. 15)

ומנך לא מנעת מפיהם

[You] did not withhold your manna from their mouths. (v. 20)

This account in Nehemiah 9 utilizes expressions similar to Ps 78:24–25 in the reference to "bread" (לחם) whose source is "heaven" (שמים), as well as a direct reference to "manna" (מן).

Across these texts, the term "manna" (מן) occurs with great regularity (Deut 8:3; 8:16; Neh 9:20); the term "bread of heaven" (לחם משמים) appears, as well (Neh 9:15). Israel is "fed" (אכל, Deut 8:3, 16) and "satisfied" (שבע, Hos 13:6) by God in the wilderness. Hosea 13:5–6 is the only text that uses this food account to accentuate Israel's rebellion (cf. Ps 78).

Summary of Parallel References to Manna

As seen in the above discussions, references to God's provision of manna in the wilderness appear in a variety of texts across the Hebrew Bible. Exodus 16 and Numbers 11 provide the most detailed descriptions of manna—including its appearance, its taste, and instructions for its preparation. All other accounts rely on two general terms to designate this divinely given food: "manna" (מן, Exod 16:31; Num 11:6, 7, 9; Deut 8:3, 16; Ps 78:24; Neh 9:20) and "bread/food" (לחם, Exod 16:4, 8, 12, 15, 22, 29, 32; Pss 78:25; 105:40; Neh 9:15; cf. Deut 8:3). When the generic term "bread/food" (לחם) is used, there is often a locational modifier included to add specificity—bread/food from "heaven" (שמים, Exod 16:4; Ps 105:40; Neh 9:15) or bread in the "wilderness" (מדבר, Exod 16:32; cf. "manna in the wilderness," Deut 8:16).

In regard to the divine provision of manna, forms of the verbal root "to satisfy" (שבע) often appear in this context (Exod 16:8, 12; Pss 78:25; 105:40; Hos 13:6). The language of manna which "rains" (מטר) from heaven appears only in Exod 16:4 and Ps 78:24. The specific language of YHWH "giving" (נתן) manna occurs in Exod 16:15, Ps 78:24, and Neh 9:15.

There is surprising diversity in the ways that the manna tradition is employed across the Hebrew Bible. Exodus 16 presents YHWH's provision of manna as both a response to Israel's hunger (v. 3; cf. Deut 8:3), as well as a test (v. 4; Deut 8:16). In Ps 105:40, the account of the provision of manna recalls YHWH's faithfulness to Israel; in Hos 13:5–6, it highlights Israel's rebellion.

Literary Analysis of Psalm 78's Depiction of Manna (vv. 23–25)

Psalm 78's record of the manna event holds two notable features—the lavish abundance of the food and the active involvement of YHWH in supplying the food. This abundance of food is accentuated through the quantity and variety of descriptors used and the uniqueness of the chosen expressions. Israel first asks YHWH for "bread" (לחם) in vv. 19b–20—here the term is used in a general way with no elaboration: "Is YHWH able to set a table in the wilderness? . . . Is he able to give bread (לחם) as well, can he provide meat for his people?" This term appears again in v. 25 as YHWH provides Israel not just with "bread" (לחם), but "bread of the mighty" (לחם אבירים). In addition, the psalmist includes three added food descriptors in rapid succession (vv. 24–25): "manna" (מן), "grain from heaven" (דגן־שמים), and "provisions" (צידה).[73] Two other expressions add to this sense of plenty—the reference in v. 23 to YHWH "opening the doors of heaven" (דלתי שמים פתח) and v. 25's language of "abundance" (לשבע). The image of the doors of the house of heaven being opened wide accentuates the magnitude of the divine response.[74] In addition, the psalmist may be employing merism here. The reference in v. 23 to food that appears out of "the heavens" forms a merism with v. 15 where Israel is said to drink from "the deeps." Israel is thus surrounded

73. This term "provisions" (צידה) appears 10x in the MT, often used for the food required for a long journey or march (Gen 27:3; 42:25; 45:21; Exod 12:39; Josh 1:11; 9:11; Judg 7:8; 20:10; 1 Sam 22:10; Ps 78:25).

74. The expression "doors of heaven" is unique to Psalm 78. However, the "windows" of heaven appear in various texts to emphasize divine destruction or divine blessing. In Gen 7:11 the "windows" (ארבות) of heaven open to bring floods; in Mic 3:10, the "windows" (ארבות) of heaven are said to open to bring blessing. In 2 Kgs 7:2, there is a similar expression of wonderment regarding the improbability of abundant provision of food. Here in the context of the Assyrian siege, the expression "windows of heaven" is used regarding improbable food supplies: "Even if YHWH were to make windows in the sky, could such a thing happen?" (הנה יהוה עשה ארבות בשמים היהיה הדבר הזה).

from below and from above by divine provisions. The second term, "in abundance" (לשבע), familiar from other manna contexts, also evokes a sense of copious provision.[75]

While the use of the term "manna" (v. 24) and references to "abundance" (v. 25) link this psalm to other manna texts (see discussion above), the psalmist employs two unique expressions for the manna—"grain from heaven" (דגן־שמים) and "bread of the mighty" (לחם אבירים). The expression "bread from heaven" (לחם . . . שמים) appears in Exod 16:4, Ps 105:40, and Neh 9:15. Here in Ps 78:24, the psalmist employs the expression "grain from heaven." The term "grain" (דגן) occurs only 40x in MT, most often in Deuteronomy, Hosea, and Nehemiah, and never in the context of the wilderness narratives. The use of the term "grain" (דגן) instead of "bread" (לחם) may be an attempt by the psalmist to evoke the appearance of the manna as being "like coriander seed" (Exod 16:31; Num 11:7).[76]

The phrase לחם אבירים (lit. "bread of the mighty") also provides a unique description of the manna. The term אביר is used infrequently in the MT (17x) and can refer to men or animals (often a metaphor for kings or enemies). BDB associates the word אבירים in Psalm 78 with angels (cf. Ps 103:20), although the link to Psalm 103 is tenuous. The LXX translates the phrase as "bread of angels."[77] While the term אבירים appears various times in the MT, it never refers directly to angels.[78] At the end of the line, the psalmist chooses an infrequent term for food, "provisions" (צידה). This term appears 10x in the MT, most often to refer to the food required for a long journey or march (Gen 27:3 [Ketiv]; 42:25; 45:21; Exod 12:39; Josh 1:11; 9:11; Judg 7:8; 20:10; 1 Sam 22:10; Ps 78:25). When taken together, the two images depict the journeying aspect of the Israelites, like an army on the move.

75. A point recognized by Anderson, who comments on this term: "To the full or satiety, enough and more than enough to satisfy the appetite of every individual; another expression borrowed from the history. See Exod. xvi. 3." Anderson, *Book of Psalms*, 330.

76. A point noted by Kirkpatrick: "Corn of heaven may allude to the granular form of the manna (Ex. xvi. 31)." Kirkpatrick, *Psalms 42–89*, 470.

77. Most modern translations follow the LXX and render the term אבירים as "angels" (NRSV, NIV11, NASB, ESV). Hossfeld translates the term more literally as "bread of the strong" but assumes that the text refers to "heavenly beings in contrast to the earthly powers of Pss 50:13 and 68:31." Hossfeld and Zenger, *Psalms 2*, 296.

78. It is, however, used for God. Kraus cites the following texts: Gen 49:24; Isa 1:24; 49:26; 60:16; Ps 132:2, 5. Kraus, *Psalms 60–150*, 128.

The active involvement of YHWH in this miracle of food is also notable. The manna account begins with YHWH "commanding" (צוה) the skies and "opening" (פתח) the doors of heaven (v. 23). The verb "to command" (צוה) occurs twice within Psalm 78. Its first occurrence is in the psalm's introduction (v. 5) where the psalmist reminds the audience that God "commanded" (צוה) Israel to teach his decrees (עדות)/laws (תורה) to their children. While in v. 5 there is no comment on Israel's actual compliance, here in v. 23, there is no doubt about nature's willing obedience to God's "command" (צוה). In vv. 24–25, YHWH's involvement in providing for Israel is highlighted by presenting YHWH as the subject of a succession of three verbs—"rained" (מטר), "gave" (נתן), "sent" (שלח). The use of the verb "to give" (נתן) in v. 24 is the second occurrence of this verb in the psalm. It appeared first in v. 20b as Israel questions God's ability to meet their physical needs in the wilderness: "Can he also give (נתן) bread or provide meat for his people?" Verses 24–25 offer a striking answer to this rhetorical question as YHWH not only "gives" (נתן) them bread but also lavishes Israel with "grain of heaven" (דגן־שמים), "bread of the mighty" (לחם אבירים), "provisions in abundance" (צידה . . . לשבע). Like the abundant flow of water from a rock (vv. 15–16), the psalmist's depiction of the manna event (vv. 23–25) paints a grand picture of YHWH's abundant wilderness provision.

PROVISION OF QUAIL (PS 78:26–28)

יסע קדים בשמים וינהג בעזו תימן:
וימטר עליהם כעפר שאר וכחול ימים עוף כנף:
ויפל בקרב מחנהו סביב למשכנתיו:

He sent out the east wind in the heavens, and by his power he led out the south wind;
He rained flesh upon them like dust, winged birds like the sand of the seas;
He let them fall within their[79] camp, all around their dwellings.

79. The MT has masculine singular suffixes on both "camp" and "dwellings." If one takes these singular suffixes as collective in nature, they would refer to Israel/Jacob. Hossfeld holds this position: "The ancient versions replace the MT's enclitic personal pronouns in the third person masculine singular, which refer to Israel/Jacob as a collective whole, with the plural, in order to avoid any possible application to God, the subject of the sentence." Hossfeld and Zenger, *Psalms 2*, 285. Tate, however, argues that the referent in this verse is in fact YHWH. In this case, "the camp is Yahweh's, in the midst of which he has his earthly dwelling place in the tabernacle." Tate, *Psalms 51–100*, 282.

Parallel References to the Provision of Quail

References to God's gift of quail occur with even less frequency within the Hebrew Bible than to divine provision of manna or water from a rock.[80] References appear only in the Torah (Exod 16:1–13; Num 11:1–34; Deut 9:22) and Writings (Pss 78:26–28; 105:40; 106:14).[81] As will be seen in the study below, Psalm 78 both adapts and innovates in its depiction of this wilderness food event.

Quail Provision in the Wilderness Narratives (Exodus–Numbers)

The divine provision of quail is mentioned twice during Israel's wilderness journey (Exod 16:1–13; Num 11:3–34). In the Exodus account, the provision of manna overshadows the quail, whose arrival in the camp is mentioned only in passing (16:13). In Numbers 11, the focus of the account is primarily on the quail, with the manna playing a secondary role to explain the reason for Israel's dietary discontent (v. 6).

Provision of Quail at Wilderness of Sin (Exod 16:1–13)

In the wilderness of Sin, the people "grumbled" (לון) with Moses and Aaron (v. 2) as they recalled their past experiences in Egypt: "If only we had died by the hand of YHWH in the land of Egypt, when we sat by pots of meat (סיר הבשר) and ate our fill of bread; for you have brought us out into this wilderness to kill this whole assembly with hunger" (v. 3). While YHWH explicitly promises "bread from heaven" (v. 4), no mention is made of meat until v. 8 when Moses announces that YHWH will bring "meat" (בשר) for Israel. This announcement is repeated in v. 12 with YHWH's specific statement to Moses about the food provision: "I have heard (שמע)[82] the complaining of the Israelites; say to them, 'At twilight

Both positions have merit. In light of the psalmist's focus on Israel's experience in these food events, I have translated the singular pronouns as collective in nature.

80. The greater frequency of references in the Hebrew Bible to the manna event may relate to the fact that this was recorded as a daily event (cf. Num 11:9), unlike the quail, which only appeared sporadically on Israel's wilderness journey.

81. Surprisingly, Neh 9:15's recital of the food events in the wilderness omits the mention of quail, focusing only on manna and water from the rock.

82. The language of YHWH "hearing" (שמע) Israel's complaint also occurs in Psalm 78's recounting of the event (v. 21).

you shall eat (אכל) meat (בשר), and in the morning you shall have your fill of bread; then you shall know that I am YHWH your God.'"[83] The arrival that evening of the promised "meat" in the form of quail (שלו) is described with language that is concise and direct (16:13a):[84]

ויהי בערב ותעל השלו ותכס את המחנה

In the evening quails came up and covered the camp.

Following this initial provision, there is no other mention of the quail in Exodus.[85]

The only lexical similarity between Exod 16:1–13 and Ps 78:26–28 occurs in the description of the location of the event, specifically that it is in their "camp" (מחנה).[86] It is noteworthy that while Exod 16:8, 12 (cf. v. 3) use the general word for "meat" (בשר), Psalm 78 uses the term שאר, a point that will be discussed in the literary analysis that follows.

Provision of Quail at Taberah (Num 11:4–34)

The narrator begins this account (v. 4a) with a foreboding declaration: "The rabble among them had a strong craving" (התאוו תאוה). The Israelites are swept into this passionate fervor and declare: "If only we had meat (בשר) to eat (אכל)! We remember the fish we used to eat in Egypt for nothing, the cucumbers, the melons, the leeks, the onions, and the garlic; but now our strength (נפש)[87] is dried up, and there is nothing at all but this manna to look at" (vv. 4b–6).[88] Following a description of

83. Israel's earlier recollection of the foods of Egypt (including "pots of meat," Exod 16:3) may be what prompts YHWH to provide not only manna but also quail.

84. As Sarna notes: "The narrative is expansive on the manna but terse with respect to the quail." Sarna, *Exodus*, 88.

85. Childs notes: "The abrupt handling of the quail leaves the narrative in somewhat [of] an unresolved tension which reflects the complex history of tradition behind the story. The balance between meat in the evening and bread in the morning at first leads the reader to picture both gifts alternating in a continuous cycle. . . . Although the text is never explicit and a certain ambiguity remains, the larger context does indicate that only the manna was understood as a continuing gift." Childs, *Book of Exodus*, 288.

86. The term מחנה ("camp") occurs 189x in the MT, with 20 percent of the occurrences within the wilderness narratives (38x). It appears only three times in the Psalms (27:3; 78:28; 106:16); only in Ps 78:28 does it refer to the quail account.

87. The term נפש (here translated "strength," more common "soul") occurs in Ps 78:18 as Israel demands "food of their soul" (אכל לנפשם).

88. Here Israel cries out for meat, yet the recollection of Egypt is primarily a litany of vegetables. The most ironic statement in this food complaint occurs at the beginning

the manna (vv. 7–9), the text notes YHWH's heated response to Israel's dissatisfaction (v. 10a): "the anger (אף) of YHWH burned (חרה) greatly."[89] Moses then turns to YHWH with his leadership frustrations (vv. 11–15) including the people's request for "meat" (v. 13). YHWH responds with a plan to diversify leadership to include a group of elders (vv. 16–17) and then turns to the subject of meat (vv. 18–20). Moses is told to tell the people of YHWH's intention to give them meat, yet this provision takes on an ironic twist. Moses tells them: "You shall eat not only one day, or two days, or five days, or ten days, or twenty days, but for a whole month—until it comes out of your nostrils (אף) and becomes loathsome (זרא)[90] to you" (v. 19–20a). This extreme provision is a direct result of Israel's rejection of YHWH and their nostalgia for Egypt (v. 20b). Moses' concern turns immediately to how to find such a large quantity of food (v. 21), as he proceeds to list off the variety of unavailable sources (flocks, herds, fish) for that much meat (v. 22). YHWH responds with an invitation for Moses to see that YHWH's words are true (v. 23), as a group of elders is commissioned (vv. 24–29) and the quail arrive (vv. 31–32). While Israel begins to eat the quail (v. 33), judgment ensues as YHWH's anger (אף) is kindled (חרה) against the people who are struck (נכה) with a very great plague. The account ends (v. 34) with a statement about the naming of the site Kibroth-hattaavah, a reference to where they "buried" (קבר) those with a great "craving" (תאוה).

The account of the arrival of the quail (vv. 31–32) is particularly descriptive: "Then a wind (רוח) went out (נסע) from YHWH, and it brought quails (שלו) from the sea and let them fall beside the camp (מחנה), about a day's journey on this side and a day's journey on the other side, all around (סביב) the camp (מחנה) about two cubits deep on the ground" (v. 31–32).[91]

---

of v. 5: "We remember the fish we used to eat in Egypt for nothing." Ashley notes: "The people remembered eating, but it was hardly *for free*. In fact, the cost of that plenty had been slavery, and the contrast drawn by the people between the plenty of slavery and the *nothing at all* (except manna) of their freedom (given by Yahweh) is seen as rebellion against God the Liberator (see vv. 18–20)." Ashley, *Book of Numbers*, 208.

89. Although Psalm 78 uses the term "anger" (אף) to describe YHWH's reaction to Israel's wilderness food rebellion, in these cases (vv. 21, 31) it is used with the verb "to go up" (עלה). The verb "to burn, be angry" (חרה) never occurs in this psalm.

90. The term זרא is a hapax, making this a second hapax used to describe Israel's discontent with their desert diet (cf. the term קלקל "miserable, worthless" in Num 21:5).

91. YHWH's promise in v. 21 of a month's worth of meat is reflected here in the large quantity of quail that appear in Israel's camp. Unlike the daily arrival of manna (as well as the two-day portion before the Sabbath day), here Israel is given a thirty-day supply of meat all in one day.

This divine response to Israel's mutinous cravings has a sarcastic edge. God promises the Israelites exactly what they requested: meat and lots of it. So much meat that, as Olson observes, "the Israelites wade hip deep in dead birds and feathers."[92] In addition, Num 11:33a provides a rhetorical flourish noting the irony of the timing of the judgment—"while the meat was still between their teeth" (הבשר עודנו בין שניהם), a classic depiction of talionic justice.

The descriptions of the quail event in Num 11:4–34 and Ps 78:26–28 contain only a few shared lexemes, including the verb "to pull out, to set out, journey" (נסע) associated with the wind (Num 11:31; Ps 78:26) and the locational details of the quail falling "all around" (סביב) the "camp" (מחנה).[93]

In the wilderness narratives, the gift of quail is presented as both an act of gracious provision (Exod 16) and a vehicle of divine judgment (Num 11).[94] In Exodus the arrival of meat in the form of quail is of secondary importance to the provision of manna—the narrator simply notes its arrival in the camp. In Numbers 11, the provision of the quail is described with grand rhetorical flourish as Israel's cravings lead ultimately to their death.

References to Quail in the Psalms

References to the provision of quail in the wilderness appear three times, all within the "historical psalms": Pss 78:26–28; 105:40, and 106:14–15.[95]

92. Olson, *Numbers*, 69.

93. The term "to pull out, set out, journey" (נסע) occurs 146x in MT (89x in Numbers; 3x in Psalms; 2x in Psalm 78). This verb is used in Numbers 11 and Psalm 78 to describe YHWH's leading of both the wind (Num 11:31; Ps 78:26) and Israel (Num 11:35; Ps 78:52). The word "all around" (סביב) appears 338x in the MT (18x in Numbers; 19x in Psalms). The word "camp" (מחנה) occurs 215x in the MT (49x in Numbers; 3x in Psalms—27:3; 78:28, and 106:16).

94. Regarding these contrasting outcomes, Olson notes: "The complaints that Israel makes to God in the book of Exodus are treated as legitimate needs: the people need water (Exod. 15:22–26), the people need food (Exod. 16), and the people need water again (Exod. 17:1–7). In each case God takes the complaint seriously and fulfills the needs of the Israelites by turning bitter water into sweet water, by providing manna and quail for food, and by causing water to flow from a rock." Olson, *Numbers*, 61. Yet, as we move into the book of Numbers, Olson observes a radical shift: "after Sinai and all the provisions God has given to the Israelites in the desert, the same needs and complaints arise, yet they take on a different complexion. Legitimate pleas for mercy become subversive acts of unfaith punishable by death" (64).

95. See chapter 6 for an extended discussion of these historical psalms.

Each of these psalms presents the quail event through a slightly different lens.

Psalm 105 depicts the quail account as the first element in a trio of divine provisions in the wilderness (vv. 40–41):[96]

שאל ויבא שלו ולחם שמים ישביעם:
פתח צור ויזובו מים הלכו בציות נהר:

> They asked, and he brought quails and satisfied them with bread from heaven.
> He opened the rock, and water gushed out; it flowed through the dry land like a river.

In this psalm, the quail are presented as an act of gracious provision where YHWH meets the needs of his people as they journey out of Egypt. Besides the provision of divine guidance in the cloud/fire (v. 39), this account of divine feeding is the only wilderness event mentioned in Psalm 105. Of particular note is the fact that the term "quail" (שלו) occurs only here in Ps 105:40 and in the wilderness food accounts (Exod 16:13; Num 11:31–32). There are no shared lexemes with Psalm 78's depiction of the specific provision of the quail.

Psalm 106 sets the account of the quail within the context of explicit rebellion where Israel has "forgotten" (שכח) God's works (v. 13):

ויתאוו תאוה במדבר וינסו אל בישימון:
ויתן להם שאלתם וישלח רזון בנפשם:

> But they had an intense craving in the wilderness and put God to the test in the desert.
> He gave them what they asked but sent a leanness in their soul.[97] (vv. 14–15)

Here Israel's desire for meat is called an "intense craving" (אוה תאוה), a description that provides a direct link to the Numbers passage (11:4, 34; cf. Ps 78:29–30). Although the tone of the passage is similar to Psalm 78, the two psalms contain no shared lexemes in the depiction of this food event.

The paired psalms of Psalm 105 and Psalm 106 present the quail account in surprisingly different guises. Psalm 105 presents the event in a

96. Here in Psalm 105, the order of the food elements (quail, manna, water from a rock) follows the ordering of events in Exodus 16–17.

97. Psalm 106 uses a unique expression רזון בנפשם (lit. "a leanness in their soul") to describe the consequences of the event (cf. Isa 10:16; 24:16; Mic 6:10).

positive light as God's gracious provision; Psalm 106 emphasizes instead the rebellious nature of Israel's request (v. 14) and its deadly outcome (v. 15). Psalm 105 resembles the Exodus account of the event (Exod 16–17) with its trio of provisions (quail, manna, water from a rock), while Ps 106:14–15 with its mention of "craving" (תאוה) resembles Numbers 11.

Additional References to Quail in the Hebrew Bible

The remaining reference to the quail account appears in Deut 9:22. In this case, the connection is made simply through the location name associated with the event—Kibroth-hattaavah:

ובתבערה ובמסה ובקברת התאוה מקצפים הייתם את יהוה

> At Taberah also, and at Massah, and at Kibroth-hattaavah, you provoked YHWH to wrath.

This listing of place-names calls to mind three events from the wilderness narratives. The ordering of these events is surprising in that Massah—an event associated with Israel's early days in the wilderness (Exod 17:1–7)—is sandwiched within the accounts of Num 11:1–3 and Num 11:4–34. Taberah recalls the events of Num 11:1–3 where the people complained of their misfortunes and a fire of YHWH "burned" (בער) against them. Massah is associated with Exod 17:7 where Israel "tested" (נסה) YHWH because of their desert thirst (cf. Deut 6:16; 33:8; Ps 95:8). And finally Kibroth-hattaavah, a location linked to the events of Num 11:4–34 (cf. 33:16, 17), where they "buried" (קבר) those with a great "craving" (תאוה).

Summary of Parallel References to Quail

These parallel passages show a variety of similar and identical expressions for this wilderness food: "meat" (בשר; Exod 16:8, 12; Num 11:18, 33 // שאר, Ps 78:27), "quail" (שלו; Exod 16:13a; Num 11:31; Ps 105:40 // עוף כנף, Ps 78:27), "craving" (אוה; Num 11:4, 34; Ps 78:29, 30; Ps 106:14). The accounts are split between positive portrayals of the event as gracious gift (Exod 16:1–13; Ps 105:40) and negative construals where the quail are a vehicle for divine judgment (Num 11:4–34; Ps 106:14–15; cf. Deut 9:22).

Literary Analysis of Psalm 78's Depiction of Quail (vv. 26–28)

Psalm 78's account of the quail event holds two striking features: its lexical choices in describing the provision of food and its abundance, and its depiction of YHWH's employment of the natural world to carry out this provision.

The psalmist shows great creativity and intentionality in the lexical choices for describing this food event. As seen in the framing of water from the rock (vv. 13–17), the psalmist here also draws on verbal repetition to connect events. In vv. 23–27, the psalmist uses the verb מטר ("to rain") to describe the arrival of both manna (v. 24) and quail (v. 27).[98] The psalmist also avoids common lexemes that would result in the audience connecting events. This lexical avoidance occurs twice in this passage, where the psalmist avoids the word בשר for quail and the word רוח for wind. As seen in the summary of parallel texts, three terms are used in the MT to describe the provision of quail: "meat" (בשר; Exod 16:8, 12; Num 11:18, 33), "quail" (שלו; Exod 16:13a; Num 11:31; Ps 105:40), and "craving" (אוה; Num 11:4, 34; Ps 78:29, 30; Ps 106:14). Instead of using the term בשר for "meat" (the primary designation found in the wilderness narratives),[99] the psalmist uses the less common term שאר.[100] This term appears in 78:20 when Israel requests bread (לחם) and "meat" (שאר) and again in v. 27 to describe YHWH's provision of "meat" (שאר) in the form of "winged birds" (עוף כנף). When the psalmist does use the term בשר, the word is a synonym for the finitude of humanity (v. 39): "He remembered that they were but flesh (בשר), a breath/breeze (רוח) that goes out and does not return." Through this lexical differentiation (בשר/שאר) the psalmist is making a clear distinction between human flesh and

98. The wilderness narratives use the verb מטר ("to rain") to describe the provision of manna (Exod 16:4), but not the quail.

99. In the wilderness narratives, the term בשר is used as a generic reference to "meat" (Exod 16:3; Num 11:4, 13, 21), as well as a specific reference to "quail" (Exod 16:8, 12; Num 11:18, 33). The term בשר appears 273x in MT (14x Exodus; 14x in Numbers; 16x in Psalms).

100. The word שאר appears only 16x in the MT, with its primary reference being one's relatives (Lev 18:6, 12, 13; 20:19; 21:2; 25:49; Num 27:11), the human body (Jer 51:35; Ps 73:26; Prov 11:17), and a reference to food in general (Exod 21:10). Leviticus 18:6 and 25:49 use the term שאר and בשר in tandem in the expression "the flesh of your relative." Micah 3:2–3 uses the terms שאר to refer to human flesh and בשר to refer to animal flesh. Proverbs 5:11 uses the two terms in parallel, both referring to human flesh.

human food in the form of animal flesh.[101] The second lexical avoidance relates to the psalmist's description of the means of divine provision (v. 26). Avoiding the usual word for "wind" (רוח), the psalmist instead utilizes the directional markers "east" (קדם) and "south" (תימן). The avoidance of the word "wind" may also be triggered by its use in v. 39 where it is used to emphasize the fleeting nature of human life. Here the psalmist employs two common words from the natural world (בשר and רוח) and uses them exclusively to depict human life, contrary to their more typical senses.

The psalmist's lexical choices in describing the abundance of the provision are also noteworthy. Instead of relying on the term "quail" (שלו),[102] the psalmist chooses to describe the provision using two other expressions—"meat" (שאר) and "winged bird" (עוף כנף). While the term "bird" (עוף) occurs in the Hebrew Bible with some regularity (73x in MT; 4x in Psalms; 0 occurrences in Exodus/Numbers), the expression "winged bird" (עוף כנף) occurs only here and in Gen 1:21. In the creation account, the expression is used for any type of bird (1:21; cf. 7:14), thus including but not limited to quail. The Genesis reference celebrates the fact that God made the "winged birds"; in Psalm 78, the focus moves to the fact that these creatures submit to the Creator's bidding.

Psalm 78 also emphasizes the copious quantity of food with two familiar expressions. In v. 27, the psalmist notes: "He rained flesh upon them like dust (כעפר), winged birds like the sand of the seas (כחול ימים)."[103] The expressions כעפר and כחול ימים are both used in the book of Genesis to describe the multitude of descendants promised in the Abrahamic Covenant: descendants "like the dust of earth" (Gen 13:16; 28:14) and "like the sand of the sea" (Gen 22:17; 32:12).[104] In Genesis, these expres-

101. As Hossfeld notes: "For 'flesh' the text consistently uses the uncommon concept שאר (vv. 20, 27) probably in contrast to human flesh, בשר, which is used in v. 39, even though Exodus 16 uses only בשר." Hossfeld and Zenger, *Psalms 2*, 296.

102. The term "quail" (שלו) occurs only 4x in MT (Exod 16:13; Num 11:31, 32; Ps 105:40). Ashley notes: "Most modern scholars agree that a bird of genus *coturnix* is meant, the most abundant of which is the common quail (*coturnix coturnix, coturnix vulgaris*), which migrates from Europe and West Asia to North Africa." Ashley, *Numbers*, 217.

103. Winds from the east—typically coming off the Arabian desert—would be as likely to bring dust/sand as they would be carrying quail. The New English Bible captures this idea in their translation of v. 27a: "He rained meat like a dust-storm upon them."

104. The expression "like the sand of the sea" is also used to describe Joseph's stockpile of grain during the famine in Egypt (Gen 41:49).

sions attempt to capture the enormity of this promise of future progeny; in Psalm 78, these expressions are now turned from contemplating offspring in the future to the abundance of food in the present.

Here in Psalm 78, the psalmist emphasizes the role of nature—in this case, the winds—in this wilderness wonder. In the Exodus account, the appearance of the quail is briefly noted (16:13a). In the Numbers account, the narrator simply acknowledges the role of the wind in this event (11:31). In Psalm 78's depiction of the quail account, YHWH's sovereign reign over the natural world gains extra prominence. Wiggins observes that in Psalm 78 "the wind appears as an agent of Yhwh, an embassy doing the divine bidding."[105] Compared with the accounts in the wilderness narratives, the psalmist underscores both nature's role and its obedience in this event. Psalm 78:26 states: "He sent out (נסע) the east wind in the heavens, and by his power he led out (נהג) the south wind." The two verbs used here for YHWH's control of the winds are "to pull out, set out, journey" (נסע) and "to drive, lead" (נהג). These two verbs appear in the same form and order in Ps 78:52 where YHWH shepherds his people out of Egypt (v. 52).[106] Linking YHWH's leading of the winds and his people Israel ("his flock") underscores the Creator's sovereign power and care for Israel.

Framing of Manna/Quail Events (Ps 78:18–31)

When viewed within the larger frame surrounding these events (vv. 18–22 // 29–31), this picture of divine provision is held in tension with the depiction of Israel's rebellion and the declaration of YHWH's wrath (vv. 18–22) that precedes it. When divine judgment comes to Israel as they are eating (vv. 29–31), this tension turns to dismay, as God's food provision is in fact the vehicle of divine judgment.

In v. 18, the narrator identifies Israel's request for food as a "test" (נסה) of YHWH. This test is further clarified in vv. 19b, 20b as Israel questions YHWH's "ability" (יכל) to provide food within their present

105. Wiggins, "Tempestuous Wind Doing YHWH's Will," 23. In this article, Wiggins explores "aeolian terminology" in the Psalms in an attempt to determine how the wind was perceived by the psalmists. He observes that "the wind is guided by divine intention. The weather in general is understood as a kind of 'barometer' of Yhwh's interaction with humankind. . . . Never is the wind understood as a neutral natural phenomenon in the Psalms—it is always a divine instrument, usually for purposes of destruction" (3).

106. These terms occur together nowhere else in the MT.

context: "Is God able (יכל) to set a table in the wilderness? . . . is he able (יכל) to give bread (לחם) as well, can he provide meat (שׁאר) for his people?" Although Israel can recall and even recite YHWH's wondrous provision of water (v. 20a),[107] they still fail to understand the significance of the event. In answers to Israel's query, YHWH does in fact set a table in the wilderness with "bread" and "meat" in abundance (vv. 23–28).

Verse 21 contains the first of two occurrences of the phrase YHWH/God "heard and was furious" (שׁמע . . . ויתעבר) in the psalm (cf. v. 59). In this first occurrence, Israel's verbal complaint is in fact inserted into the psalm (vv. 19–20); in the second occasion, when Israel's rebellion takes the form of idolatry and pagan worship, the specific "verbal" defiance is omitted (v. 59). Verse 21 explicitly notes that Israel's rebellion calls forth a reaction of divine "fury" (עבר), "fire" (אשׁ), and "anger" (אף). In v. 22, the narrator associates Israel's response as a failure to "trust, believe" (אמן) and "trust" (בטח).[108] Directly following the description of Israel's rebellion and YHWH's anger (vv. 18–22), the psalmist depicts divine food provision (vv. 23–29)—not divine judgment. This divine banquet scene creates a tension in the text. How should one read these food events? Are these stories of gracious provision,[109] or is the food a manifestation of divine judgment?[110] I am inclined to view it as both.[111]

The scene of divine provision closes with a depiction of Israel consuming food and being consumed by divine judgment (vv. 29–31). Here Israel is described with both a full stomach (v. 29) and a full mouth (v. 30).[112] Two aspects of v. 30 are noteworthy. First, the phrase לא־זרו מתאותם. The

107. Psalm 78:20a: "Even so, he struck the rock so that water gushed out and torrents overflowed" (הן הכה צור ויזובו מים ונחלים ישׁטפו). Israel's description actually intensifies the miracle. They recall "gushing" waters and "overflowing" wadis while the psalmist's initial description of the event (v. 16) relies on more common verbs to describe the movement of the waters (יצא "to go out" and ירד "to go down").

108. In Psalm 78, the verb בטח "to trust" occurs only here in v. 22. However, the verb אמר "to trust, believe" occurs 4x, all in the negative (vv. 8, 22, 32, 37).

109. In light of the emphasis on YHWH's abundant supply of food, this view has strong merit.

110. Tanner notes: "God's response in anger is to give the people exactly what they asked for in the first place." DeClaissé-Walford et al., *Book of Psalms*, 623.

111. Derek Kidner offers a helpful compromise: "God's reply to the challenge of 19f. was in fact a fiery 'No' to the spirit of the demand, and a prodigious 'Yes' to the substance of it." Kidner, *Psalm 73–150*, 283.

112. Some scholars include v. 29 with the food events that precede it. However, Watson, identifying a chiasm (tetracolon) with the repeated word "craving" (תאוה), links vv. 29–30 together. Watson, *Classical Hebrew Poetry*, 342.

verb זור is similar to the noun "loathsome" (זרא) used in Num 11:20 to describe the appetite-depleting result of a months' supply of quail ("it will become loathsome to you," היה לכם לזרא). Most translations render this word "to be a stranger," although the translation "not loathsome to them" captures this scene more clearly.[113] Second, the use of the general word אכלם to describe what Israel had ingested. Nasuti speculates that this word choice is "perhaps in order to include both the quails and the manna" as objects of the people's sinful demands.[114]

The frame closes with an explicit description of divine judgment (v. 31). The psalmist is able to create an inclusio of judgment (vv. 21, 31a) by repeating the same phrase—YHWH's "anger rose" (אף עלה)—before and after the food provision. The account concludes with a satirical jab at the recipients of divine judgment (v. 31b). The psalmist describes the fallen as משמניהם (literally "their fattest ones") and בחורי ישראל (the "young men of Israel"). The word משמן, often translated "strong" or "noble,"[115] is from the root משן "to be fat." The second term used for those killed is בחורי ישראל ("young men of Israel"). The irony of this phrase becomes apparent when seen in the context of the earlier description of the proliferation of quail. In v. 27, the psalmist captures the abundance of the quail in language similar to YHWH's promise of abundant progeny who would be "as dust" (כעפר) and "as the sand of the sea" (כחול ימים). Yet here in v. 31, it is the "young men of Israel" (בחורי ישראל)—the hope of the covenant promise of descendants—who in fact die as a result of the food rebellion.

Conclusion: Psalm 78's Depiction of the Manna/Quail Events (vv. 23–28)

Psalm 78's description of the provision of manna and quail in the wilderness (vv. 23–28) emphasizes the sheer abundance of this divine gift of food. The psalmist's literary skill is manifested through the adoption

113. See also Greenstein, "Mixing Memory and Design," 206.

114. Nasuti, *Tradition History and the Psalms of Asaph*, 130n86.

115. Most modern translations choose some variation on the idea of nobility or strength. Beth Tanner chooses "nobles," noting: "Fatness has a positive meaning of nobility or strength, as indicated in a related Arabic word." DeClaissé-Walford et al., *Book of Psalms*, 620n14. I would argue that this lexical movement away from the literal meaning flattens the rhetorical force of the text, trimming the richness (fat) out of the text.

of new expressions ("grain of heaven," "bread of the mighty"), adapting existing expressions (food "still in their mouths" עוד . . . בפיהם; cf. Num 11:33, עודנו בין שניהם, "still between their teeth"), and repurposing common phrases ("dust"/"sand of the sea") for new purposes. The psalmist presents YHWH as actively involved in the provision of food, even summoning the created world as servants in these wilderness food events. The manna/quail account coheres through the use of verbal repetition (מטר, "to rain," vv. 24, 27) and a balanced three-verse depiction of each event.[116] By placing the manna/quail events back to back with no intervening commentary, the psalmist is able to magnify the abundance of this divine food provision.

THE RHETORICAL USE OF FOOD IN PSALM 78:15–31

Seen within the literary frame (vv. 15–31), YHWH's provision of water/manna/quail in the wilderness draws its rhetorical power by continuously reversing expectations related to the physical, sensory, locational, social, and patterned dimensions of food. Each of these dimensions will be addressed below, followed by a consideration of their compounded rhetorical force when they appear together.

The Physical Dimension of Food in the Wilderness Account

The physical dimension of food is being subverted in this food account in that instead of preserving life, food consumption leads to death. The psalmist notes: "But before their craving was loathsome to them, while the food was still in their mouths, the anger of God rose against them and he killed the fattest among them and laid low the young men of Israel" (vv. 30–31). Two aspects of this scene are striking. First, the psalmist pictures Israel with full stomachs ("they ate and were well satisfied," v. 29) and full mouths (v. 30) at the time of their deaths. Here, the food that should have been a means to sustain life becomes a vehicle for death as what Israel desires consumes their very lives. Second, the psalmist adds an ironic flourish that echoes the narrator's depiction of the food event in

116. Each also begins with the identification of nature's involvement in the food event (vv. 23, 26).

Numbers 11.[117] In Ps 78:30b, the poetic phrase "while the food was still in their mouths" (עוד אכלם בפיהם) has a striking resonance with the narrative recounting "while the meat was still between their teeth" (הבשר עודנו בין שניהם) found in Num 11:33a. Here in Psalm 78, the psalmist once again draws upon the events of the wilderness narratives yet captures their content with a unique literary finesse.

The Sensory Dimension of Food in the Wilderness Account

The psalmist highlights the sensory dimension of food throughout the passage (vv. 18–31), particularly through the language of anticipation of food consumption, as well as the fulfillment of these food desires. The manna/quail events open (v. 18) with a reference to Israel's appetite (אכל לנפשם). In vv. 19–20, Israel's food desires are articulated as desiring a banquet of "bread" (לחם) and "meat" (שאר). In vv. 23–28, YHWH abundantly provides these foodstuffs, with the result (v. 29) that the people "ate and were well satisfied" (ויאכלו וישבעו מאד). The unique use of the modifier מאד with these verbs of food consumption captures the excessive quantity of food provided[118] and underscores YHWH's extravagant response to Israel's earlier query (v. 19). The repetition of the term "craving" (vv. 29b, 30; cf. Num 11:4) emphasizes Israel's insatiable appetite, while the reference to the death of the "fattest" (משמן) captures the results of this unrestrained eating (v. 31). Commenting on the irony of the account, Hakham notes: "He slew those who had eaten of the quails, had stuffed themselves, and had become fat from having eaten so much. The psalmist uses the word במשמניהם, in the sense of 'the people who had become fat.' This is a derogatory term implying that they had eaten so voraciously that their flesh had turned into fat."[119] In this ironic turn, judgment takes the form of Israel's initial request,[120] and comes while the taste of manna and quail is "still in their mouths" (עוד . . . בפיהם).

117. This depiction in Exod 11:33 is a piquant account of judgment: "But while the meat was still between their teeth, before it was consumed, the anger of YHWH was kindled against the people, and YHWH struck the people with a very great plague."

118. Nowhere else in the MT does the modifier מאד occur with either of these two verbs.

119. Hakham, *Psalms with the Jerusalem Commentary*, 196. For a critique of this view, see DeClaissé-Walford et al., *Book of Psalms*, 620n14.

120. As Kirkpatrick observes: "God punishes men by answering their prayers, a truth which even heathen moralists recognized." Kirkpatrick, *Psalms 42–89*, 471.

The Social Dimension of Food in the Wilderness Account

Israel's speech in vv. 19–20 is replete with irony. One aspect of their speech that is particularly ironic is their reference to Israel's relationship to YHWH as "his people" (עמו). The inclusion of this relational marker in a speech about food emphasizes Israel's expectation for YHWH as the *paterfamilias* to be concerned about the welfare of his family/clan.[121] As Cohen observes: "In these words was the sting of their grumble: if we are His people, as He claims, then He should make ample provision for us!"[122] Their accusation is a rhetorically loaded challenge to motivate YHWH to action.

The Locational Dimension of Food in the Wilderness Account

Psalm 78's recounting of the water events in the wilderness (vv. 15–16) focuses on the sheer abundance of divine provision. However, the psalmist closes the account (v. 17) by reminding the audience that the context of these miracles is in a dry desert land (ציה), a "land of drought."[123] The word used here, ציה, is a rare term, occurring only 16x in the MT. Instead of the more common word מדבר (cf. 78:15, 19, 40, 52), here the psalmist makes an intentional choice of a word for rhetorical effect. For with this word, the narrator acknowledges the very real threat associated with this wilderness environment. As Alexander observes, this term "may here be used to suggest the idea that they foolishly and wickedly provoked God in the very situation where they were most dependent on him for protection and supplies."[124] Here in an unlikely place (ציה, "a dry land") from an unlikely source (צור/סלע, "a rock"), the Most High (עליון) is at work providing for Israel's basic needs.[125]

121. Instead of the image of *paterfamilias*, Gillmayr-Bucher find the image of YHWH as king to be the dominant social metaphor underlying this account of food-provision. Gillmayr-Bucher, "How Does Food Shape History?," 91–93.

122. Cohen, *Psalms*, 252.

123. Kirkpatrick's literal translation of ציה. Kirkpatrick, *Psalms 42–89*, 468.

124. Alexander, *Psalms*, 329.

125. As Goulder aptly notes: "To anyone even thinking about desert travel the first concern is water; and in vv. 15–16 God provides *drink in abundance as out of the depths*." Goulder, *Psalms of Asaph and the Pentateuch*, 114.

In addition, the recognition of the locational dimension of the manna/quail events underscores the dramatic irony of Israel's demand for food in vv. 19–20. Similar to the miracle of God's provision of water from a rock in a "dry land" (ציה, v. 17), here Israel's location—"the wilderness" (מדבר, v. 19)—is of central importance for recognizing the rhetorical force of their demand for food. The psalmist is clear that it is not Israel's hunger that prompts them to call out for God's provision of food; it is a skepticism regarding God's ability to provide for their needs. In the wilderness, an environment of scarce natural food sources, Israel requests a lavish meal. The specific inclusion of the location of the meal underscores Israel's brash "test" (נסה, v. 18) of God's "ability" (יכל) to provide for their desires.

The Patterned Dimension of Food in the Wilderness Account

The narrator also draws on the patterned dimension of food. This can be observed particularly within Israel's verbal demand for food (vv. 19–20): "Is God able to set a table in the wilderness? Even so, he struck the rock so that water gushed out and torrents overflowed. Is he able to give bread as well, can he provide meat for his people?" This speech appears in none of the parallel passages and is not required to move the storyline forward. The argument flows naturally from the narrator's statement of Israel's treasonous food discontent (v. 18) to YHWH's response of fury/anger (v. 21). The question remains: Why does the psalmist insert this speech into the psalm? I believe that this verbal request (vv. 19–20), seen through the lens of expected etiquette at a formal meal, creates a context of situational irony that explains the violent response of the host (YHWH) that results from his guests' (Israel) abandonment of their expected role.

As noted in chapter 3, hospitality/formal meals involve social scripts for the role of guest and host. Formal meals function under an agreed-upon etiquette and a heightened set of expectations that govern their social interaction. With the acceptance of the invitation, the roles of host and guest are established and expectations are assumed for the time period of their interaction. While in the context of the wilderness, YHWH assumes the role of host and Israel as guest, with the natural world serving as YHWH's attendants.

Israel's speech in vv. 19–20 identifies three aspects of the expected table etiquette that has been either dismissed or breached by Israel. First, Israel expresses dissatisfaction with the host's provisions. In vv. 15–16, YHWH provides abundant water for Israel. Yet in v. 20, we hear their dissatisfaction with this divine table service: "Even though he struck the rock so that water gushed out and torrents overflowed, can he give bread as well, can he provide meat for his people?" Second, Israel makes specific requests of their host instead of trusting their host to meet their needs. In v. 19, Israel asks that the host "set a table" (לערך שלחן) for them; in v. 20, Israel requests specific foods to be present at the meal—"bread" (לחם) and "meat/flesh" (שאר). This expression "to set a table" (לערך שלחן) occurs only 7x in MT. In three cases (Pss 23:5; 78:19; Prov 9:2), the host of this meal is a divine figure.[126] In Prov 9:2, Lady Wisdom "sets a table" for the naïve to seek refuge there. In Ps 23:5, the psalmist celebrates YHWH's provision of a table "in the presence of his enemies" (נגד צררי). However, in Ps 78:19, Israel questions YHWH's ability to act for their good—a direct reversal of Psalm 23's expression of trust. For Israel, this "table" that Israel demands is a feast set with "bread" (לחם) and "meat" (שאר). The specific request for "meat" must be considered both in light of the immediate context of their wilderness environment and the general expectations of a diet within the ancient world. With the insecurity of food resources in the wilderness, animals are better kept alive for their renewable resources (milk, cheese, wool/hair). In addition, Israel's request for meat would be heard as a demand for a luxury that would have been rarely enjoyed by the average Israelite living in the land of Canaan. Here in the inhospitable context of the wilderness, Israel's demand for extravagant hospitality would have been jarring to the ears of the original audience of the psalm.

Third, Israel brings shame on their divine host by questioning his ability to provide for the guests at his table. In addition to questioning YHWH's ability to provide, the final word of the speech challenges the host's relationship to his guests. Here Israel refers to God (אל) in the third person, further accentuating the relational distance between the speaker and the intended divine recipient of their request. When Israel questions God's care for "his people" (עמו), this relational dissonance is magnified.

Seen through the conventions of hospitality, YHWH's violent behavior flows naturally from Israel's blatant disrespect and disregard for their

126. The remaining four instances involve human participants at a meal (Isa 21:5; 65:11; Ezek 23:41) or the preparation of the table for the Bread of Presence (Exod 40:4).

host. As in formal meals where roles have been breached, here we see hospitality revert to hostility as the security provided through the formal conventions of hospitality ceases. The fact that this speech is presented as a "test" of YHWH (v. 18) heightens the irony of the encounter.[127] The nature of the relationship of host and guest requires that each respect the complementarity of their roles. When a guest is disrespectful of the host or chooses to withhold honor due to the host, the relational structure that these roles provide no longer exists, and all privileges associated with the status of guest are revoked. In addition, the slighted host is free to relinquish his role as host and may revert to hostility to protect his honor. Seen within the light of the conventions of a formal meal, the resulting violence on the part of YHWH (vv. 21, 31) is the end result of breached table etiquette. For now, as Pitt-Rivers observes about the laws of hospitality, "once they are no longer host and guest they are enemies."[128]

The Multidimensional Force of Food Language in Psalm 78:15–31

As seen in the discussion above, the psalmist draws upon a variety of food dimensions in this depiction of the wilderness food account. The repeated references to the setting of these food events as the "wilderness" remind the audience of Israel's vulnerability and the scarcity of naturally occurring food sources in this barren land. In a context lacking in fertile fields and pasturelands, Israel asks for bread and meat. The psalmist is quick to note that Israel's request is not driven by physical hunger but by appetite/craving and doubt. Here, Israel doubts YHWH's ability to provide, bringing shame upon their host. This relational distance is emphasized as Israel refers to God in the third person, reminding God of his responsibilities to care for "his people" (עמו). While YHWH exceeds Israel's food expectations by allowing them to indulge their craving (תאוה) for bread and meat, the tables are turned as this meal ends in death for the fattest (משמן) and finest among them. By drawing upon

127. Jacobson classifies this instance of direct discourse (vv. 19–20) in the broader category of "enemy quotation." He assumes that the speakers here are the sons of Ephraim and this quotation proves evidence for why God rejected the northern tribes. Jacobson argues that the enemy quotation can serve as "instruction" for the audience by way of showing how not to speak and how not to act. Jacobson, *"Many Are Saying,"* 37–38, 58–59.

128. Pitt-Rivers, "Stranger," 29.

multiple dimensions of food at the same time, the psalmist highlights Israel's disordered heart (v. 8). By appealing to the audience's emotional, visceral, and intellectual sensibilities, the psalmist issues an invitation to the audience to consider and even enter into this scene of divine provision and human rebellion.

RHETORICAL ANALYSIS OF PSALM 78'S DEPICTION OF THE WILDERNESS FOOD EVENTS (VV. 15–31)

Two aspects of the wilderness food account (vv. 15–31) draw the audience toward a confident trust in the possibility that YHWH can intervene again in the present. First, YHWH responds to Israel's need in surprising and gracious ways in the midst of desperate circumstances. Second, YHWH shows his active care and sovereign power to meet Israel's needs.

Throughout this wilderness section (vv. 13–31), the psalmist presents a series of reversals in expected responses. In light of Israel's sin against YHWH (v. 17), YHWH still provides for Israel's request for a "table in the wilderness" (vv. 23–28). Throughout this section, the psalmist uses a variety of literary techniques to capture the extravagance of YHWH's food provisions. The psalmist coins original expressions to describe the events (e.g., "bread of the mighty," "grain of heaven"), relies on modifiers for intensification (e.g., v. 15 "caused them to drink abundantly"; v. 29 "ate and were very satisfied"), and turns to merism to describe provisions from below (e.g., water coming from the deeps) and above (e.g., manna from the heavens). The linking of the two water events and the two food events also intensifies the abundance of these wilderness wonders.[129] While the wilderness narratives often simply note the food's appearance in Israel's midst, the psalmist exhibits particular interest in describing the food itself—the mechanics of its arrival and its abundant quantity. In doing so, the psalmist directs the audience's attention toward the emotional and physical significance of these moments of divine provision. The rhetorical force of the psalmist's depictions of the abundance of the wilderness food elements moves the audience to a deeper appreciation of YHWH's gracious care for his people.

129. This occurs with the use of the verb "to cleave" (בקע) that draws together two water events: the opening of the Red/Reed Sea (v. 13) and water from a rock (v. 15). This also occurs with the verb "to rain" (מטר) used for two food events: manna (v. 24) and quail (v. 27).

Throughout the wilderness food account (vv. 15–31), the psalmist stresses YHWH's active involvement and sovereign power to provide for the needs of his people. In the wilderness frame, no human agents are associated with this act of provision. Without the need for specific human leadership, this scenario could be repeated at any moment. In addition, the psalmist presents the natural world responding to God's command and entering as willing servants. In v. 23, God "commands" the skies and opens the heavens to provide food for humanity. In v. 26, God "led out" (נסע) the east winds and "guided" (נהג) the south winds to bring Israel quail to eat. Creation's willing obedience to bring about YHWH's commands reminds the audience of YHWH's sovereign control in the world.

CONCLUSION

Psalm 78's account of the wilderness food events (vv. 15–31) provides a picture of YHWH's gracious care for Israel, even in the midst of their doubt and rebellion. The psalmist goes to great lengths to emphasize the abundance of this divine provision of food. YHWH's sovereign power over the created order is shown through the natural world's obedient participation in this provision. Rocks bring forth water; the heavens pour forth grain; and the winds report for service. Food language, in all its various dimensions, is exploited for rhetorical effect, as the psalmist seeks to capture the attention and ignite the imagination of the audience as a means to experience YHWH's wilderness wonders.

5

Destruction of Food Supplies in Egypt (Psalm 78:43–51)

INTRODUCTION

FOLLOWING AN EXTENDED CONSIDERATION of Israel's "forgetful" rebellion and YHWH's mindful compassion (78:32–42),[1] the recital next turns to the Egyptian plagues (vv. 43–51). The plague account continues for nine verses (vv. 43–51)—a description second in length to the wilderness food account (vv. 15–31).[2] Similar to the wilderness food account, the psalmist departs from a purely chronological retelling, both in the position of the plague account within the recital and in the ordering of the plagues. The plagues which take place in Egypt (78:43–51) are moved to the end of the wilderness frame where only two "events" remain to be recounted—YHWH's pastoral guidance and protection of Israel (vv. 52–53a) and the closing of the Red/Reed Sea on Israel's enemies (v. 53b).

Three food elements are explicitly described in Psalm 78's account of the plagues in Egypt—water (v. 44), agriculture (vv. 46–47; possibly

1. Food references in this section of the psalm will be considered in chapter 6.

2. When compared with the other events depicted in the historical recital, these two food accounts receive the most attention. Leaving the "wilderness frame" (vv. 13–53), the recital becomes more general, offering few clearly identifiable events from the historical narratives. The only other "events" that the psalmist describes in extended detail are YHWH's judgment in response to Israel's disobedience and misdirected worship in the land (vv. 59–64) and YHWH's choice of David as Israel's shepherd-king (vv. 70–72).

v. 45), and livestock (v. 48; possibly vv. 49–50).[3] In order to appreciate the specific literary and rhetorical choices made by the psalmist in the presentation of the plagues, one must first consider other depictions of these events within the Hebrew Bible—namely, the book of Exodus and the Psalms. Seen within this context of similar material, the distinct literary contributions of Psalm 78 become more pronounced. After the discussion of the plagues related to agriculture (vv. 46–47), attention will be given to the plague/s of flies/frogs (v. 45) and its possible agricultural connection. Following the discussion of the plague of livestock (v. 48), consideration will be given to vv. 49–50 as a possible livestock-related plague. Next, the plague account as a whole will be addressed, with particular attention given to its rhetorical use of food language, as well as the rhetorical intention of this section of the psalm. The chapter concludes by considering the rhetorical intention of the psalmist's sequencing of food events in the wilderness frame of Psalm 78 (vv. 13–53).

GENERAL INTRODUCTION TO THE PARALLEL REFERENCES TO THE EGYPTIAN PLAGUES

Only three passages in the Hebrew Bible contain an extended list of the plagues of Egypt:[4] Exodus 7–11,[5] Ps 78:44–51, and Ps 105:26–38.[6] Although there is substantial overlap in the accounts, the descriptions of the plagues in these three texts vary in number, sequence, and content.[7]

3. An analysis of the plagues with a clear reference to agricultural and livestock destruction will be followed by a consideration of the plagues that may be "possible" references to food events.

4. References to the Egyptian plagues as a whole appear across the Hebrew Bible. The phrase "signs and portents" (אתות ומופת) occurs in Exod 7:3 at the start of the plague account (cf. Deut 4:34; 6:22; 7:19; 26:8; 29:2; 34:11; Jer 32:20–21; Pss 78:43; 105:27; 135:9; Neh 9:10; cf. Deut 13:1, 3; 28:46; Isa 8:18; 20:3). In Exodus, the language of "pestilence" (דבר) is used specifically to describe the plague against livestock (9:3, 15). Its other uses in the Hebrew Bible designate divine judgment, not the Egyptian plagues in particular. Two additional terms—מגפה (Exod 9:14) and נגף (Exod 11:1)—seem to refer to the plagues in general, with the verb נגף ("to plague, strike") used to describe the infestation of frogs (8:2) and the death of the firstborn (12:23, 27; as a noun in 12:13).

5. Psalm 78 parallels Pentateuchal material identified as both P (Exod 14:16, 21 // Ps 78:13; Exod 16:8, 12 // Ps 78:29) and non-P (the majority of material in Exod 7–12). See Noth, *History of Pentateuchal Traditions*, 267–69.

6. Psalm 135:8–9 and 136:10 make mention of the plagues, but only to the death of Egypt's firstborn.

7. Possible rhetorical motives for the various inclusions and arrangements of the

These differences become apparent as one compares the accounts in the chart below:

Exodus	Psalm 78	Psalm 105
		Darkness (9)
1. Water to Blood	Water to Blood (1)	Water to Blood (1)
	Swarms of Flies (4)	
2. Frogs	Frogs (2)	Frogs (2)
3. Gnats	–	Swarms of Flies, Gnats (4, 3)
4. Swarms of Flies	see above	
5. Animal Pestilence	see below	–
6. Boils	–	–
	Locusts (8)	
7. Hail	Hail (7)	Hail (7)
	Animal Pestilence (5)	
8. Locusts	see above	Locusts (8)
9. Darkness	–	see above
10. Death of Firstborn	Death of Firstborn (10)	Death of Firstborn (10)

When compared with Exodus 7–11 and Psalm 105, Psalm 78's listing of the plagues is striking in its reordering of the individual plagues and its omission of the plagues of gnats, boils, and darkness.[8] Scholars typically explain the psalmist's plague omissions based on theories of sources available to the psalmist. While this theory may explain what is absent from the psalmist's account, it fails to address the second distinctive of Psalm 78's account, namely the psalmist's ordering of the plagues, an order that diverges significantly from the proposed Yahwist/J source. While scholars have considered rhetorical motivations for the presentations of the plague accounts in Exodus and Psalm 105,[9] there is a lacuna in regard to Psalm 78. A lacuna that this study seeks to address.

specific plagues have been considered by scholars, specifically the plague lists in Exodus and Psalm 105. For Exodus, see Fretheim, "Plagues as Ecological Signs," 385–96. For Psalm 105, see Lee, "Genesis I and the Plagues Tradition," 257–63; Stinson, "Praise the LORD," 99–109.

8. For this discussion, the account of the plagues in Exodus 7–11 will serve as the base text for comparing the number and order of the plagues.

9. On Exodus, see Fretheim, "Plagues as Ecological Signs," 385–96; on Psalm 105, see Lee, "Genesis I and the Plagues Tradition," 257–63.

This chapter argues that the order and descriptions of the plagues in Psalm 78 reflect the psalmist's intention to show a deliberate dismantling of Egyptian food supplies beginning with water sources (v. 44), agricultural supplies (vv. 46–47; cf. v. 45), then sources of meat (v. 48; cf. vv. 49–50). The discussion begins with an analysis of the language used to describe the destruction of explicit food elements (v. 44, 46–47, 48) and then considers the less obvious food-related plagues to argue for their possible consideration as examples of food destruction.

DESTRUCTION OF EGYPT'S WATER SUPPLIES (PS 78:44)

ויהפך לדם יאריהם ונזליהם בל ישתיון:

> He turned their rivers to blood, so that they could not drink of their streams.

Parallel References to the Plague of "Water to Blood"

There are only three references in the Hebrew Bible to the plague of "water to blood": Exod 7:14–25, Ps 105:29, and Ps 78:44. The account in Exodus and Psalm 105 will be discussed in turn, noting any shared lexemes with Psalm 78. As will be seen in this study, Psalm 78 and Psalm 105 share a variety of common lexemes with the Exodus account, but each emphasizes contrasting aspects of this plague.

Plague of "Water to Blood" in the Exodus Account

In the Exodus account, the plague of "water to blood" (Exod 7:14–25; cf. 4:9)[10] appears as the first of a series of "signs and portents" (אתות ומופת) done to convince Egypt of YHWH's sovereignty (v. 17) and to persuade Pharaoh to allow the Israelites to depart into the wilderness to worship YHWH (v. 16). YHWH tells Moses to approach Pharaoh in the morning by the waters of the Nile. The narrative is set up in three stages: the

10. Before Moses journeys back to Egypt, YHWH offers the sign of "water to blood" as evidence that YHWH has spoken to Moses (Exod 4:9).

announcement of the plague (vv. 14–16), the command to Aaron (vv. 17–18), and the resulting actions (vv. 19–25).

In Exod 7:17–18, YHWH details a series of events that will follow from the striking of the Nile River—the water in the Nile will turn to blood, the fish will die, the waters will become foul and undrinkable. In vv. 19–20, this pronouncement of destruction is followed by a second command, this time directed to Aaron, that extends this sign to encompass all the waterways of Egypt. The comprehensive nature of the sign is striking. Here YHWH employs five different words for waterways in Egypt, as well as household water storage.[11] The impact of the plague is emphasized throughout the account through the repeated references to Egypt's primary water source, the Nile River (יאר, vv. 15, 17, 18 [3x], 20 [2x], 21 [3x], 24 [2x], 25). The remainder of the account (vv. 20–25) describes the results of Moses' and Aaron's actions.

Psalm 78:44's closest lexical parallels occur in the result statements in Exod 7:20b (cf. v. 17) and Exod 7:21a (cf. v. 18) with the verbs "to turn" (הפך) and "to drink" (שתה), and the nouns "Nile, river" (יאר) and "blood" (דם):[12]

ויהפכו כל המים אשר ביאר לדם

Exod 7:20b: and all the water in the river was turned into blood

ולא יכלו מצרים לשתות מים מן היאר

Exod 7:21b: so that the Egyptians could not drink its water

The clustering of these key terms is restricted primarily to the plague account in Exodus and Psalm 78. References to the turning (הפך) of the Nile (יאר) occur only in Exod 7:17, 20, and Ps 78:44. Besides the references to the "turning" (הפך) of the Nile to "blood" (דם) in Exod 7:17, 20, Pss 78:44, and 105:29, the only other occurrence of something "turning"

11. Exod 7:19–20: "Take your staff and stretch out your hand over the waters of Egypt (מימי מצרים)—over its rivers (נהרתם), its canals (יאריהם), and its ponds (אגמיהם), and all its pools of water (כל מקוה מימיהם)—so that they may become blood; and there shall be blood throughout the whole land of Egypt, even in vessels of wood and in vessels of stone (ובעצים ובאבנים)."

12. The verb "to turn" (הפך) occurs 94x in the MT (4x in Exodus; 10x in Psalms, 3x in Ps 78). The verb "to drink" (שתה) occurs 222x in the MT (12x in Exodus; 5x in Psalms). The term "river, Nile" (יאר) occurs 64x in the MT (25x in Exodus; 1x in Psalms—78:44). The word "blood" (דם) occurs 361x in the MT (29x in Exodus; 21x in Psalms).

(הפך) to "blood" (דם) occurs in Joel 3:4 [ET 2:31]. Here the moon turns to blood on the day of YHWH.

References to Plague of "Water to Blood" in the Psalms

The only other reference to the plague of turning water to blood occurs in Pss 78:44 and 105:29:

ויהפך לדם יאריהם ונזליהם בל ישתיון

> Ps 78:44: He turned their rivers to blood, so that they could not drink of their streams.

הפך את מימיהם לדם וימת את דגתם

> Ps 105:29: He turned their waters into blood, and caused their fish to die.

Both Psalms 78 and 105 highlight the occurrence of "waters" turning to blood. However, in Psalm 105, the psalmist uses a generic term, "waters" (מים), while Psalm 78 uses a more specific term for these waters—"Nile, river" (יאר). Unlike Psalm 78, Psalm 105 focuses on the disruption of the water ecosystem and the resulting death to the fish that inhabit the waters—a detail also included in the Exodus account. In Psalm 105, the plague of water turned to blood is the second listed plague to befall Egypt. Here, unlike its place at the head of Psalm 78's listing, the plague of water turned to blood follows the plague of darkness.

Summary of Parallel References to Plague of "Water to Blood"

The Exodus account of the plague of water-turned-blood provides a detailed description of the water event's disturbance of the Nile ecosystem and the disruption to the lives of the Egyptians who no longer have ready access to fresh water. Psalms 78 and 105 seem to draw from various aspects of the Exodus material and present two perspectives on this event. While Psalm 78 is similar to the Exodus account in placing this plague at the head of the sequence, Psalm 105 has it following the plague of darkness. While both Psalms 78 and 105 refer to the "turning" (הפך) of waters to "blood" (דם), Psalm 105 alone follows Exodus in stressing the implications of this event as it plays out in the ecosystem with the death of fish.

In addition, Psalm 105 opts for a more general reference to "waters" (מים) instead of the more specific term "Nile" (יאר; cf. Exod 7:19, Ps 78:44).

Literary Analysis of Psalm 78's Depiction of the Plague of "Water to Blood" (v. 44)

Two aspects of Psalm 78's depiction of the water-turned-blood event are particularly noteworthy: its use of paired terms within the depiction of the event and its intra-textual links with the earlier wilderness food account (vv. 15–31). In Ps 78:44, the psalmist pairs the terms "Nile, river" (יאר) and "stream" (נזל), both in the plural. The singular form of יאר is used primarily to refer to the main river of Egypt, the Nile. The plural form of יאר, used here in Psalm 78, appears only sporadically and can be used in a generic sense of "waters," although the term is used in Exodus to describe the lesser waterways that flow into/out of the Nile itself (Exod 7:19). The use of the plural "their rivers" (יאריהם) may be an attempt to create a balanced parallel with the plural "their streams" (נזליהם). The second word, "stream" (נזל), is a low-frequency term, occurring only 5x in the MT and not used in the Exodus plague account.[13] Here in Psalm 78's first plague, a literary pattern begins to develop of using paired terms.[14]

In addition, the psalmist employs an intra-textual link to the wilderness water event (v. 16) through the term "stream" (נזל), here used for the waters of Egypt (v. 44). The psalmist first employs this term in v. 16: "He made streams (נזלים) come out of the rock and caused waters to flow down like rivers." In this wilderness context, YHWH draws out "streams" (נזל) from an unexpected source (סלע, a rock) to provide drink in a dry land. In its second use (v. 44), YHWH makes the Egyptian "streams" (נזל) that flow from the Nile—a predictable and abundant water source—undrinkable (בל־ישתיון). This repetition of the term נזל gains significance from its low frequency (5x in MT) and because of the variety of words that could have been used to describe the waters of the Nile. For example, the Exodus account includes the common words "waters" (מים; cf. Exod 7:15, 17, 18, 19, 20, 21, 24; Ps 105:29) and "river" (נהר; cf. Exod 7:19),

13. The term נזל occurs in Exodus to describe the Reed/Red Sea and its parting (15:8). The word appears twice in Psalm 78 (vv. 16, 44), as well as in Isa 44:3 and Prov 5:15.

14. As will be seen in this chapter, the psalmist often utilizes paired terms, combining a low frequency term with a high frequency word or a specific term found in the Exodus account.

as well as less common words such as "pool" (אגם; cf. Exod 7:19) and "reservoir" (מקוה; cf. Exod 7:19). As noted in the previous chapter, the psalmist often uses the repetition of a particular lexeme to draw events together.[15] Here, the repetition of such an uncommon term as "stream" (נזל) heightens the likelihood of intentionality. Seen in this light, the psalmist presents the water plague as an inversion of the water miracle of the wilderness.

DESTRUCTION OF EGYPT'S AGRICULTURE (PS 78:46–47)

ויתן לחסיל יבולם ויגיעם לארבה:
יהרג בברד גפנם ושקמותם בחנמל:

> He gave to the caterpillar their produce, and their labor to the locust.
> He slew their vines with hail, and their sycamores with frost.[16]

Parallel References to the Destruction of Egypt's Agriculture

Disruption of agriculture through natural forces or enemy occupation is mentioned frequently in the Hebrew Bible.[17] However, references to God's specific destruction of Egyptian agriculture—particularly through locusts and hail—appear only in Exod 9:18–10:20, Ps 78:46–47, and Ps 105:32–35. As will be seen below, Psalm 78's depiction of these plagues shares little in common with the Exodus account or the account in Psalm

15. This occurs with the use of the verb "to cleave" (בקע) that draws together two water events: the opening of the Red/Reed Sea (v. 13) and water from a rock (v. 15). This also occurs with the verb "to rain" (מטר) used for two food events: manna (v. 24) and quail (v. 27).

16. The term חנמל is a hapax, and its meaning is uncertain. The LXX translates it παχν, "hoarfrost."

17. References to famine conditions in Israel occur with surprising regularity in the Hebrew Bible (e.g., Gen 12:10; 26:1; 42:6; 2 Sam 21:1; 1 Kgs 18:2; 2 Kgs 4:38; 2 Kgs 6:25; Ruth 1:1; Neh 5:3). In addition to crop failure by climactic factors, agricultural devastation may occur through pestilence or by invading armies. A particularly striking description occurs in Judg 6:3–5, which depicts the invasion of Midianite and Amalekite armies as a hungry locust horde. A similar picture exists in Joel 1:2–4, although here there is ambiguity in regard to the identity of the destroyers—human or insect.

105 besides the basic terminology of the plagues themselves: "locusts" (ארבה) and "hail" (ברד).[18]

Destruction of Egypt's Agriculture in the Exodus Account

In the Exodus account of the plagues, two primary culprits are associated with agricultural destruction—hail (9:13–35) and locusts (10:1–20).[19] In the Exodus account, these plagues appear consecutively and, as a result, bring about comprehensive destruction of the agricultural substructure in Egypt.[20]

In the Exodus account, the plague of the hail (9:13–35) is the first plague to bring about destruction on a cataclysmic scale. In Exod 9:22, YHWH declares that the plague of hail will fall on and destroy every living thing that remains in the fields—"humans and animals and every plant of the field" (על האדם ועל הבהמה ועל כל עשב השדה). The announcement (v. 18) and the narrator's report (v. 24) both emphasize the plague's magnitude[21] and uniqueness.[22] In v. 23, the hail is said to "rain" (מטר) down on the land of Egypt, accompanied by "thunder" (קול) and "fire" (אש). Since this plague affects both agriculture and livestock, comments here will be restricted to the agricultural dimension of the plague, and a discussion of its effect on livestock will be delayed until the following section.

The specific agricultural destruction caused by the hail plague is described in Exod 9:25 as the hail struck down (נכה) "all the plants of the field" (כל־עשב השדה) and shattered (שבר) "every tree in the field" (כל עץ השדה). Further clarification on the extent of the destruction is given at the conclusion of the account, where the narrator notes that the

18. Psalms 78 and 105 also share the lexeme גפן ("vine"), which does not occur in the Exodus account.

19. Exodus 8:20 [ET 8:24] notes that the land was "ruined" (שחת) as a result of the flies. This may or may not be a reference to agricultural destruction.

20. Meyers notes that the Exodus narrative gives expanded emphasis to these two plagues including "vivid details, far more than are given for other sign-and-wonders." Meyers, *Exodus*, 85. The enormity of the destruction of these two plagues is stressed throughout the account. Fretheim observes the extravagant repetition of the word "all" (כל) to describe the decimation of the land by the locusts (Exod 10:5, 6, 12, 13, 14, 15; a total of 11x). Fretheim, "Plagues as Ecological Signs," 391.

21. The text uses the expression "very severe" (כבד מאד; vv. 18, 24) to describe the hail.

22. Twice the narrator identifies the plagues as a "never before seen" occurrence in Egypt's history (9:18, 24).

"flax and barley" (הפשתה והשערה) were struck down by the hail, while the "wheat and rye" (החטה והכסמת) were not struck down because of their later harvest times (vv. 31–32). When Pharaoh pleads for the hail to stop (v. 29), Moses replies that the thunder and hail will cease "so that you may know that the earth is YHWH's" (למען תדע כי ליהוה הארץ)—an explicit statement about YHWH's control over the natural world. As one considers Psalm 78's account of this plague, the only shared term with the Exodus description is the word "hail" (ברד).[23]

The Exodus account of the locust's destruction of agriculture (10:1–20) follows immediately after the hail plague. YHWH stresses the magnitude of the event—"very severe" (כבד מאד, 10:4)—and the uniqueness of the destruction.[24] The locust plague is explicitly described as a completion of the destruction begun by the plague of hail: "they shall eat the rest of what has escaped—what is left to you by the hail" (v. 3). Unlike the other plagues, the locusts arrived in a two-step process. Exodus 10:13 notes that YHWH "led out an east wind" (נהג רוח קדים) that blew for a day/night;[25] and in the morning, the east wind had brought the locusts. Exodus 10:15b pictures the locusts' destruction as the comprehensive decimation of all the agriculture in the land:

> ויאכל את כל עשב הארץ ואת כל פרי העץ אשר הותיר הברד
> ולא נותר כל ירק בעץ ובעשב השדה בכל ארץ מצרים:

> And they ate all the plants in the land and all the fruit of the trees that the hail had left; nothing green was left, no tree, no plant in the field, in all the land of Egypt.

The fourfold repetition of the modifier "all" (כל) highlights the utter ruin experienced in the land of Egypt. Unlike the divine distinction that saves Israel's livestock from hail (8:26), no distinction is made here between the fields of the Egyptians and the fields of Israel (i.e., land of Goshen). This

23. The word "hail" (ברד) occurs only 29x in the MT (17x in Exodus associated with the plague; 6x in Psalms including Ps 78:47, 48, and Ps 105:32).

24. In Exod 10:6, YHWH describes it as "something that neither your parents nor your grandparents have seen, from the day they came on earth to this day." When the locusts arrive (v. 14), the narrator notes that there have never been so many creatures seen before: "such a dense swarm of locusts as had never been before, nor ever shall be again." When the locusts appear, they cover the land so that it appears dark (10:15). Locusts may have been a natural occurrence in the land of Egypt. However, it is the magnitude of the number of locusts appearing together that would have been so shocking.

25. Cf. Ps 78:26 where the language of "leading" (נהג) the "east wind" (קדים) also appears; however, in this case the winds bring quail to Israel in the wilderness.

lack of differentiation may have a pragmatic purpose in the fact that Israel would not be present to gather in the harvests in light of their imminent departure. The destruction of Israel's agriculture may also have served as motivation for the Israelites to leave Egypt and its assumed agricultural security. The locusts' destructive power is also emphasized by the repetition of the verb "to eat" (אכל; 10:5, 12, 15). As Durham observes, this is a "disaster that makes the starvation of the Egyptians people a terrible probability."[26] The only shared vocabulary in the Exodus account and Psalm 78 is the term "locust" (ארבה).[27]

References to the Destruction of Egypt's Agriculture in the Psalms

Only two psalms explicitly mention the destruction of Egyptian agriculture through the plagues of hail and locusts: Ps 78:46–48 and Ps 105:32–35.

In Psalm 105, the psalmist includes hail as the sixth plague in the account, following after darkness (v. 28), water-to-blood (v. 29), frogs (v. 30), flies (v. 31a) and gnats (v. 31b). In vv. 32–33, the plague of hail is described in the following manner:

נתן גשמיהם ברד אש להבות בארצם:
ויך גפנם ותאנתם וישבר עץ גבולם:

> He gave them hail for rain and fiery flames throughout their land.
> He struck their vines and fig trees and shattered the trees of their country.

The psalmist's account opens (v. 32) with a description of the destructive agents associated with this plague—"hail" (ברד) and "fiery flames" (אש להבת)—and closes (v. 33) with a list of the agricultural items destroyed—vines (גפן), fig trees (תאנה) and trees (עץ). Psalm 105 uses similar language to the Exodus account for the agents of destruction—"hail" (ברד) and "fire" (אש)—as well as how and what is destroyed: plants are "struck" (נכה, v. 33; cf. Exod 9:25) and trees are shattered (שבר עץ, v. 33; cf. Exod 9:25). Like Exodus, the psalmist gives specificity to the types of products affected by the hail. The psalmist's inclusion of "their vines and fig trees"

26. Durham, *Exodus*, 136.

27. The term "locust" (ארבה) occurs only 24x in the MT (7x in Exodus plague account; 3x in Ps—Pss 78:46; 105:34; 109:23).

(גפנם ותאנתם) may serve to heighten the significance of this agricultural loss since these terms are often paired in the Hebrew Bible to picture a state of prosperity and security.[28] The only vocabulary shared by Psalm 105 and Psalm 78 in the depiction of this plague are the terms "hail" (ברד) and "vine" (גפן).

In Psalm 105, the plague of locusts follows directly after the hail.[29] Psalm 105:34–35 reads:

אמר ויבא ארבה וילק ואין מספר:
ויאכל כל עשב בארצם ויאכל פרי אדמתם:

> He spoke, and the locusts came, and young locusts without number;
> they ate up all the plants in their land and ate up the fruit of their ground.

Here the psalmist employs a similar pattern to the hail plague with a description of the destructive agents, followed by a listing of the agriculture destroyed. In v. 35, the psalmist presents the agricultural destruction in terms very similar to the Exodus account of the locust: "they ate all the plants in the land" (ויאכל כל עשב בארצם; cf. Exod 10:15: ויאכל את כל עשב הארץ), and they ate "the fruit of the ground" (פרי אדמתם; cf. Exod 10:15 "the fruit of the trees" כל פרי העץ). The psalmist's use of the term "locust" (ארבה, v. 34; cf. Exod 10:4, 12, 13, 14, 19) and the comment on the immensity of the locust horde account (אין מספר) also resemble the Exodus account.[30] The only shared vocabulary with Psalm 78 is the term "locust" (ארבה).

Summary of Parallel References to the Destruction of Egypt's Agriculture

Psalm 105 shares a variety of similarities to the account in Exodus of agricultural destruction by the plagues. Both Exodus and Psalm 105

28. This expression occurs 39x in MT. This reference to "vines and fig trees"—typical products of Canaan—seems out of place in this Egyptian scene of destruction, a point noted by Holm-Nielsen, "Exodus Traditions in Psalm 105," 30n16.

29. Psalm 105 follows the ordering of the Exodus account beginning with the plague of hail (vv. 32–33; cf. Exod 9:13–35) followed by the plague of locusts (vv. 34–35; cf. Exod 10:1–20). This order is in contrast to Psalm 78, where the events are reversed.

30. The expression "without number" (אין מספר) may be an economic way to poetically capture the lengthier descriptions of the locust horde found in Exod 10:1–20.

present the plague of hail before the locust plague. Both are concerned with similar aspects of the destruction, most notably the magnitude of the locusts and the fiery presence of the hail.

Literary Analysis of Psalm 78's Depiction of the Destruction of Egypt's Agriculture (vv. 46–47)

Psalm 78's depiction of the agricultural destruction caused by the locusts and hail shows similar tendencies to the water-to-blood plague, namely, paired terms and intra-textual links with the earlier wilderness food account (vv. 15–31). Throughout the description, the psalmist draws on words that have relatively low frequency in the MT.[31] In addition, the psalmist also employs a hapax in the word translated "frost" (חנמל, v. 47). A common practice of the psalmist is the use of paired terms, which may account for the choice of several of these more obscure terms. In the depiction of agricultural destruction (v. 46), the psalmist pairs the less common word "caterpillars" (חסיל) with a more common term, "locusts" (ארבה),[32] as well as a curious pairing of two low-frequency terms: "their produce" (יבולם) and "their labor" (יגיעם). In 78:47, the psalmist pairs the less common "sycamores" (שקמה) and the more common "vines" (גפן),[33] as well as the hapax "frost" (חנמל) with the more common word "hail" (ברד), which occurs 29x in the MT.

Intra-textual links to the wilderness food events described earlier occur through the verbs "to give" (נתן) and "to slay" (הרג). Until this point in the psalm, the verb "to give" (נתן) has appeared solely in the context of food provision. In v. 20, Israel questions YHWH's ability to "give" (נתן) bread; in v. 24, YHWH responds to Israel's complaint by "giving" (נתן)

31. For example, the psalmist's description includes words such as "caterpillars" (חסיל ; 6x in MT) and "sycamores" (שקמה; 7x in MT), as well as "produce" (יבול; 13x in MT) and "labor" (יגיע; 16x in MT).

32. The term "caterpillar" (חסיל) occurs only 6x in the MT. The term "locust" (ארבה) occurs 24x in the MT. The linking of locusts and caterpillars occurs in two other contexts. They appear together as the two types of locusts announced in Joel 1:4; 2:25 and in Solomon's invocation at the newly completed temple: "If there is famine in the land, if there is plague (דבר), blight, mildew, locust (ארבה), or caterpillar (חסיל)" (1 Kgs 8:37a; cf. 2 Chr 6:28).

33. The term "sycamore" (שקמה) occurs 7x in the MT. The term "vines" (גפן) occurs 55x in the MT. These terms appear together nowhere else in the Hebrew Bible. The term "sycamore" is often used rhetorically to signify the commonplace nature of this tree in Israel (1 Kgs 10:27; 2 Chr 1:15; 9:27).

not just bread, but "grain from heaven" (דגן־שמים). In the plague account, YHWH again "gives" (נתן) food, but here he gives food gained through human labor (יגיע) to a pair of unlikely guests, the caterpillars and locusts.[34] A second link occurs with the verb "to slay" (הרג). At the end of the wilderness food account (v. 31), YHWH "slays" (הרג) the fattest (משמן) of Israel after they have gorged themselves on God's provision. Here in v. 47, it is not food-filled humans who are struck down, but food supplies intended for humans—vines and sycamores. This picture of violence now directed at plant life heightens the intensity of this agricultural loss.

Consideration of Surrounding Plagues (Ps 78:45–47)

Psalm 78's picture of agricultural destruction reverses the ordering of several of the plagues found in Exod 9:13—10:20 and Ps 105:32–35. In Psalm 78, the plague of locusts (v. 46) is positioned before the plague of hail (v. 47). In this new location, the locust plague (v. 46) follows on the heels of the plagues of flies and frogs (v. 45):

ישלח בהם ערב ויאכלם וצפרדע ותשחיתם:
ויתן לחסיל יבולם ויגיעם לארבה:

> He sent to them flies, which devoured them, and frogs, which destroyed them.
> He gave to the caterpillar their produce, and their labor to the locust. (vv. 45–46)

With this move, all the plagues with creatures as agents are assembled together—flies/frogs in v. 45 followed by caterpillars/locust in v. 46.[35]

Within this new literary proximity, the audience is invited to consider the effects of the flies/frogs within the context of agricultural destruction brought on by the locusts, as well as the hail.

In the MT, the lexemes "swarm of flies" (ערב) and "frog" (צפרדע) occur only in the Egyptian plague accounts (Exod 7:26—8:11 [ET 8:1–15]; 8:16–26 [ET 8:20–32]; Pss 78:45; 105:30–31). The term "swarm of flies" (ערב) occurs 9x in the MT (Exod 8:17, 18, 20, 25, 27 [ET 8:21, 22, 24, 29, 31]; cf. Pss 78:45; 105:30). The term "frog" (צפרדע) occurs 13x in the MT

34. The verb "to give" (נתן) occurs 5x in Psalm 78 (vv. 20, 24, 46, 61, 66). The final two references occur in the context of the land, vv. 61 and 66.

35. In the Exodus account and Psalm 105, the plague of locusts is separated from the plagues of the frog, gnats, and flies. See plague chart at the beginning of the chapter.

(Exod 7:27–8:5, 7–9 [ET 8:2–9, 11–13]; Pss 78:45; 105:30). The appearance of these two terms across all three accounts increases the likelihood of an awareness of a common plague tradition.

In the Exodus account, the plague of flies occurs as the fourth plague and frogs as the second plague—with the gnats as the intervening plague (see chart at the start of the chapter). While the Exodus account does not explicitly associate flies and frogs with agricultural ruin, the context of their destruction does have an implicit association with food supplies. In Exod 7:28 [ET 8:3], YHWH promises to "plague, strike" (נגף) the Egyptian territories with frogs. These frogs are said to appear primarily in domestic contexts (i.e., palace, bedchamber, bed), as well as arenas associated with cooking and food preparation ("in your ovens and kneading bowls," בתנוריך ובמשארותיך). This infestation within cooking areas would likely lead to the contamination of Egyptian food supplies as well. In Exodus 8, flies are said to "fill" (מלא) the "ground" (אדמה; 8:17 [ET 8:21]) and "destroy" (שחת) the "land" (ארץ; 8:20 [ET 8:24]), but the particular aspects of this destruction is omitted. Psalm 105 also includes the plagues of frogs (v. 30) and flies/gnats (v. 31). The psalmist notes that the frogs swarm the land and appear in the king's bedchamber (v. 30). In Psalm 105, the flies/gnats simply "come" (בוא) into the territories, and their destructive power is omitted (v. 31).

In Psalm 78:45, the psalmist explicitly comments on the actions of the flies (ערב) and frogs (צפרדע). The flies "eat" (אכל) and the frogs "ruin" (שחת) the Egyptians. In the Exodus account of the plagues, the verb "to eat" (אכל) is used repeatedly to describe the locusts' destruction of agriculture (Exod 10:5, 12, 15). Psalm 78:45's use of "to eat" (אכל) to describe the effects of the flies—creatures who like the locusts also feed on plant life (nectar, plants, fruit, dry food stores)—paints this creature in the same light as the locusts of the Exodus account that are sent to consume Egypt's food supplies. The use of the verbs "eat" (אכל)/"ruin" (שחת) seems an odd choice if the psalmist simply wanted to describe the general nuisance of these insects and reptiles. However, when seen in the context of the locust plague that follows (vv. 46), there may be hints that the destruction of agricultural supplies may in fact begin with the flies and frogs. In addition, the psalmist uses the verb "ruin" (שחת) to describe the resulting crisis caused by the frogs. Thus, the magnitude of the frogs' harm makes the contamination (and by extension destruction) of food supplies a possible scenario.

By arranging the plagues of explicit agricultural destruction (locusts and hail) with creatures (flies/frogs) who "eat and ruin" (אכל/שחת), the psalmist may be grouping these plagues around their destructive consequences, as seen in the chart below:

	Divine Action	Destructive Agent	Action of Agents	Object of Action
v. 45	sent (שׁלח)	swarms of flies frogs	ate (אכל) ruined (שׁחת)	them them
v. 46	gave (נתן)	caterpillars locusts	– –	produce fruit of labor
v. 47	destroyed (הרג)	hail frost	– –	vines sycamores

Moving from the possibility of general agricultural destruction by flies/frogs (v. 45), to destruction of agricultural products by the caterpillars/locusts (v. 46), to destruction of specific crops by hail/frost (v. 47), the psalmist presents a tightening circle of specific agricultural ruin.

DESTRUCTION OF EGYPT'S LIVESTOCK (PS 78:48)

ויסגר לברד בעירם ומקניהם לרשפים:

> He gave over their animals to the hail,[36] and their livestock to thunderbolts.

Parallel References to the Destruction of Egypt's Livestock

Destruction of livestock is an outcome of three of the plagues of Egypt—livestock pestilence (Exod 9:1–7), hail (Exod 9:13–35), and the death of the firstborn (Exod 11:1–10). Outside the book of Exodus, only Ps 78:48 (cf. vv. 49–50) and Ps 135:8 explicitly mention the death of livestock as an aspect of the Egyptian plagues. As will be seen below, Psalm 78 shares only the most basic lexemes with Exodus's account of the death of livestock: "livestock" (מקנה) and "hail" (ברד).

36. There are manuscript variants regarding the word "hail" (ברד). Two Hebrew manuscripts and Symmachus have the word "pestilence" (דבר) here. However, MT, LXX, Syr, Targum all have the word "hail" (ברד).

Destruction of Egypt's Livestock in the Exodus Account

In the Exodus account, there are three plagues associated with the death of Egyptian livestock—livestock pestilence (Exod 9:1–7), hail (Exod 9:13–35), and the death of the firstborn (Exod 11:1–10).[37] The livestock pestilence appears as the fifth plague and is uniquely associated with "the hand of YHWH" (יד־יהוה), unlike the other plagues that involve a specific action performed by Moses or Aaron (Exod 9:3, 15). In Exod 9:3, this plague is described as "very severe" (כבד מאד) since it will cause the death of all livestock (מקנה) found in the fields—specifically "the horses, the donkeys, the camels, the herds, and the flocks" (בסוסים בחמרים בגמלים בבקר ובצאן).[38]

Following the sixth plague (boils; cf. Exod 9:8–12), YHWH recalls the plague of cattle pestilence (דבר) in the introduction to the plague of hail (9:15): "For by now I could have stretched out my hand (יד) and struck you and your people with pestilence (דבר), and you would have been cut off from the earth." This divine declaration of restraint at the sparing of human life has an expressed theological purpose—that Pharaoh and the Egyptians would see YHWH's power and that his Name would be proclaimed to all the earth (v. 16).

In the seventh plague (9:13–35), the livestock (מקנה) in the field as well as anything found there—humans (אדם) or domestic animals (בהמה)[39]—will be killed by the hail (9:19; cf. v. 25). The language used here for animals switches from the term "livestock" (מקנה) to the more common "domestic animal" (בהמה). In the opening pronouncement of the plague, Egypt's "livestock" (מקנה) out in the fields is the main focus of the plagues' destruction. The account switches to the term "animals" (בהמה) later in the depiction of the plague and its destructive effect on "humans and animals" (האדם והבהמה).

37. In Exodus, animals (בהמה), as well as humans, are affected by two plagues that do not lead to death: the plagues of gnats (8:13–14 [ET 8:17–18]) and plague of boils (9:9, 10).

38. Israel's livestock is spared from both the plague of cattle pestilence (9:1–7) and the plague of hail (9:13–35). In both cases, the plagues are described as "very severe" (כבד מאד; pestilence, 9:3; hail, 9:18, 24). As Israel is leaving Egypt (Exod 12:38), the narrator notes that besides the multitude that joined them, there was "livestock in great numbers, both flocks and herds" (וצאן ובקר מקנה כבד מאד). The expression used here "in great numbers" (כבד מאד) is the same as the "very severe" nature of the plagues that killed Egypt's own livestock—an ironic reversal of sorts.

39. The expression מאדם ועד־בהמה ("from humanity to domestic animals") may be a merism to express the totality of destruction.

The tenth and final plague also mentions the death of livestock, but here the word used is "domestic animal" (בהמה). In Exod 11:5, YHWH pronounces: "Every firstborn in the land of Egypt shall die, from the firstborn of Pharaoh who sits on his throne to the firstborn of the female slave who is behind the handmill, and all the firstborn of the animals (בהמה)." This promise is repeated later in 12:12: "I will strike down every firstborn in the land of Egypt, from humans to animals (מאדם ועד־בהמה)." The result statement (12:29) follows much later in the narrative where the text notes that the death included "all the firstborn of animals" (כל בכור בהמה). In these accounts of livestock death in Exodus, only the terms "livestock" (מקנה) and "hail" (ברד) appear in Psalm 78's account.

References to the Destruction of Egypt's Livestock in the Psalms

Psalm 105's account of the plagues omits all references to livestock death. Only Psalm 135 mentions the death of animals in the Egyptian plagues (vv. 8–9):

שהכה בכורי מצרים מאדם עד בהמה:
שלח אתות ומפתים בתוככי מצרים בפרעה ובכל עבדיו:

> He struck down the firstborn of Egypt, both man and animals;
> He sent signs and portents into your midst, O Egypt, against Pharaoh and all his servants.

Here, in this very short rendition of the plague account, the death of animals and humans provides the paramount example of the "signs and portents" of Egypt. Psalm 135 has no shared lexemes with Psalm 78's account of animal-based plagues.

Summary of Parallel References to the Destruction of Egypt's Livestock

The death of Egyptian livestock plays a significant role in three of the Exodus plagues, although in two of the plagues only a small percent of the population of the livestock is affected: those in the fields (Exod 9:13–35, plague of hail) and firstborn of the animals (Exod 11:1–10; 12:29–32, death of firstborn). Only the livestock pestilence has a wide-ranging effect on the animal population. Psalm 135 specifically mentions the death of animals in the final plague, although this detail is omitted in Psalms 78 and 105.

Literary Analysis of Psalm 78's Depiction of the Destruction of Egypt's Livestock (v. 48)

Psalm 78's depiction of the destruction of livestock in the hail plague exhibits both paired terms and intra-textual links within the plague account itself.[40] Two sets of paired terms are used in v. 48. In each case, the psalm draws on a word common to the Exodus account and links it with a second word with lower frequency. This occurs with the pairing of the term "livestock" (מקנה) with "animals" (בעיר).[41] The psalmist also pairs a higher frequency word, "hail" (ברד),[42] with a low frequency word, "flash, plague" (רשף).[43] The pairing of the terms רשף / ברד has led scholars to speculate about the possibility that the term "hail" (ברד) is a corruption of the word "pestilence" (דבר), a result of the transposition of the daleth.[44]

Intra-textual links within the plague account (vv. 43–51) occur with both the noun "hail" (ברד) and the verb "to give over" (סגר). The reference to "hail" (ברד) in v. 48 provides a direct link to v. 47's depiction of the destruction of agriculture also by hail (ברד). This depiction parallels Exodus, where both agriculture and livestock are affected by the plague of hail. A link also occurs through the verb "to give over" (סגר) found in the opening of v. 48 and reoccurring at the close of v. 50. The verb "to give over" (סגר) occurs 83x in the MT and does not appear in the Exodus plague account (Exod 7–11). Within Psalm 78, this verb סגר is used 3x (vv. 48, 50, 62), with a clear reference to livestock in its first occurrence

40. This literary convention was also used in the earlier depictions of agricultural destruction caused by locust and hail plagues.

41. The term "livestock" (מקנה) appears 76x in the MT (13x in Exodus; 1x in Psalms, Ps 78:48). Within Exodus, the term appears both in the livestock pestilence (6x; 9:3, 4, 6, 7) and hail plague (3x; 9:19, 20, 21). The term "animals" (בעיר) occurs only 6x in the MT (Gen 45:17; Exod 22:4 [ET 5]; Num 20:4, 8, 11; Ps 78:48).

42. The noun "hail" (ברד) appears 29x in the MT (17x in Exodus; 6x in Psalms). All occurrences in Exodus refer directly to the plague of hail.

43. The term רשף ("flash, plague") occurs 7x in the MT (Deut 32:24; Hab 3:5; Pss 76:4; 78:48; Job 5:7; Song 8:6).

44. This reading is supported by two Hebrew manuscripts and Symmachus. Supporters of this view often note the paired terms "pestilence" (דבר)/"flash" (רשף) are used in Hab 3:5 to describe God's judgment: "Before him went pestilence (דבר), and plague (רשף) followed close behind."

(v. 48) and a clear reference to people in v. 62. Further discussion of these intra-textual links will continue below.

Consideration of Surrounding Plagues (Ps 78:48–50)

Psalm 78:49–50 radically departs from the style of the poetry that precedes it. Here the tightly structured lines used to describe the first five plagues disappear. Instead of bicolons with a parallel structure of an opening verb and paired objects, the text moves to tricolons:

ישלח בם חרון אפו עברה וזעם וצרה משלחת מלאכי רעים:
יפלס נתיב לאפו לא חשך ממות נפשם וחיתם לדבר הסגיר:

> He let loose on them his fierce anger / wrath, indignation, and distress / a company of destroying angels.
> He made a path for his anger / he did not spare them from death / but gave their animals over to the pestilence.

With the mention of "anger" (אף), this description resembles aspects of the depiction of divine fury against Israel in the wilderness (cf. vv. 21, 31). This description also employs several lexemes appearing in the psalmist's earlier account of the Egyptian plagues[45] and the wilderness food account.[46] The only common vocabulary with the Exodus plague account is the word "pestilence" (דבר).

There is much scholarly speculation and very little agreement about these verses.[47] The scene depicted in vv. 49–50 resembles no event record-

45. The verb "to send" (שלח) is also used with the plague of flies (v. 45), and the verb "to give over" (סגר) is also used for the death of cattle in the hail plague (v. 48).

46. The verb "to send" (שלח) is also used in v. 25 to describe the arrival of "provisions" (צידה) in the wilderness. The verb "to be angry" (עבר) describes God's response to Israel's doubts regarding his ability to provide food.

47. Some scholars view vv. 49–51 simply as a depiction of the death of the firstborn. This position is held by Anderson, who notes: "Here we find an account of the final plague, the death of Egypt's firstborn, the climax of the series of punishments (Exod. 11:1–12:36)." Anderson, *Book of Psalms*, 572. Clifford views vv. 49–50 as a transition between the hail plague and the death of the firstborn: "Instead of a specific sixth plague, there are two tricola (vv 49–50) portraying divine wrath against Egypt and providing a transition to the slaughter of v 51." Clifford, "In Zion and David a New Beginning," 134. Lee argues that "the tradition of Yahweh's punishment of the Assyrians has been incorporated into the recitation of the slaying of the Egyptian firstborn in Ps. 78.49–51 with the purpose of reaffirming the power and might of Yahweh to intervene on behalf of Israel." Lee, "Context and Function of the Plagues Tradition," 87. Briggs sees these verses as coming from the hand of a later glossator. He attributes a stylistic motivation to the inclusion. He notices that "the divine anger directed against the enemies of His

ed in the Exodus plague account or in Psalm 105's recital of the plagues. Its only common term with the Exodus plagues is the word "pestilence" (דבר)—a term used to describe the death of livestock (Exod 9:3, 15). The referent for this pestilence in vv. 49–50 is also unclear. The description includes only one specific object, their lives (חיתם), which can refer to either animals or humans.

However, vv. 49–50 exhibit enough significant connections to v. 48 that they can be considered as a possible referent to the plague of "livestock pestilence." Two aspects of the psalmist's description in vv. 49–50 lead in this direction. First, the term "pestilence" (דבר) is used in the Exodus plague account exclusively for the livestock pestilence (9:3, 15). Since each new plague in Psalm 78 has been clearly identified using terms from the Exodus account to identify the plague,[48] the reference to דבר would follow this pattern. In addition, the Exodus account lacks a description of how the livestock perish in this pestilence. Exodus 9:3 simply emphasizes that this plague is brought about by "the hand of YHWH" (יד־יהוה). In addition, the Exodus account stresses that the "pestilence" (דבר) brought against livestock was intentionally withheld from Pharaoh and the Egyptians (Exod 9:14).

A second aspect of the description in v. 50 that associates this event with the possible destruction of livestock is the use of the verb "to give over" (סגר). As noted in the literary analysis, this verb is used in v. 48 for YHWH's destruction of animals (בעיר) and livestock (מקנה) by hail and thunderbolts. In v. 50, the object of the verb סגר is "living thing, animal" (חיה).[49] By repeating this verb in vv. 48 and 50, where the objects of the verb are both terms used for animals, the psalmist may be intentionally drawing together these two plagues.[50] As seen in the wilderness food account, the psalmist often employs verbal links to draw together events.[51] The psalmist may be using the same technique here to draw two animal-focused plagues together.

---

people is in striking antithesis to the restraint of His anger toward His people, though by a different author." Briggs and Briggs, *Critical and Exegetical Commentary on Psalms*, 188.

48. This occurs with the use of common lexemes for the plagues of blood (דם), frogs (צפרדע), flies (ערב), locust (ארבה), and hail (ברד).

49. BDB considers Ps 78:50's use of חיה as a "doubtful" generic reference to "life."

50. The LXX coordinates these two references by using the phrase "their cattle" (τα κτηνη αυτων) in both vv. 48 and 50, but the verbal repetition does not occur.

51. This was seen with the verb "to cleave" (בקע) to link two water events (Red/Reed Sea and water from a rock, vv. 13, 15) and with the verb "to rain" (מטר) to link two food

FRAMING OF THE EGYPTIAN PLAGUE ACCOUNT (PS 78:43–51)

For some scholars, the question of the psalmist's selection of these plagues is solved by the proposed Yahwist/J source that would have served as the source document at the time of the composition of the account.[52] However, this hypothesis fails to address the selection *and arrangement* of the plagues included in the psalmist's account.[53] In what follows, a proposal will be made for Psalm 78's intentional arrangement and selection of the plagues as a systematic dismantling of Egypt's food supplies—water resources, agricultural supplies, then livestock/meat—an order that has already been established in the wilderness food account.

When one compares the account of the plagues in Psalm 78 to the one found in Exodus, one finds both continuity and discontinuity. The major instances of continuity occur in its description and placement of the plagues of water-turned-blood and the death of the firstborn. Psalm 78 places the plague of water-turned-blood as the first plague against Egypt, similar to the account in Exodus (contra Ps 105). The psalmist also concludes the plague list with the death of the firstborn, similar to the Exodus account and Psalm 105. In addition to the ordering of the first and last plagues, the psalmist uses a number of shared terms with the first and last plagues in the Exodus account. In the water-turned-blood plague, the psalmist shares vocabulary with Exod 7:20b (cf. v. 17) and Exod 7:21a (cf. v. 18) in the words "to turn" (הפך), "Nile, river" (יאר), "blood" (דם), and "to drink" (שתה)—a point noted earlier in the chapter. Psalm 78's depiction of the final plague—death of the firstborn—also shares a significant number of lexemes with the account found in Exod

events (manna and quail, vv. 24, 27).

52. Houtman offers a helpful categorization of the three proposed sources and their presence in the Exodus plague account: "Not all three are assumed to be present to the same extent: I (J, E, P); II (J, P); III (P); IV (J); V (J); VI (P); VII (J, E); VIII (J, E); IX (E); X (J, E, P). The bulk of the text is from J. His version contains seven plagues. E and P have each five plagues." Houtman, *Exodus*, 14–15. Thus, the J (Yahwist) source would reflect only plagues I (Nile), II (frogs), IV (flies), V (livestock pestilence), VII (hail), VIII (locusts), X (death of firstborn): the same seven plagues found in Psalm 78.

53. A variety of creative explanations exists for Psalm 78's variations from the presentation in Exodus. Hoffmeier claims "liturgical license." Hoffmeier, "Egypt, Plagues in," 374. Tate assumes a lapse in memory: "The recital shows part of what the Israelites did not remember." Tate, *Psalms 51–100*, 293. McCann concludes that "the psalmist's concern is less with the past than with the present and the future." McCann, "Book of Psalms," 992.

12:12b (cf. v. 29) through the words "to strike" (נכה), "all" (כל), "firstborn" (בכור), and "Egypt" (מצרים):

והכיתי כל בכור בארץ מצרים

> Exod 12:12b: "and I will strike down all the firstborn in the land of Egypt."

ויך כל בכור במצרים ראשית אונים באהלי חם

> Ps 78:51: He struck down all the firstborn in Egypt, the first issue of their strength in the tents of Ham.

Regarding these lexical parallels found in the description of the death of the firstborn, Greenstein notes: "However the psalmist may deviate from the Torah's text in retelling of the plagues story, he forges an intractable link at the end of the series. No Israelite would miss the association of the psalm's *vayyakh kol bekhor bemitsrayim*, 'he stuck every firstborn in Egypt' (v. 51), a nearly verbatim echo of Exod. 12:29: *vaYHWH hikka kol bekhor be'erets mitsrayim*."[54] These lexical links are all the more striking in light of the sparse lexical parallels in the descriptions of the rest of the plagues.[55]

The lexical discontinuity from Exodus in the remainder of the plagues stands in stark contrast to the strong frame provided by the opening and closing plagues. Two aspects of this discontinuity will be addressed below: ordering and selection. In the central section of the psalmist's plague account (vv. 45–50), there are three changes from the ordering of the plagues found in Exodus. The psalmist transposes the flies (v. 45a) before the frogs (v. 45b); locusts (v. 46) before hail (vv. 47–48); hail (vv. 47–48) before livestock pestilence (vv. 49–50).[56] The triple occurrence of transposed elements exhibits a consistency in the psalmist's handiwork.[57] Of these changes, the psalmist's reordering of the hail and locust accounts may offer the strongest clue as to the psalmist's rhetorical motivations in this section of the psalm. Even if one does not hold to the

54. Greenstein, "Mixing Memory and Design," 207.

55. As seen earlier in this chapter, the psalmist's only significant lexical links to the Exodus account are through the terminology used to identify each of the plagues: blood (דם), frogs (צפרדע), flies (ערב), locust (ארבה), hail (ברד), and pestilence (דבר).

56. Greenstein also observes this transposition. Greenstein, "Mixing Memory and Design," 207.

57. Of the three changes, the switch in the ordering of the plagues of flies and frogs exhibits no apparent significance in the patterning of the account except for the fact that it fits into a larger pattern established by the author.

position that the focus of the destruction of the flies/frogs is primarily agricultural (see argument above), the psalmist clearly presents the locust plague (v. 46) as an act of agricultural destruction that continues into the following verse with the destruction of agriculture through the hail (v. 47). In addition, if one reads vv. 49–50 as the plague on livestock, then the destruction of livestock begun by the hail in v. 48 simply continues with another plague against animals in the livestock pestilence (vv. 49–50). Thus, we find a clear separation of agricultural destruction (vv. 46–47; cf. v. 45) and death of livestock (v. 48; cf. vv. 49–50).

Unlike the other plagues in the psalmist's account, the hail plague is the only one to have a dual aspect to its destruction, in this case, agriculture (v. 47) and livestock (v. 48). The psalmist's ordering of the destruction caused by the hail is reversed from the order found in Exodus which highlights the hail's effect on livestock, with the agricultural dimension of the plague following as a secondary result. By reordering the destructive arenas of the hail to first address agriculture, then livestock, the psalmist is using the hail plague as the bridge between the agricultural destruction initiated by the locusts and the destruction of livestock caused by the pestilence. Seen in this way, the psalmist is then intentionally reorganizing the plagues around what is being destroyed—agricultural products (by flies, frogs, locusts, hail) then livestock (by hail, livestock pestilence).[58] When the plagues are seen within this paradigm of the destruction of agriculture and livestock, the omitted plagues also follow an intentional pattern. The plagues of gnats, boils, and darkness are missing from the psalmist's account because they do not destroy agriculture or cause animal deaths. In this reading of the psalmist's plague account, one does not need to propose a hypothesized source text to explain the absence of these three plagues.

This proposal for the shaping of Psalm 78's depiction of the plague account offers a rhetorically motivated solution that explains both the selection and arrangement of the plagues. While much work has been done on the rhetorical shaping of both the Exodus plague account and the depiction of the plagues in Psalm 105, this proposal offers a way forward for considering the shape of Psalm 78's plague account.

58. Greenstein finds a similar movement in the psalm. Yet for him, the rhetorical significance lies solely in its cohesion to the Exodus plotline: "The psalmist's sequence does make rhetorical sense and can be explained as a takeoff on the Torah. In the psalm the plagues begin with an assault on Egypt's water (blood) and its land and vegetation (flies, frogs, locusts, and hail); then they escalate in severity by attacking its livestock (cattle plague) and its people killing the firstborn." Greenstein, "Mixing Memory and Design," 207. Greenstein assumes that v. 48's reference to "hail" should be amended to "pestilence."

THE RHETORICAL USE OF FOOD IN PSALM 78:43–51

Within the plague account (vv. 43–51), YHWH's destruction of Egyptian food supplies draws its rhetorical power by reversing expectations related to the physical, locational, and patterned dimensions of food. Each of these dimensions will be addressed below, followed by a consideration of the rhetorical force of the convergence of food language in the psalmist's portrayal of the Egyptian plagues.

Physical Dimension of Food Destruction in Egyptian Plagues

Water events head both the account of food provision in the wilderness (vv. 15–16) and the account of food destruction in the plagues in Egypt (v. 44). This key positioning of water events may reflect the vital concern for maintaining hydration in order to sustain life. Without a consistent source of water, Egypt's basic existence is threatened. Thus, YHWH's water-based miracles were powerful ways to capture the attention of the audience through the everyday need for water.

Locational Dimension of Food Destruction in Egyptian Plagues

The locational dimension of these "signs and portents" is often overlooked by scholars. However, the psalmist repeatedly calls attention to the location of the plagues by emphasizing that this destruction of water and food resources is happening in "Egypt" (מצרים, v. 43, 51), in "the fields of Zoan" (שדה צען, v. 43) along the banks of the Nile River (יאר, v. 44).[59] Beginning in the book of Genesis, Egypt is associated with stable

59. The psalmist seems to be using locational markers to frame this section of the recital. The plague account begins in v. 43 with two locational markers: "Egypt" (מצרים) and "fields of Zoan" (שדה צען). Unlike the earlier reference in v. 12 to "the land of Egypt" (ארץ מצרים), here in v. 43 the psalmist employs only the term for the nation. The psalmist closes the plague account (v. 51) with another reference to the nation, here referring to the death of the firstborn in Egypt (מצרים). The psalmist's choice of the term "Nile, river" (יאר) in v. 44 may reflect a concern for establishing locational specificity, similar to the reference to "fields of Zoan" (שדה צען). The psalmist also frames the account with a move from agricultural to domestic locations. In v. 43, the events are said to unfold "in the fields of Zoan" (שדה צען; cf. v. 12); in v. 51, the final plague moves

food supplies (Gen 12:10; cf. 26:2; contra Gen 41–47, where a seven-year famine strikes Egypt). This agricultural stability rests in the constancy of the Nile River, both its water supply and its annual flooding that creates a context for agricultural productivity.[60] When YHWH turns the Nile to blood, this change threatens the stability of the whole regional ecosystem. In addition, the destruction of the agricultural food supplies in Egypt—a location known internationally as a refuge in times of famine—heightens the dramatic tension of the text.

Patterned Dimension of Food Destruction in Egyptian Plagues

As shown in this chapter, the ordering of the plagues in Psalm 78 follows neither the account in Exodus nor the account in Psalm 105. The psalmist instead orders and arranges the plagues by what is being destroyed—water sources (v. 44), agriculture (vv. 45–46, possibly v. 45), livestock (v. 48, possibly vv. 49–50), and human life (v. 51). This disruption of food supplies by YHWH shattered assumptions about Pharaoh's ability to protect and maintain the cosmic order. Knierim, arguing for the role that agriculture plays in depicting this cosmic order, contends: "Agriculture, conceived theologically, is that form of human activity in which humans on earth are integrated into the cosmic life-cycle which owes its creation and existence to Yahweh."[61] In ancient Egypt where the ruling pharaoh was considered a deity himself, a disruption in stable agricultural patterns reflected an assumed disruption in the cosmic order. In Exod 9:29, Moses announces that the hail will stop and that by nature returning to its rightful ordering (Exod 9:29), Pharaoh/the Egyptians would come to know "that the earth is YHWH's" (כי ליהוה הארץ). Thus, the cyclical

---

into the dwellings of the Egyptians (i.e., "the tents of Ham" אהל־חם). There is debate over the proper translation for the expression "fields of Zoan" (שדה צען). Kidner argues that "the *fields* would be better translated 'the country round' or 'the region of.'" Kidner, *Psalm 73–150*, 282. In light of the psalmist's concern with the destruction of agriculture, Zoan's "fields" is a more precise and preferred translation (cf. Ruth 1:1, 6).

60. Hilary Marlow notes: "The river Nile was (and still is) subject to an annual inundation lasting for a period of approximately six weeks, during which the surrounding flood plain was covered with a layer of rich alluvial silt, and irrigation pools and channels were replenished. It was following this annual flooding that the winter crop was sown." Marlow, "Lament over the River Nile," 235.

61. Knierim, "Cosmos and History in Israel's Theology," 197.

nature of agricultural production provides a ready structure for depicting both cosmic order and, in the case of the plagues, cosmic disorder.

The Multidimensional Force of Food Language in Psalm 78:43–51

As seen in the discussion above, the psalmist draws upon a variety of food dimensions in this recital of the Egyptian plagues. The reference to the setting of this destruction as "the fields of Zoan" reminds the audience of this unexpected turn of events in the lush and fertile lands along the Nile River. Here the psalmist presents evidence for YHWH's sovereign power by systematically dismantling the security of Egypt's food supplies. Instead of the security of water supplies from the Nile, the Egyptians are forced to search for clean water. Agriculture and livestock, mainstays of Egypt's economy, are decimated. And in this destruction, YHWH shows his cosmic rule over creation itself. By drawing upon multiple dimensions of food at the same time, the psalmist is able to magnify the disorder that Egypt experiences in the plagues.

RHETORICAL ANALYSIS OF PSALM 78'S DESCRIPTION OF THE DESTRUCTION OF EGYPT'S FOOD SUPPLIES (VV. 43–51)

Three aspects of the Egyptian plague account (vv. 43–51) encourage the audience to embrace a confident trust in YHWH's power to intervene in their present circumstances. First, YHWH overturns locational expectations. Second, YHWH is directly involved in dismantling Egypt's food supplies—no human agents are present. Third, the natural world readily serves as YHWH's stewards.

In the depiction of the plagues in Egypt, the psalmist repeatedly reminds the audience of YHWH's power to change current circumstances. The psalm's plague account is an explicit example of YHWH's power to destabilize environments. The psalmist's description is also an implicit recognition of YHWH's ability to restore environments as well. If YHWH can make the ever-fertile Nile delta into a wasteland, could YHWH not also provide for the rain-reliant fields of Canaan?

Unlike the Exodus account and the recital in Psalm 105, Psalm 78's depiction of the plague account involves no human agents. In the Exodus account, many of the plagues commence with a symbolic act performed by either Moses or Aaron.[62] While the Exodus narrative makes it clear that YHWH is the one who brings the plagues, Moses and Aaron play a significant role in the announcement and commencement of the plagues. In Ps 105:26–27, Moses and Aaron are both mentioned in the context of the "signs and portents" (אתות ומופת) of the plagues (vv. 26–27).[63] Unlike the Exodus and the Psalm 105 accounts of the plagues, Psalm 78 pictures YHWH as the sole agent, without mediator or spokesperson. Throughout the plague account, the psalmist stresses YHWH's active involvement and sovereign power in this scene of judgment on Israel's enemies. By not including human agents, the psalmist depicts a scenario not dependent on human initiative or leadership. It is a reversal of fortune brought about solely by the hand of YHWH.

Considering the role of nature in the psalmist's plague account, one finds that the natural world is often sent as envoys or servants of YHWH. In Psalm 78, creation itself participates and cooperates with YHWH's commands. As Tanner observes: "The impact here is to stress again what God had done to save the Israelites from their captors and to demonstrate that God's weapon is the creation. This tells all listening that God is truly the Creator, for creation obeys God's command."[64] In the wilderness food accounts, the psalm describes how nature plays a role in bringing food, as the skies rain food and the winds bring quail. Yet in the plague account, the psalmist pictures God's creatures (flies, frogs, locusts, caterpillars) on a different mission, a mission uniquely designed for them. They are sent to eat. Thus, in the midst of bringing about judgment on Israel's enemies, the Creator is providing for creation's needs.[65]

62. In this account, Aaron lifts his staff and strikes the water (7:20); stretches out his hand over the waters (8:6); stretches out his hand with his staff and strikes the dust (8:17). Moses throws soot of a kiln in the air (9:8); stretches out his staff toward heaven (9:23); stretches out his staff over the land (10:13); stretches out his hand toward heaven (10:22).

63. Moses and Aaron are not, however, mentioned once the actual plagues are recounted (vv. 28–38). YHWH becomes the active agent.

64. DeClaissé-Walford et al., *Book of Psalms*, 624.

65. The psalmist's depiction of the plagues only introduces the creatures and the destruction that they bring. In the Exodus account, some of these creatures meet a quick death. The frogs who are not in the Nile River die and are piled in heaps (8:13); the east wind that brought the locusts now drives them into the Red/Reed Sea (10:19). In addition, all the fish in the Nile River die in the first plague (7:21). In Psalm 78, no creatures are harmed in the portrayal of this account.

THE PROVISION AND DESTRUCTION OF FOOD WITHIN THE WILDERNESS FRAME (PS 78:13–53)

One of the structural aspects of the psalm that has challenged scholars is the placement of the Egyptian plagues near the end of the wilderness account. In a psalm that urges the audience to recount God's wonders (v. 4) and not forget the works of God (v. 6), why does the psalmist choose to depart from a strictly linear account of history? Chronologically the plagues should be set at the start of the account, following the psalmist's first reference to "the land of Egypt, the field of Zoan" (v. 12). In addition, why does the psalmist include a detailed listing of the plagues when a simple reference to "the signs and portents" of Egypt would suffice as a summary of the events?[66]

In light of its substantial length and its curious placement, one is moved to assume that Psalm 78's inclusion of the plague account fills a rhetorical purpose in the psalm greater than a rote recitation of historical events. Nasuti argues that the lengthy account of the plagues is an attempt to balance the extended account of the food miracles earlier in the psalm. Nasuti contends: "At the same time, however, it is clear that this section is part of the author's original composition and not something added by a later redactor, since its additional length helps to compensate for the extended character of the first half of the main body of the psalm."[67] Instead of simply balancing the composition, the psalmist's ordering, depiction, and placement of the Egyptian plagues can be understood as a foil for the wilderness food account presented earlier in the text (vv. 15–31).

This literary connection between the psalmist's presentation of the wilderness food account and the Egyptian plagues has been acknowledged by other scholars. Marc Girard has argued for a structural parallel between the "miracles of water" in vv. 12–16 (Opening of the Red/Reed Sea // Water from a Rock) and vv. 43–53 (Waters of Nile to Blood //

66. This phrase is used not only in Ps 135:9 but also in Neh 9:10, where one might expect a longer listing of this event. See also instances in Deuteronomy (4:34; 6:22; 7:19; 26:8; 29:3; 34:11), Jeremiah (32:20–21) and Psalms (135:9).

67. Nasuti, *Tradition History and the Psalms of Asaph*, 89. Hossfeld assumes that the plague account is a secondary addition to the psalm and sees careful work on the part of the redactor in embedding this passage within an existing psalm. He asserts that the placement of the plagues at this point in the psalm is an attempt to keep it during the lifetime of the exodus generation since "beginning with v. 52 the text moves swiftly from Israel's being led in the wilderness to the occupation of the land by the second generation." Hossfeld and Zenger, *Psalms* 2, 288.

Closing of the Red/Reed Sea).[68] In this case, the placement of the provision of water from a rock (vv. 15–16) as the first food event (contra Exod 16–17, Ps 105) shows an intentional ordering of the wilderness food events to parallel the Egyptian plagues.

As noted earlier, a variety of intra-textual links within Psalm 78 draw together the wilderness food account (vv. 12–31) and the plague account (vv. 43–51). These examples occur mainly through the use of verbal links between the two accounts. One finds an example of this in v. 46 where YHWH "gives" (נתן) Egypt's crops to the locust; yet earlier in v. 20, Israel questions YHWH's ability to "give" (נתן) them food in the wilderness (cf. v. 24). Intra-textual links occurs in v. 47 when YHWH "slays" (הרג) Egypt's vines and sycamores with hail just as he "slays" (הרג) the fattest (v. 31) in the wilderness. Links also occur in vv. 45–46 where the trio of verbs—"send" (שלח), "ate" (אכל), "gave" (נתן)—are used to refer to the approach of the plagues of flies, frogs, and locusts. This verbal set also appears in the manna account in vv. 24b–25: "He gave (נתן) them the grain of heaven. Each ate (אכל) the bread of the mighty; he sent (שלח) them provisions in abundance."[69] A final link occurs with the term "streams" (נזלים) when YHWH pollutes the "streams" (נזלים) of Egypt (v. 44), although in the wilderness he makes "streams" (נזלים) flow in abundance (v. 16).

Terence Fretheim notes that the pairing of the plague and food events is evident in the Exodus account. He argues that God's provision of water and provision of food in the wilderness were acts of "recreation" following the "de-creation" caused by the plagues:

> For example, the result of the first plague was that "they could not drink the water" (7:24). When, in 15:23, "they could not drink the water," the bitter water is made sweet and potable. . . . Or, whereas God "rained" (*mtr*) hail upon Egypt, destroying the food sources (see 9:18, 23), in 16:4 God "rains" bread from the heavens. Or, as locusts "came up" (*'lh*) and "covered" (*ksh*)

68. Girard finds a complex concentric structure to the psalmist's presentation of the wilderness account (vv. 12–53). In addition to the parallel of water miracles, he also finds a parallel structure in the psalmist's inclusion of two "miracles of food" (the manna in vv. 23–25 and the quail in vv. 26–29). Girard argues that the food miracles (manna/quail) hold the center position of the section. He does not, however, expand on the other plagues' purpose. Girard, *Psaumes redécouverts*, 359–61. Jean-Luc Vesco follows Girard's structural divisions. Vesco, *Psautier de David traduit et commenté I*, 702–3.

69. A point noted by Emanuel, "Psalmists' Use of the Exodus Motif," 67.

> the land (10:14–15), destroying the food, so in 16:13 the quails "came up" and "covered" the camp, providing food.[70]

Many of the lexical and thematic links that Fretheim finds in the Exodus account also appear in Psalm 78. Surprisingly, Psalm 78 describes the wilderness food events found in vv. 12–31 with language more typical of the plague events. In Ps 78:24, 27, manna and quail "rain down" (מטר) on Israel, reminiscent of the hail that "rained down" (מטר) on Egypt's crops (9:18, 23). In Ps 78:20, Israel remembers how YHWH "struck" (נכה) the rock to bring water (Ps 78:20); while in the Exodus account, YHWH "struck" (נכה) Egypt's livestock/crops (Exod 9:25, 31, 32) and the first-born (Exod 12:12, 13, 29). In Ps 78:26, YHWH sent out the "east" (קדים) and "led" (נהג) the south winds to bring the quail which becomes food for Israel, where in Exodus, YHWH "led" (נהג) the "east" (קדים) wind to bring the locusts that destroy Egypt's food (Exod 10:13).

By moving the Egyptian plagues to the end of the wilderness account, the psalmist is able to invite the audience to reconsider Israel's failure to comprehend the significance of YHWH's "wonder" of food provision for a second time—now in light of Egypt/Pharaoh's inability to be convinced by the "signs and portents" of the plagues. A consistent feature of the Exodus plague account is the fact that Pharaoh's "heart was hardened" (לב + חזק/קשה/כבד) and the signs performed in his presence did not achieve their logical effect of changing his heart toward YHWH/the Israelites. Psalm 78 paints a picture of Israel whose "heart was not steadfast" (לא־הכין לבו) (vv. 8, 37). In the psalmist's recital of the plagues, neither Pharaoh nor the Egyptians is directly mentioned. This omission may in fact be rhetorically motivated. It is as if the psalmist invites the audience to reconsider Israel's own rebellious heart as they have also been given "wonders" to build their trust in YHWH. As with Egypt in the "signs and portents" of the plagues, so for Israel in their experience of the "wonders" in the wilderness, the psalmist acknowledges that these miraculous events did not change their hearts (v. 37).

The additional support for the intentional juxtaposition of the wilderness food account and the Egyptian plagues comes from an ancient theological reflection of these events. In the Wisdom of Solomon, the Exodus plagues and the wilderness food events are used to present two views, God's treatment of the righteous and God's treatment of the wicked

70. Fretheim, "Plagues as Ecological Signs," 395.

(here typified by Egypt).[71] In Wis 11:6–8, the narrator pairs the water events of the Nile-turned-blood with God's provision of water from a rock. In Wis 16:1–4, the animal plagues are contrasted with God's provision of delicacies of quail meat. In Wis 16:15–29, the destruction of crops in Egypt is contrasted with God's provision of manna in the wilderness. The Wisdom of Solomon makes explicit the parallels that are implicit in Psalm 78.

Lastly, the psalmist's depictions of the wilderness food event and the plague account exhibit a similar means of provision and a similar progression in that provision. In both the manna/quail account and the plague account, YHWH employs similar agents as a means of provision. In the manna/quail account, he utilizes the wind and clouds as he brings provision from the heavens. In the plague accounts, he now brings destruction from above as he employs weather (hail, lightning) and flying creatures (flies and locusts) to bring judgment. And as was shown in this chapter, God's provision and destruction follows a similar progression and pattern moving from water sources (rock // Nile) to crops (heavenly grain/bread // vines and sycamores) to meat sources (meat/winged bird // livestock), and in both accounts, human death is the last event (the fattest and young men of Israel // firstborn of Egypt).

CONCLUSION

Through the ordering and depiction of the plagues, as well as the placement of these events within the larger wilderness account (vv. 13–53), the psalmist is able to present the Egyptian plagues (vv. 44–51) as a foil for the wilderness food account (vv. 15–31). Instead of following a strict listing of the destructive agents associated with the Egyptian plagues, the psalmist instead orders the account based on what aspect of the food supply is being destroyed. Seen in this way, the selection and ordering of the plagues presents a systematic dismantling of food supplies—water resources (water-to-blood), agricultural supplies (flies, frogs, locust, hail), then livestock (hail, livestock pestilence). And by placing the Egyptian plagues after the wilderness food events, the psalmist is able to present the plagues as an antithesis of YHWH's wilderness food provision.

71. For a discussion of the use of the Exodus tradition, see Cheon, *Exodus Story in the Wisdom of Solomon*.

While chapters 4 and 5 considered the psalmist's literary and rhetorical choices in the presentation of the two key food accounts in the wilderness frame (vv. 13–53), the following chapter will expand the scope of discussion to include the psalmist's use of food language across the composition as a whole. In addition, Psalm 78's use of food language will be considered in light of the Psalm collections most closely related to it by content—the historical psalms (Pss 105, 106, 135, 136)—and by context—the Asaph Collection (Pss 50, 73–83).

6

Psalm 78's Use of Food Language

Considering Its Associated Collections (Historical Psalms and the Asaph Collection)

INTRODUCTION

CHAPTERS 4 AND 5 identified Psalm 78's literary similarities to and differences from the Hebrew Bible's other depictions of the wilderness food events and the Egyptian plagues. While displaying instances of some common language and themes to these other depictions, it was shown that Psalm 78 offers a unique presentation of these events through its emphasis on YHWH's extravagant provision of food for Israel in the wilderness (vv. 15–16, 23–28) and in its depiction of the Egyptian plagues as a systematic dismantling of food supplies (vv. 44–50).

This chapter expands the study of Psalm 78 to consider instances of food language across the composition. It begins with a general survey of the variety of examples and uses of food language within the psalm and specifically considers the rhetorical use of food dimensions for describing Israel's experience of life in the land (vv. 54–72).[1] In order to

1. See chapters 4 and 5 for discussions of the rhetorical use of food dimensions occurring within the wilderness frame (vv. 13–53).

identify Psalm 78's distinct uses of food language, the chapter turns to the collections in the Psalter with which it is most closely identified. This begins with a study of the "historical psalms" (Pss 105, 106, 135, 136), a collection of psalms that relate to Psalm 78 through *content*—psalms with an extended historical recital. It then considers the Asaph Collection (Pss 50, 73–83), a set of psalms that are related to Psalm 78 through occupying the same immediate literary *context* (Pss 73–83) and/or the common designation לאסף (Pss 50, 73–83). The aim of this study is to highlight Psalm 78's rhetorical distinctives, as well as expand the reader's awareness of the use of food language within the Psalter.

PSALM 78'S USE OF FOOD LANGUAGE

Besides describing two food-related events in Israel's history (wilderness food and Egyptian plagues),[2] the psalmist also utilizes food language in the wilderness frame (vv. 13–53) to depict Israel's rebellion (vv. 19–20, 29–30), to describe YHWH's specific judgment (v. 31), to reflect on the human condition (v. 39), and to offer an image of Israel's dependence on YHWH (v. 52–53). In addition, food language also appears within Israel's experience of life in the land (vv. 54–72) to picture death in warfare (v. 63), to illustrate YHWH's surprising intervention (v. 65), and to give evidence for David's leadership potential (vv. 70–72). As seen in this simple listing of examples, food language appears with remarkable regularity across the composition.[3]

2. The psalmist includes specific depictions of divine provision of water from a rock, manna, and quail (vv. 15–16, 23–28), as well as divine destruction of water supplies, crops, and livestock in Egypt (vv. 43–50).

3. I would be remiss if I did not add the references to Ephraim (lit., "the fruitful ones") that appear in v. 9 and in v. 67. The use of this tribal eponym provides another possible food reference in light of the fact that the land given to Ephraim was some of the most fertile land in Canaan. As Wenham notes: "'Ephraim' perhaps originally meant 'fertile land' or 'pasture land,' certainly an apt description of the land that the tribe of Ephraim would inherit. But Joseph relates Ephraim to the verb פרה 'be fruitful,' a key term in Genesis (cf. 1:22, 28; 8:17; 26:22; 35:11), especially in the promises (17:6, 20; 28:3; 48:4)." Wenham, *Genesis 16–50*, 398. Although this tribal name has the potential for rhetorical use (cf. Hos 9:16; 14:9), the psalmist refrains from any explicit rhetorical play in these references.

Food Language in the Wilderness Frame of Psalm 78 (vv. 13–53)

In the wilderness frame (vv. 13–53), Psalm 78's first food reference occurs in vv. 15–16 where God gives Israel abundant water to drink. The source of this water—wilderness "rocks" (צרים) / "a rocky crag" (סלע)—challenges Israel's expectation regarding food distribution.[4] Ironically, this divine provision for Israel's need for water in a wilderness context (ציה, "a dry land," v. 17) leads only to Israel's willful testing (נסה) of God's ability to provide for their desires. Here Israel's sin lies not in forgetting God's abundant provision of water,[5] but in their verbal challenge regarding God's ability to provide food for his people (vv. 19b–20):

> Is God able to set a table in the wilderness? (היוכל אל לערך שלחן במדבר)
> Is he able to give bread as well? (הגם לחם יוכל תת)
> Can he provide meat for his people? (אם יכין שאר לעמו)

The food miracles that follow are YHWH's direct answer to these rhetorical questions. For in vv. 23–28, God commands, creation responds, and Israel is fed.

In v. 29, the psalmist highlights the fact that Israel's legitimate need for physical nourishment in the wilderness had turned into an insatiable craving (תאוה) in the midst of their unrestrained consumption of YHWH's provisions. Dramatic irony saturates the depiction of the consequences of their actions. The psalmist notes in v. 30 that while "the food

4. Reversal of expectation is a common occurrence throughout Psalm 78's depiction of divine provision of food during Israel's wilderness journey. In this context, rocks bring water (vv. 15–16), the heavens rain grain (v. 24), and the winds deliver quail to Israel's "doorstep" (v. 27–28).

5. As discussed in chapter 4, the psalmist's quotation of Israel's description of the water miracle (v. 20) uses different terms than the earlier depiction by the psalmist; but similar to the psalmist, Israel's response emphasizes the striking abundance of this provision. Israel's vivid memory of God's provision of water provides the ironic frame for their lack of trust in God's ability to provide food. This theme of remembering and forgetting runs throughout Psalm 78. However, commentators often fail to recognize that in Psalm 78, Israel remembers almost as often as they forget. While Israel is called to "not forget" (v. 7), the sons of Ephraim do in fact "forget" (v. 11), and later we find that Israel "does not remember" (v. 42) God's power. However, in the wilderness Israel also "remembers" that God is their rock and redeemer (v. 35) and here in v. 20 they recall with great detail the previous water miracle. See Marco Pavan for an extended study of the theme of remembering in Book 3 of the Psalter, with particular interest in Psalm 78. Pavan, *He Remembered That They Were But Flesh*, 223–335.

was still in their mouths" (עוד אכלם בפיהם), YHWH killed the fattest (משמן) among them (v. 31).[6]

In the central wilderness section (vv. 32–42), the psalmist offers a picture of Israel's rebellion that lacks any historical references linking it to a specific wilderness event.[7] In the midst of Israel's tripartite rebellion (vv. 36–37a),[8] God acts in unexpected ways. Instead of direct divine judgment, the psalmist announces God's compassion (רחום) and details his merciful response to Israel (v. 38; cf. Exod 34:6). This announcement of forgiveness and divine restraint is followed by the motivation for God's actions (v. 39): "He remembered (זכר)[9] that they were but flesh (בשר),[10] a passing breeze/breath that goes out and does not return (שוב)."[11] Here God's compassion is rooted in the remembrance of humanity's need to be sustained by its Creator. As Gärtner notes: "The remembrance of God the creator is highlighted in Ps 78:38f., which refers to the fallibility of

6. See chapter 4 for an extended discussion of this account.

7. Hossfeld also acknowledges the change in the recital: "The fourth strophe, vv. 32–39, begins, similarly to its predecessors, with the depiction of the continuing sin of Israel, but then devotes itself not to a description of events, but to a depiction of the fate and behavior of Israel, as well as God's astonishing reaction of mercy. The special feature of this strophe is theological reflection." Hossfeld and Zenger, *Psalms 2*, 290. Hossfeld makes a break at v. 39 where I continue this section to v. 42.

8. Here the psalmist notes: "But they flattered him with their mouths (פה); they lied to him with their tongues (לשון). Their heart (לב) was not steadfast toward him" (vv. 36–37a).

9. BDB (s.v. זכר) identifies four texts where God is the subject of the verb זכר followed by a clause with כי and "extenuating circumstances": Job 7:7; 10:9; Ps 78:39; 103:14; see also 89:48. In each case, humanity's finite condition is in view. In Job 7:7, Job calls God to remember (זכר) his life is but a "breath" (רוח) that does not "return" (שוב). In Job 10:9, Job calls God to remember (זכר) that God fashioned him like clay and questions whether God will "return" (שוב) him to "dust" (עפר). A similar argument appears in Ps 103:13–16. Here YHWH's compassionate response (רחם; cf. Ps 78:38) is rooted in the fact that he knows how we are formed, he "remembers" (זכר) we are "dust" (עפר). In each of these examples, it is humanity's dependency on its Creator that becomes the evidence for pleading for God's compassionate response.

10. The use of the term "flesh" (בשר) here is in contrast to the term שאר (meat/flesh) used in the wilderness food account to describe Israel's request for meat and the quail consumed by humans (vv. 20, 27). See discussion in chapter 4.

11. Remembering (זכר) and turning/returning (שוב) are key themes in this section of the psalm. In vv. 34–35 the psalmist notes that Israel turns (שוב), seeks God, and remembers (זכר) that God was their rock and redeemer. Here in vv. 38–39, God "turned back" (שוב) from his anger and remembered (זכר) that Israel was but a breath/wind that goes out and does not "return" (שוב). In vv. 41–42, Israel returns again (שוב) to test God as they did not "remember" (זכר) his power at work in the past. These repeated phrases lead me to extend the reflection from v. 32 to v. 42 (contra Hossfeld, Clifford).

humankind, which is designated as 'flesh' and transient 'breath' or 'wind.' But precisely in this creaturely status to which the fallibility of man is bound—as made clear by Israel's actions in history (Ps 78:17–27)—God remembers his people."[12] The psalmist's picture of God as Sustainer of his creation, offering forgiveness in the past, invites a present hope as well.

In the closing section (vv. 43–53) of the wilderness frame, the psalm continues with a depiction of God's "signs" (אות) and "portents" (מופת) that occurred in Egypt and in the fields of Zoan (v. 43; cf. vv. 44–51). The psalmist's departure from a chronological recounting of events in Israel's history is most strongly felt in this return to Egypt (cf. v. 12) following Israel's journey through the wilderness (vv. 13–42).[13] As shown in chapter 5, Psalm 78's depiction of the "signs and portents" in Zoan's fields is presented as a systematic dismantling of Egypt's food supplies (water, crops, livestock), a mirror image of the divine provision of food supplies (water, manna, meat) in the wilderness.

The wilderness section of the psalm concludes with a picture of YHWH leading (נסע) and guiding (נהג) Israel as a "flock/sheep" (עדר/צאן) safely through the wilderness (vv. 52–53a).[14] This choice of pastoral imagery to describe Israel also has ironic value in light of the recent destruction of Egypt's own livestock (מקנה/בעיר, vv. 48).[15]

12. Gärtner, "Historical Psalms," 378–79. See Kraus for a similar position. Kraus, *Psalms 60–150*, 128.

13. Scholars have sought various explanations for this move back to Egypt in Ps 78:43–51. As argued in chapter 5, I believe that in this return the psalmist is able to accentuate the reality Israel had recently left in Egypt where the countryside was ravaged by the plagues, leaving polluted waterways and fields stripped of the harvest. Thus, the psalmist is able to capture some of the same irony found in the wilderness narratives that depict Israel's mis-memory of their eating habits in Egypt (i.e., Exod 16:3; Num 11:5). Israel's dissatisfaction with YHWH's provision and the forgotten reality of agricultural devastation in Egypt both heighten the dramatic irony of their wilderness rebellion depicted in vv. 17–20.

14. The verb pair "lead" (נסע) / "guide" (נהג) is used earlier to describe YHWH's employment of the winds (v. 26) to bring "meat" (שאר) for Israel in the wilderness (v. 26). In both instances, YHWH's sovereign involvement in the created world is on display.

15. Here in vv. 52–53, the focus is on YHWH's protective care of Israel in the midst of danger, not necessarily on the provision of food for his flock. And yet as seen in Ps 23:1–3, these two features of a shepherd's care are intrinsically linked.

Food Language in the Land-Based Section of Psalm 78 (vv. 54–72)

The use of food language continues into the land-based section of the psalm (vv. 54–72) but with a diminished frequency. Each of the examples in this section will be considered, with particular attention given to the presence of intra-textual links. This section closes with a discussion of the psalmist's rhetorical use of food dimensions—namely, the physical, sensory, and locational dimensions of food.

Survey of Food References in Psalm 78:54–72

Food language continues to be used by the psalmist as Israel enters into the land. Once Israel enters the land (vv. 54–72), they again test (נסה) and rebel (מרה) against God (vv. 56; cf. vv. 17–18, 40–41). And here in the land, God once again "heard" (שמע) and "was furious" (עבר, v. 59; cf. v. 21) although now Israel's rebellion is associated with high places (במות) and idol (פסיל) worship (v. 58). In v. 63, God's response is described as a fire that "consumes" (אכל) Israel's young men (בחור).[16] Later in v. 65, YHWH's sudden engagement with Israel's circumstances is compared to one awaking (יקץ) from sleep,[17] a warrior roused (רון) from the stupor of wine (יין). While YHWH is often pictured as "awaking" in order to come to Israel's aid,[18] the added notion that YHWH could be in something like

16. The death of the "young men" (בחור) is also recorded as a consequence of Israel's rebellion in the wilderness food events (v. 31).

17. Here in Psalm 78, the psalmist utilizes the *qal* verb יקץ ("to awake"; cf. *hiphil* קיץ). The verb יקץ is also used of Noah's "awaking" (יקץ) from a wine-induced sleep (Gen 9:24) and Elijah's taunt against the prophets of Baal where he questions if their god needs to be "woken" (יקץ) from sleep (1 Kgs 18:27). See Mrozek for a helpful discussion of YHWH's initiative in Psalm 78 (contra 1 Kgs 18 and Ps 44). He notes: "This awakening is either requested (1 Kings 18, 27; Ps 44, 24) or takes place spontaneously (Ps 78, 65). . . . In Ps 78 God appears as a hero who awakens (78, 65) and gets up on his own." Mrozek, "Motif of the Sleeping Deity," 418–19.

18. For a consideration of the related theme of the psalmist's plea for YHWH to "arise" (עירה) and "contend" (ריב), see Jacobson, "Perhaps YHWH Is Sleeping," 129–45. Jacobson makes only a brief—and quite sarcastic—comment on YHWH's drinking habits in Psalm 78 (pp. 131–32). Batto briefly mentions Psalm 78. He notes: "The image of God awakening from sleep in Ps 78, 65 may also derive from the sleeping deity motif; the allusion to wine and the possibility of a drunken stupor image make this uncertain, however." Batto, "Sleeping God," 171n49.

a wine-induced slumber is a rhetorically rich depiction of this scene of reversal of fortune in Israel's experience of divine judgment.[19]

The psalm concludes with a repetition of a pastoral image that was used earlier in the psalm (vv. 70–72; cf. vv. 52–53). Here David is described as being taken from the sheepfolds (מכלאת צאן), from tending the nursing ewes (עלות),[20] to now "shepherd" (לרעות) a different sort of flock, namely Israel/Jacob (v. 71).[21] The psalm closes with a repetition of this vocational charge, as David is called to "shepherd" (רעה) and "lead" (נחה; cf. v. 53 used of YHWH) them.

Literary Analysis of Psalm 78's Depiction of Life in the Land (vv. 54–72)

In the land-based section of the psalm (vv. 54–72), the psalmist relies on intra-textual links to draw together the events of the wilderness and the land in order to consider their similarities, as well as provide literary scaffolding for the composition as a whole. This comparison of Israel's experience in the wilderness and the land occurs through referencing Israel's disobedience in the land (v. 56) with the verbs "test" (נסה) and "rebel" (מרה), a pair of terms used repeatedly in the wilderness frame to describe Israel's errant behavior (vv. 17–18, 40–41). In addition, the expression God "heard" (שמע) and "was furious" (עבר) is used twice in the psalm. In the first instance, it occurs as a response to Israel's verbal expression of doubt regarding God's ability to provide food in the wilderness (v. 21). In the second instance, it follows Israel's active expression of doubt regarding God's ability to provide in the land—here seen in their embrace of high places (במות) and idol (פסיל) worship (v. 58). The fact that no verbal exclamation occurs in this land context—and the psalmist still repeats the verb "to hear" (שמע)—forges a link between Israel's rebellions in the wilderness and in the land. Literary scaffolding also occurs through the inclusion of shepherding images at the close of the wilderness frame

19. This picture of military reversal in the land echoes the spiritual reversal witnessed by Israel in the wilderness—in vv. 65–66 YHWH delivers Israel from oppression of enemies, and in v. 39 Israel is delivered from the consequences of their sin (כפר עון).

20. The book of Samuel also depicts David as a shepherd king who feeds his flock (e.g., 2 Sam 6:19; cf. 2 Sam 9:1–13).

21. The emphasis on David's pedigree as a shepherd would not have been surprising in the ancient world. For an account of the use of "Shepherd" as a title for royalty and deity within Mesopotamia and Egypt, see Vancil, "Sheep, Shepherd," 1188–89.

(vv. 52–53a) and the close of the land-based section of the psalm (vv. 70–72). At the conclusion of the psalm, David's role as shepherd, as one who "leads" (נחה) his people in the land (v. 72), is verbally linked with YHWH's role as shepherd who "leads" (נחה) his people in safety in the wilderness (v. 53a; cf. v. 14).

The Rhetorical Use of Food in Psalm 78:54–72

Three dimensions of food undergird the examples of food language found in the land-based section of Psalm 78. These dimensions include the physical dimension of food consumption bringing life, the sensory dimension of food consumption's associations with perception, and the locational dimension of food production as a regionally specific enterprise.

Physical Dimension of Food

In the land-based section of the psalm (vv. 54–72), the physical dimension of food is linked with divine judgment in v. 64. In a scene of enemy oppression, fire "devours" (אכל) Israel's young men (v. 63) and priests fall by the sword (v. 64). While "eating" (אכל) is stock imagery in the Psalter for the destructive force of fire (cf. Pss 18:9; 21:10; 50:3), it becomes noteworthy in a psalm filled with other occurrences of food language.[22]

Sensory Dimension of Food

The sensory dimension of food is emphasized in the image of YHWH awaking from wine (יין) to engage in battle on Israel's behalf (v. 65). This image is rooted in alcohol's ability to dull the senses and impair one's ability to respond to the circumstances at hand. Here in v. 65, the psalmist uses food language to offer a shocking picture of Israel's perceived divine inattention.

22. The lexeme אכל occurs 7x in Psalm 78. The only other lexemes used with this kind of frequency are אלהים (8x) and ישראל (7x). All other lexemes occur five times or less. See Pavan's appendix E for a list of lexemes and their occurrences in Psalm 78 compared to Book 3 of the Psalter. Pavan, *He Remembered That They Were But Flesh*, 409–14.

Locational Dimension of Food

The locational dimension of food undergirds the closing picture of David (vv. 70–72). Here the psalmist celebrates that David's prior job was in husbandry (vv. 70–71), an essential occupation related to food production in Canaan. David's direct engagement with his flock—i.e., "from the sheepfolds" (מכלאת צאן)—and his attentiveness to their needs—i.e., from tending "the nursing ones" (מאחר עלות)—are presented as essential qualifications for his new leadership role. By learning to care for the basic needs of his animal flock, David is now called "to shepherd" (לרעות) Israel/Jacob. This agrarian image of leadership provides a fitting close to a psalm saturated in food language.

Psalm 78 is remarkable in its sustained use of food language across the composition. However, there are further rhetorical implications to Psalm 78's food language that can be recognized when it is viewed in the midst of and in light of other psalms.

PSALM 78 AND THE HISTORICAL PSALMS (PSS 105, 106, 135, 136)

As noted in chapter 2, Psalm 78 has proved elusive to scholars who have sought to categorize this psalm by genre. Kraus notes: "Psalm 78 is in many respects a unique piece in the OT."[23] However, most scholars—including Kraus—acknowledge that on the basis of content, Psalm 78 can be described broadly as a "historical psalm."[24] The body of Psalm 78 (vv. 13–72)[25] is a lengthy recital of events drawn from Israel's historical traditions. One finds a similar focus on historical traditions in Psalms 105, 106, 135, and 136.[26] Although one could expand this list to include

23. Kraus, *Psalms 60–150*, 122.

24. Kraus, *Psalms 60–150*, 122. Adele Berlin prefers the language of psalms "invoking traditions about Israel's past"—a nuanced nod to the problems of historicity and the imposition of modern notions of what constitutes history. Berlin, "Interpreting Torah Traditions in Psalm 105," 21.

25. As seen in chapter 2, there is debate regarding where Psalm 78's historical recital begins. For instance, Campbell argues that the recital begins in v. 9, while Clifford argues for v. 12. Because v. 12 seems to be a continuation of the argument about faulty memory of the ancestors, I begin the actual recital at v. 13.

26. Although there are a variety of ways that one can establish the boundaries for determining the category of "historical psalms," I follow one of the general trends in Psalms studies. See Gärtner, "Historical Psalms," 373; Gillingham, "Psalm 105 and 106," 452; Berlin, "Interpreting Torah Traditions in Psalm 105," 20.

any number of psalms that recount events from Israel's history,[27] these five psalms explicitly focus on a series of events that form a continuous account of history.[28] This common use of historical recital provides a cohesive unity to these five psalms.[29]

Rhetoric and Food Language in the Historical Psalms

When comparing these five recitals, one finds great diversity in style and intent, even though the psalms are often describing the same events within Israel's history. As Mays notes: "Though the psalms seem based on the narrative as it is recorded in these books [Genesis-Samuel], each version is selective and distinctive in the way it tells the story."[30] He continues: "The different versions illustrate the creative ingenuity employed in shaping the material of Israel's traditions about its past."[31] In his study of Psalms 78, 105, 106, 136,[32] Walter Brueggemann emphasizes the rhetorical richness of these recitals. By moving the focus from "history" to "historical recital," he argues that this designation "immediately shifts our attention to speech, rhetoric, communication, and eventually literature."[33] The rhetorical richness of these psalms is the center point of the following investigation.

Psalms 105, 106, 135, and 136 all employ food language to varying degrees and for differing purposes. For each, I will provide a short

27. See the recent works by Ramond, whose list expands to include Pss 78, 81, 95, 105, 106, 114, 135, 136, and Klein, whose list includes Pss 78, 105, 106, 114, 135, 136. Ramond, *Leçons et les enigmes du passé*, 428; Klein, *Geschichte und Gebet*, 401.

28. See Jasper, who notes: "But only in Pss. lxxviii, cv, cvi, cxxxv, and cxxxvi is there an attempt to give a chronological and consecutive record of the events." Jasper, "Early Israelite Traditions and the Psalter," 51.

29. Fensham offers a helpful designation for the category of historical psalms: "Our choice of material is determined by parts of Scripture which give a fairly extensive description of history and which present the history as a unity. It is a presentation of history in a fixed chronological order or scheme. Only when this is the characteristic, can we talk of Psalms of history." Fensham, "Neh. 9 and Pss. 105, 106, 135 and 136," 36. Fensham omits Psalm 78 from his discussion on the assumption that it is preexilic.

30. Mays, *Psalms*, 254. Mays considers Pss 78, 105, 106, and 136 in this category.

31. Mays, *Psalms*, 254.

32. Brueggemann excludes Ps 135 from his study, although he notes: "Of the others, Psalm 135 might well be included. My argument, however, is not affected by the inclusion or exclusion of other examples. I have proceeded to make my argument in reference to the clearest examples." Brueggemann, *Abiding Astonishment*, 67n11.

33. Brueggemann, *Abiding Astonishment*, 13.

introduction to the psalm, followed by a discussion of its rhetorical use of food language. I will conclude this section by reflecting on Psalm 78's rhetorical use of food language as seen in the midst of and in light of this group of historical psalms.

Psalm 105

Psalm 105's historical recital spans Israel's history from God's covenant with Abraham to Israel's entry into the land of Canaan. In this hymn of praise,[34] the deeds of YHWH take center stage, with little focus on Israel's response. The psalm is bookended with celebrations of YHWH's mindfulness (זכר, vv. 8, 42) to his covenant promise of land (vv. 8–11; 42–44).

Food language appears in three contexts in Psalm 105—Israel's experience in Canaan (v. 16), their exodus from Egypt (vv. 33, 35), and their journey through the wilderness (vv. 40–41). In v. 16, the psalmist notes that Israel's departure from Canaan is linked to a "famine" (רעב) in the land (v. 16a), a time when God "broke every staff of bread" (כל־מטה־לחם שבר).[35] Within Psalm 105's account of the Egyptian plagues, the destruction of agricultural food supplies receives the most attention.[36] Verse 33 describes how hail destroyed Egypt's vines (גפן), fig trees (תאנה), and the trees of the region (עץ גבול). Verse 35 notes that the locusts "ate up" (אכל) all the plants (עשב) of the land and the fruit (פרי) of their ground. Lastly, Psalm 105 describes God's provision of food and water in the wilderness (vv. 40–41). Here in v. 40, Israel asks and YHWH brings food—"quail" (שלו), "bread of heaven" (לחם שמים), and abundant water (מים) from a "rock" (צור).

Within Psalm 105, food language is used across the psalm to depict a series of reversals. It has been well noted that the covenant promise of

34. Mays observes: "In form and function, Psalm 105 is a hymn of praise. . . . Verses 1–6 are the extended summons to praise, and verses 12–45 compose the content of praise." Mays, *Psalms*, 338.

35. The expression—"to break" (שבר) the "staff of bread" (מטה לחם)—is rare, occurring only four other times in the MT (Lev 26:26; Ezek 4:16; 5:16; 14:13). This image of bread as the physical support of daily life draws from the daily caloric value of grains in the ancient Israelite diet. See chapter 3 for a discussion of the "locational" dimension of food and the role of grains within the ancient Israelite diet.

36. Unlike the single-verse descriptions of the other plagues, the psalmist extends the depictions of the plagues of hail (vv. 32–33) and locusts (vv. 34–35) for two verses—the first verse introduces the agent of destruction and the second the resulting agricultural devastation.

land runs through Psalm 105.[37] What has not been given due notice is the rhetorical uses of food language—particularly reversals—that appear at key junctures in the psalmist's discussion of land.[38] The first reversal of expectation occurs with the direct association of YHWH with the famine in Canaan (v. 16) following quickly after the celebration of the divine promise of this land (v. 11).[39] The destruction of the Egyptian crops (vv. 34–35)—particularly the "fruit of their ground" (פרי אדמתם)—by locusts "without number" (אין מספר) reverses the fertility language used earlier in the psalm for God's people.[40] YHWH's provision of food for Israel (vv. 40–41) follows the destruction of Egypt's own food supplies (vv. 32–35). This reversal emphasizes YHWH's power over the created order. YHWH—who can bring (בוא) locusts to eat up the grass of Egypt's land (ארץ) and the fruit of their ground (אדמה)—can also feed his people by bringing (בוא) quail and bread from heaven (שמים).[41] Besides bringing bread from above, YHWH can also make waters "gush" (זוב) and rivers "flow" (הלך) below in a dry desert land (ציות). Finally, Israel's experience

37. References to land (ארץ) appear with noted frequency (vv. 7, 11, 16, 23, 27, 30, 32, 35, 36, 44, with an additional occurrence as the referent of the pronoun in v. 12). In addition to the word ארץ the psalmist uses the terms "territory/borders" (גבול) in vv. 31 and 33 and "ground" (אדמה) in v. 35. The theme of "land"—so central to God's promise to Abraham—continues into the plague account, where there is a repeated emphasis on the location of the events—within the land (ארץ, vv. 32, 35, 36) and territory (גבול, vv. 31, 33) of Egypt. Both Clifford and Ceresko see the concept of land as key to the argument of the psalm as a whole. Clifford, "Style and Purpose in Psalm 105," 420–27; and Ceresko, "Poetic Analysis of Ps 105," 20–46.

38. Ceresko's study of irony in Psalm 105 offers a helpful foray into the use of irony and lexical and dramatic reversals present in the psalm, particularly the section on Joseph in Egypt (vv. 16–24) and the psalmist's use of the term ארץ. His recognition of the psalmist's interest in "land" opens up a larger arena of consideration, for the psalmist's concern extends beyond land as space or place to what grows out of it—i.e., food. Besides Ceresko's essay, I am not aware of any other studies on irony or reversals in Psalm 105.

39. The Genesis account of these events does not attribute divine cause for the famine that propelled Israel into Egypt (cf. Gen 42:5; 43:1, 5; 45:6; 47:13).

40. The psalmist notes that Israel was but "few in number" (מתי מספר) while in the land of Canaan (v. 12), but YHWH made his people "very fruitful" (פרה . . . מאד) once they settled in Egypt (v. 24). While the language of fertility used for Israel is itself a reversal of fortune, the use of the same language for agricultural decimation offers an ironic reversal as well. Ceresko uses the language of "distant parallels" to describe the psalmist's technique of delayed repetitions. Ceresko, "Poetic Analysis of Psalm 105," 27.

41. Vesco observes YHWH's sovereign control of food supplies in a similar kind of reversal between Psalm 104 and Psalm 105: "Le pain peut sortir de la terre (Ps 104,14, 15) ou descendre des cieux (Ps 105,40)." Vesco, *Psautier de David traduit et commenté II*, 970.

of bread—their lack of bread (v. 16, the broken "staff of bread") in Canaan and their unexpected supply of bread (v. 40, "bread of heaven") on their wilderness journey provides a bread-themed inclusio for their journey into and out of Egypt. In Psalm 105, YHWH's sovereign control of food supplies in Canaan (v. 16), in the land of Egypt (vv. 24–35) as well as in the wilderness (vv. 40–41) drives home one of the key themes of the composition: YHWH's sovereign power over all the earth (v. 7).

Psalm 106

Psalm 106's historical recital covers the period from Israel's exodus from Egypt to their settlement in the land of Canaan and concludes with their reality of exile (v. 47; cf. v. 27).[42] The psalm resembles a hymn, but also bears traits of a complaint.[43] The central focus of the psalm's recital is a series of events that highlight Israel's disobedience and lack of faith in YHWH. The theme of divine remembrance closes the psalm (v. 44–45). Here YHWH regards Israel's distress (v. 44), remembers (זכר) his covenant, and relents because of his covenant love (חסד) for Israel (v. 45).

Food language appears in five of the seven wilderness episodes described in the psalm (vv. 14–15, 17, 20, 28, 32).[44] The first reference (vv. 14–15) describes what appears to be the divine provision of quail in the wilderness (cf. Num 11:4–23, 31–34); however, no food items are described. Instead the psalmist notes in v. 14 that Israel "had an intense craving" (ויתאוו תאוה).[45] In response to this craving (v. 15), YHWH "gave them their request" (ויתן להם שאלתם) but sent on them a "wasting disease"

42. As Kraus notes: "The historical situation into which the psalm is to be placed emerges very clearly in vv. 27 and 47. God's people are scattered to all the lands, have suffered the Babylonian exile, and pray for 'being gathered from among the nations.'" Kraus, *Psalms 60–150*, 317.

43. Allen observes: "The limitations of the form-critical method are evident from the fact that Ps 106 has been regarded as a hymn (Kraus, *Psalmen*, 900) and as a communal complaint (C. Westermann, *Praise*, 57, 141; cf. H. Gunkel, *Die Psalmen*, 464–65). An assessment depends on the relative weight given to elements of praise and complaint." Allen, *Psalms 101–150*, 49.

44. Kraus lists the seven episodes as the exodus tradition (vv. 7–12), the craving at the feeding with quail (vv. 13–15), Dathan and Abiram (vv. 16–18), the golden calf (vv. 19–23), the complaining in the desert (vv. 24–27), Baal-Peor (vv. 28–31), and the waters of Meribah (vv. 34–35). Kraus, *Psalms 60–150*, 316.

45. This same expression is used in Num 11:4 (cf. Ps 78:29–30) in the context of the provision of quail.

(lit. "a leanness into their soul," רזון בנפשם).[46] In the second reference (v. 17), divine judgment is described as the earth "opening" (פתח) and "swallowing" (בלע) Dathan.[47] In the third reference (v. 20) which details the golden calf incident (cf. Exod 32), the psalmist muses: "they exchanged their glorious One for an image of an ox which eats grass" (וימירו את כבודם בתבנית שור אכל עשב).[48] The fourth reference (v. 28) describes Israel's rebellion at Baal-Peor (cf. Num 25) where Israel "ate sacrifices to the dead" (ויאכלו זבחי מתים). The last food reference (v. 32) mentions "the waters of Meribah" (מי מריבה), although YHWH's provision for Israel's thirst is never described, only Israel's rebellion and Moses' rash words (cf. Num 20:2–13).

Within Psalm 106, the psalmist relies on reversals throughout these individual episodes of human rebellion and divine judgment. In both references to the wilderness food events (Israel's "craving" in vv. 14–15 and the "waters of Meribah" in v. 32), the psalmist avoids depicting food provisions or their actual consumption. In vv. 14–15, the psalmist accentuates the fact that the satisfaction of Israel's desires ends instead in bodily distress (lit., "a leanness in their soul"). Commenting on this reversal of expectations, Curtis notes: "The people's inappropriate request (v. 14), the result of their greed, rebounded against them. God *did* give them what they asked, but the result was not what they wanted."[49] And at the waters of Meribah, no one actually drinks. The only times anyone actually eats in the psalm are in the contexts of worship gone wrong. In the wilderness, Israel replaced "their glorious One" (כבודם) for an image of a grass-eating (אכל עשב) beast (v. 20). Here the infinite Creator is replaced with a finite creature—an ox with a prodigious appetite.[50] And in Baal-Peor (v. 28),

46. The phrase רזון בנפשם is challenging to translate. The word "leanness" (רזון) occurs only 3x in the MT (Ps 106:15; Isa 10:16; Mic 6:10). The closest parallel to Ps 106 occurs in Isa 10:16 where the prophet describes how YHWH will send "leanness on the fattest/stoutest" (במשמניו רזון) of the warriors.

47. In the account in Num 16:32, the earth is further anthropomorphized and is given a mouth: "The earth opened its mouth and swallowed them" (ותפתח הארץ את פיה ותבלע אתם).

48. Here we find food language used for the natural process of food consumption in the animal world.

49. Curtis, *Psalms*, 211.

50. Vesco puts the accent on the transitory nature of the ox's food supplies: "Or cette gloire a été échangée contre un boeuf qui a besoin d'herbe pour se nourrir. Le participe présent 'mangeur d'herbe' est méprisant. Il faut au boeuf, pour se nourrir, de l'herbe qui rapidement se dessèche, le symbole meme du transitoire voué rapidement à la destruction et à la mort (Is 37, 27; Ps 92, 8; 102, 5, 12)." Vesco, *Psautier de David traduit et commenté II*, 1006.

Israel joins in at the table for the dead; but here the tables are turned and this meal ends in death (v. 29).[51] In Psalm 106, the vocabulary of eating (אכל, בלע) is used only in the contexts of rebellion and judgment (vv. 17, 20, 28); and in the wilderness food accounts (vv. 14–15, 32), actual food is nowhere to be seen. Here in Psalm 106, ironic reversal is a key component of the psalmist's scathing critique of Israel's life and worship.

Psalm 135

After a call to praise (vv. 1–3), Psalm 135 enters into a litany of reasons for Israel's praise to YHWH (vv. 4–21). Only five of the twenty-one verses constitute the historical recital (vv. 8–12) which highlights YHWH's defeat of Israel's enemies (both in Egypt and on their entry into Canaan) and a celebration of the gift of land to Israel.[52]

There is only one food reference in Psalm 135. In the depiction of the final Egyptian plague (v. 8), the psalmist notes: "He struck the firstborn of Egypt—man (אדם) and beast (בהמה)." This explicit mention of the death of "beasts" (בהמה) is a unique inclusion within the historical psalms to describe the final Egyptian plague. Similar to the Exodus account, the psalmist here uses the "man" (אדם)/"beast" (בהמה) merism to describe the totality of destruction (cf. Exod 11:5; 12:29).

Psalm 136

Psalm 136 is a companion hymn of praise linked to Psalm 135. Following a short introduction (vv. 1–4), Psalm 136 offers an extended historical recital (vv. 5–22) that includes the great "wonders" (פלא) of YHWH in creation (vv. 5–9), Israel's deliverance from Egypt through the plagues and protection at Red Sea (vv. 10–15), guidance through the wilderness (v. 16), and YHWH's defeat of kings and the giving of their lands to Israel (vv. 17–22). In the final verses (vv. 23–25), the psalm shifts from third person to first person as the psalmist now includes the audience in the recital of YHWH's deeds for his people.[53] In these verses, the psalmist

51. As Kraus notes: "Israel has therefore entered the communion of the מתים. In the process, death as a penalty has come upon the evildoers (v. 29; cf. Num. 25:5; 1 Cor. 10:8)." Kraus, *Psalms 60–150*, 320–21.

52. The briefness of the recital leads some scholars to omit this psalm from the list of historical psalms.

53. Mays notes: "These items appear to be the voice of the postexilic community

offers praise to YHWH who remembered (זכר, v. 23) their low estate and delivered (פרק, v. 24) them from their enemies and who now "gives food" (נתן לחם, v. 25). The psalm ends (v. 26) with an exclamation of praise to the "God of heaven" (אל השמים).

Psalm 136's sole mention of food appears as the final evidence for Israel's praise (v. 25): "he gives food to all flesh" (נתן לחם לכל בשר). The subject of the reference "all flesh" (כל־בשר) is ambiguous—referring to humanity or to all God's creatures.[54] Closing this litany of praise with a reference to YHWH's present provision of food is a striking finale. Psalm 136 opens with a reference to YHWH's creation of the world (vv. 5–9; heavens, earth, sun, moon, stars) and closes with a statement of praise to this same Creator who sustains his creation by giving them food (v. 25).[55] Regarding this inclusio, Zenger notes: "With this the psalm returns to the vision already sketched in vv. 4–9, alluding to Genesis 1, of the good creator God (for the 'gift' of nourishment to all the living things, cf. Gen 1:29–30)."[56] The final line of the psalm reinforces this theme as the God of heaven is praised for maintaining his covenant love forever.

Psalm 78 in the Midst of the Historical Psalms

Within this collection of historical psalms, food makes history. Whether this is telling food stories or telling stories using food language, the psalmists rely on food in their recitals of Israel's past and present. As one considers the collection as a whole, one finds some common trends in the use of food language.[57]

Food plays a powerful thematic role in Israel's recitals of their past. In each of these psalms, we find that the psalmist uses food language to accentuate the major themes within the larger recital, whether this is YHWH's sovereignty (Ps 105) or Israel's rebellion and divine judgment (Ps 106), the destruction of enemies in the past (Ps 135) or YHWH's care as Creator and Sustainer in the present (Ps 136). As one considers Psalm 78, one finds that the central theme of confident trust (כסל, v. 7) is developed

---

confessing that they are the beneficiaries of the LORD's hesed in their time." Mays, *Psalms*, 420.

54. Curtis, *Psalms*, 250.

55. A point also recognized by Gärtner, "Historical Psalms," 393.

56. Hossfeld and Zenger, *Psalms* 3, 509.

57. In the discussion that follows, I will consider the other historical psalms before turning to Psalm 78.

in a variety of recollections told in the language of food. This is seen in God's involvement in the past through his provision of food (vv. 15–16, 23–28), his forgiveness rooted in his compassionate understanding of humanity's finitude (vv. 38–39), his shocking intervention on Israel's behalf bringing about deliverance from enemies (v. 65–66), and his guidance through various means and in a variety of settings (vv. 52–53, 70–72; cf. v. 14). If the purpose of Psalm 78 is to build confident trust (v. 7a) by remembering the deeds of YHWH (v. 7b) so that Israel can keep YHWH's commands (v. 7c), then one finds that food language is being consistently used to bring about this life-empowering confident trust.

The language of divine remembrance appears in four of the five historical psalms (Pss 78, 105, 106, 136). In Psalm 105, YHWH's remembrance of the covenant promise of land opens and closes the recital (זכר, vv. 8, 42). In Psalm 106, divine remembrance of the covenant causes YHWH to act in covenant love (חסד) toward Israel (v. 45). Psalm 136 celebrates YHWH as a God who remembered (זכר, v. 23) Israel in its distress, and who also delivered them from their enemies (v. 24). Psalm 78 recounts God's compassionate response toward Israel in the midst of their rebellion in the wilderness; here YHWH's response is rooted in the remembrance of humanity's frailty and finitude (v. 39). In each of these psalms, divine remembrance calls forth action on the part of YHWH—provision of land (Ps 105), a posture of covenant love (Ps 106), deliverance (Ps 136), and forgiveness (Ps 78). I would propose that reciting instances of YHWH's remembrance of and engagement with Israel's plight in the past is a means to instill hope in an uncertain present.

These historical recitals also draw upon the physical and locational dimensions of food for rhetorical effect. Psalms 78, 105, 106, and 136 draw on the physical dimension of food to accentuate YHWH's sovereign role in the preservation of life. Psalms 78 and 105 draw on the locational dimension of food by celebrating the provision of food in unexpected places—water in a dry land, food in a wilderness setting. In addition, unexpected scarcity also occurs in the contexts of assumed abundance. Both Psalms 78 and 105 depict the destruction of food supplies along the fertile Egyptian Nile. Psalm 105 is unique in describing the severity of a prolonged famine in Canaan that brings about forced migration. These reversals of food fortunes highlight God's sovereignty through both the provision and withholding of food supplies. In a postexilic context, the reversal of fortune theme is a powerful rhetorical trope for bringing hope when Israel's unknown future is filled with questions of God's presence in their current reality.[58]

Recent scholarship has argued that the Psalter's historical recitals reflect a community coming to terms with their postexilic realities in the land.[59] In this context, food—both its presence and absence—provides a powerful avenue to construe the past as paradigmatic for the present. While Psalms 78, 105, 106 tells stories of God's food provision in the past,[60] Ps 136:25 celebrates God's provision of food *at all times*. Telling stories of God's abundant provision in the past can give hope for a future reality when food supplies in the present may be scarce because of socio-economic realities.[61]

The physical dimension of food is also employed for rhetorical effect to describe the reality of divine judgment. Psalm 106:15 describes an ironic twist where the satisfaction of Israel's cravings ends instead in "leanness" (רזון). Psalm 78:31 also emphasizes the consequences of Israel's greedy eating with the death of the "fattest" (משמן) in their midst. Both psalms innovate with food language to depict the ironic conclusion of a meal that should have brought life but instead brings death.

These food events also become the context for revealing intentions and motivations. In the historical psalms, Israel's request for food (שׁאל, "to ask") is associated with a variety of motivations and responses. In Ps 105:40, the verb שׁאל "to ask" appears as a simple request by Israel and

58. Although not specifically discussed above, each of the psalms refers to Israel entering the land of Canaan (78:54–55; 105:44; 106:34–35; 135:11–12; 136:21–22). While food provisions are not mentioned in any of these accounts, the book of Joshua makes clear that the entry into the land was in fact a food event. Joshua 5:11 notes: "The manna ceased on the day they ate the produce of the land, and the Israelites no longer had manna; they ate the crops of the land of Canaan that year." This simple editorial note highlights the food potential of the land of Canaan; however, it is noteworthy that within the historical psalms, the provision of food in the land of Canaan is never explicitly developed. Psalm 105:44b may be referring to agricultural land: "they inherited the toil of the peoples" (עמל לאמים יירשו). This verse closes out the recital and offers no other information about its referent. Psalm 106's lengthy description of life in the land (vv. 34–46) lacks any food language or references to food events. Neither Psalm 135 nor Psalm 136 develops Israel's experience in the land.

59. See the works of Judith Gärtner, Anja Klein, Susan Gillingham, and Sophie Ramond cited throughout this chapter.

60. The recipients of these past provisions of food are not limited to humans alone. In the depiction of the Egyptian plagues in Ps 78:45, the swarms of flies (ערב) are sent to "eat" (אכל); in Ps 105:34–35, it is the locusts/caterpillars (ארבה/ילק) that are sent to "eat" (אכל) through Egypt's agricultural supplies.

61. This could include taxation, mortgaging of fields and crops, as well as the commandeering of food (e.g., Neh 5:3–5).

is followed by an immediate provision of food by YHWH. In Ps 106:14–15, the noun שְׁאלה "request" is used in connection with Israel's testing (נסה) of YHWH over their rebellious cravings (אוה). In Ps 78:18, Israel's asking for food appears in the context of "testing" (נסה) of YHWH. Psalm 136—similar to Psalm 105—pictures YHWH's gracious provision of food; however, here YHWH gives food to all flesh, even before they ask (Ps 136:25).

Psalm 78 in Light of the Historical Psalms

As seen in its use of food events and food language, Psalm 78 fits firmly in the tradition of the larger collection of historical psalms. However, Psalm 78 shows three key distinctives.

First, Psalm 78 emphasizes the extravagance of both divine provision of food and its destruction. Compared with the other historical psalms, Psalm 78 places proportionally greater emphasis on the wilderness food accounts and the destruction of food supplies in Egypt. Within Psalm 78's historical recital, the wilderness food events extend to seventeen verses (vv. 15–31). Psalm 105 describes YHWH's provision of food with only two verses. Psalm 106's recital includes Israel's "craving" (תאוה) in the wilderness (vv. 14–15) and their arrival at the waters at Meribah (vv. 32–33), but in each case actual food and drink are never described. In Psalms 135 and 136, the wilderness food events do not even appear in the recital. As discussed in chapter 4, Psalm 78 depicts these food events with extravagant detail and literary artistry. Thus for the psalmist, the wonder of YHWH's food provision in the wilderness is of central importance to its recital of history. Psalm 78 shows a heightened interest in the Egyptian plague accounts, utilizing ten verses (vv. 12, 43–51) to describe these events. Psalm 105 employs a similar commitment to recounting the plagues (vv. 27–36) but gives the wilderness food events a diminished emphasis (vv. 40–41). Both Psalms 135 and 136 refer to the Egyptian plagues (the "signs and portents" of Egypt) but only describe the final plague of the death of the firstborn (Pss 135:8–9; 136:10).[62] Thus we find in Psalm 78 a dual concern with presenting the wilderness food accounts and the Egyptian plagues as the hallmark events within the wilderness frame (vv. 13–53).

62. In Ps 106:7, the psalmist acknowledges that their fathers in Egypt did not consider YHWH's "wonders" (נפלאות), but never explicitly refer to the plagues.

A second distinction is Psalm 78's use of food language to describe both Israel's experience in the wilderness (vv. 13–53) and their experience in the land (vv. 54–72). This consistent use of food language in the land-based section of the psalm highlights the psalmist's rhetorical use of food language in an intentional and consistent manner.

A third distinctive is Psalm 78's utilization of each of the five dimensions of food language. As seen above, the historical psalms often draw from the physical and locational dimensions of food. Psalm 78, however, also employs the sensory, social, and patterned dimensions of food for rhetorical effect. In addition, while the other historical psalms may innovate with food language to depict food events (primarily within the wilderness context), Psalm 78 employs food language across the psalm to describe a variety of non-food events. Thus, one finds that Psalm 78 employs food language with a greater frequency than any of the other historical psalms.

When one considers Psalm 78 in the midst of the historical psalms, one finds a similar concern with telling stories of food events, often relying on the theme of reversal. However, Psalm 78 shows a remarkable interest in depicting not just the food events but describing in detail the actual foods consumed or destroyed. Not only does Psalm 78 depict literal foods but it also draws on the language of food to describe Israel's journey both through the wilderness and into the land.

PSALM 78 AND THE ASAPH COLLECTION (PSS 50, 73–83)

In addition to its association through content with the historical psalms, Psalm 78 also fits contextually within the Asaph psalms, a collection spanning Books II and III bearing the common title לאסף (Pss 50, 73–83).[63] Outside the Psalter, the name "Asaph" appears as one of the Levites appointed by David as a chief musician (1 Chr 15:17–19; 16:4–5). In addition, Ezra 3:10 notes that the Asaphite guild of musicians was active even after the exile participating in the dedication of the second temple.[64]

63. For extended discussions of the collection as a whole, see Goulder, *Psalms of Asaph and the Pentateuch*; Nasuti, *Tradition History and the Psalms of Asaph*; Illman, *Thema und Tradition in den Asaf-Psalmen*; Jones, "Psalms of Asaph." The more recent work has been done by Jacobson, *Memories of Asaph*.

64. There is not, however, enough evidence to connect the Asaph psalms directly to the individuals mentioned in 1 Chronicles and Ezra. DeClaissé-Walford et al., *Book*

This psalm collection is made up of a variety of genres, with many psalms that defy a general classification. Despite their difference in form, the Asaph psalms exhibit many common features that tie the collection together. These features included the use of unique divine names, a concern for history, and the judicial nature of the psalms.[65] Another common trait of the collection is the frequent references to "Joseph" (Pss 77:16; 78:67; 80:2; Jehoseph, 81:6) and the shepherd/sheep motif (Pss 74:1; 77:21; 78:52–53, 70–72; 79:13; 80:2). While there is a variety of opinions regarding the date of individual psalms within this collection, most scholars acknowledge the sense of imminent threat (e.g., Ps 83) or reality of trauma (e.g., Pss 74, 77, 79, 80) that pervades the collection. In light of this underlying tenor of distress, scholars are inclined to date the collection to the Babylonian exile in the sixth century.[66]

Rhetoric and Food Language in the Asaph Collection

Scholars have regularly noted the sheep/shepherd motif as a unifying characteristic of the Asaph Collection (Pss 74:1; 77:21; 78:52–53, 70–72; 79:13; 80:2).[67] However, this image drawn from the arena of food production—in this case, husbandry—is just one of the many uses of food language in the collection. In fact, the Asaph Collection is notable for its quantity of food references, as well as the remarkable range[68] and unique descriptions of the food provisions mentioned.

---

of Psalms, 582. The question of "authorship" based on psalm titles is a long-standing debate and not central to the argument in this study. I simply recognize the titles as one of many similarities that link this collection of psalms.

65. Delitzsch, *Biblical Commentary on the Psalms*, 123. The collection's concern for history is explored in detail in Karl N. Jacobson's monograph entitled *Memories of Asaph: Mnemohistory and the Psalms of Asaph*.

66. Firth notes that "there are enough datable references within the Asaph psalms to indicate that the exile was a significant trigger for the development of the canonical collection. Not all of the psalms necessarily originated with the exile, but the main collection (Pss 73–83) appears to be shaped by concerns generated by the fall of Jerusalem." Firth, "Asaph and Sons of Korah," 25. Goulder is a lone voice who holds to the view that the collection arose out of the northern shrines in Israel (Shechem, Bethel) in the 720s BCE in the midst of the rising threat of Assyrian invasion. Goulder, "Asaph's History of Israel," 81.

67. Delitzsch, *Biblical Commentary on the Psalms*, 124; Goulder, "Asaph's History of Israel," 74; Illman, *Thema und Tradition in den Asaf-Psalmen*, 39.

68. Of Goody's food categories, the Asaph Collection employs food language from four of his five categories (i.e., production, distribution, consumption, and disposal). An expansion of Goody's category of "disposal" is present at the end of the collection

Within the Asaph Collection, nine of the twelve psalms employ at least one use of food language (Pss 50, 74, 75, 77, 78, 79, 80, 81, 83).[69] In the study below, I will focus on seven of these psalms (Pss 50, 74, 75, 79, 80, 81, as well as 78) and offer only a brief mention to the other two (Pss 77 and 83), which include only one passing food reference each.[70] For each of the psalms, I will provide a basic introduction followed by a discussion of its rhetorical use of food language. I will conclude this section by reflecting on Psalm 78's rhetorical use of food language as seen in the midst of and in light of the Asaph Collection.

Psalm 50

Psalm 50 heads the list of Asaph psalms, although it appears alone in Book 2. Within the context of Book 2, Psalm 50 functions as a bridge between the psalms of the Sons of Korah (Pss 42–49) and a collection of Davidic psalms (Pss 51–72).[71] The psalm fits comfortably in its current location based on its lexical links to Psalm 49[72] and thematic links to

(Ps 83:10) where Israel's enemies are described as "dung on the ground" (דמן לאדמה)—the end-product of food consumption used to depict the end of human life. The word דמן appears only in association with corpses left on the ground (2 Kgs 9:37; Jer 8:2; 9:22; 16:4; 25:33)—the image of humans as refuse. The only missing category is the language of food preparation.

69. Psalm 73:10 refers to draining or drinking "the waters of fullness" (מי מלא). Tate assumes that it is a metaphor for abundance, although he notes that "the verse is too uncertain in meaning to claim very much for it." Tate, *Psalms 51–100*, 229n10b. Alter, following Kraus, emends the text to read "they lap up their words," but acknowledges that "the text has almost certainly suffered mangling in scribal transmission here." Alter, *Book of Psalms*, 254.

70. Psalm 77's recollection of God's wonders at the Red/Reed Sea (vv. 10–20) closes with the image of Israel as "a flock" (צאן). Here the focus is on God's protection and guidance provided through the agency of Moses and Aaron (v. 21): "you led your people like a flock" (נחית כצאן עמך). The only reference to food language in Psalm 83 is its reference to Israel's enemies as "dung" (דמן), an implied reference to food disposal (v. 10).

71. Following the lead of Gerald Wilson, McCann notes: "It is not clear why Psalm 50 is separated from the other Asaph psalms, unless perhaps the editors of the psalter wanted representatives of both Levitical collections (that is, Korah and Asaph) to introduce the Davidic collection (Psalm 51–72), since representatives of both Levitical collections follow the Davidic collection (see Psalms 73–83; 84–85; 87–88)." McCann, "Book of Psalms," 881. Spero offers an unconvincing argument that this psalm is the work of the original Asaph and is included in Book 2 because of Asaph's close association with David. Spero, "Was Psalm 50 Misplaced?," 26–31.

72. Delitzsch observes a lexical link between Ps 49:2 and Ps 50:7 with a call to the "people" (עם) to "hear" (שמע). Delitzsch, *Biblical Commentary on the Psalms*, 122.

Psalm 51.[73] Psalm 50 presents itself as a prophetic oracle,[74] possibly spoken within the context of a celebration of covenant renewal.[75] The psalm breaks into three main sections: theophany and summons (vv. 1–6), a judgment speech about right worship (vv. 7–15), and judgment speech on right living with a final exhortation (vv. 16–23).

Food language appears in each of the three sections of the psalm (v. 3, 9–15, 22).[76] The psalm opens with a theophany where God is pictured in the context of a storm and "consuming" (אכל) fire (v. 3).[77] Food language is the most developed in the judgment speech about right worship (vv. 7–15). This speech contains an extended discourse on sacrifice and Israel's misconceptions about divine eating habits (vv. 9–13).[78] The argument begins by establishing that God has no need for Israel's household livestock (פר [bull] and עתודים [goats], v. 9).[79] Verses 10–11 focus on God's sovereignty over the created world, particularly the creatures from the forests, hills, heights, and fields. As v. 12 emphasizes: "If I were hungry, I would not tell you, for the world is mine, and all that is in it."[80] The discourse ends with a divine sarcastic quip: "Do I eat the flesh of bulls[81] or

73. Firth finds a thematic link between Psalm 50 and Psalm 51 in that both downplay the importance of sacrifice compared with heartfelt praise. He notes: "Psalm 50 encourages the nation to see worship as being more than just the cult, just as Psalm 51 does for the individual." Firth, "Asaph and Sons of Korah," 25.

74. Regarding the prophetic context of the discourse, Kraus observes: "Worth noting is the fact that there are words of Yahweh in the first person present in all three parts [vv. 1–6, 7–15, 16–23]." Kraus, *Psalms 1–59*, 488.

75. Craigie and Tate, *Psalms 1–50*, 363.

76. As will be seen in the Asaph psalms in Book 3, the sustained use of food language is a notable feature in the Asaph Collection as a whole. Psalm 50, with its extended discourse on food, fits well within this collection. One does not find the same prevalence of food language in the Psalms of the Sons of Korah that precede Psalm 50 or in the Davidic psalms that follow it.

77. The image of a consuming fire (אש אכלת) also appears in the theophany on Sinai (i.e., Exod 24:17) and is used elsewhere as a description of God himself (e.g., Deut 4:24; cf. Heb 12:29).

78. Gudme offers a helpful consideration of Psalm 50's divine proclamation within the context of various other texts addressing sacrifice as food for the deity in the Hebrew Bible. Gudme, "'If I Were Hungry,'" 172–84.

79. The language used here for Israel's sacrificial animals stresses their domestic contexts—"from your house" (מביתך) and "from your folds" (ממכלאתיך).

80. As Kraus notes: "To the Creator and Lord of the world all animals belong. No one can give anything to God that he would not already have owned long ago." Kraus, *Psalms 1–59*, 494.

81. Here the psalmist departs from the earlier pairing of "bulls" (פר) and "goats" (עתודים) in v. 9 and changes to בשר אבירים (lit. flesh of the mighty) and the blood of

drink the blood of goats?" (v. 13).[82] The final food reference occurs in v. 22 with a divine challenge to those who forget God to be on guard, "lest I tear (טרף) you to pieces with no one to deliver."[83]

Throughout Psalm 50, the psalmist masterfully uses food language to realign Israel's perspectives on the sacrificial system and God himself. The central section of the psalm (vv. 7–15) emphasizes that God does not need Israel's sacrifices, but Israel does. Echoing the sarcasm found in the psalm, Craigie jests: "God possessed already all the animals of the world, birds and beasts, domestic and wild (vv. 10–11). He had no pressing need for an extra steer or a couple of billy-goats, as if he were running short of provisions (v. 13)."[84] Here in Psalm 50, the psalmist is also critiquing Israel's naively anthropomorphic picture of God as one who needs Israel's sacrifices for nourishment. As Kraus notes: "The guilt of Israel consists of this, that the people had forgotten (v. 22) the majestic reality of their God."[85] To a people who had reduced the divine to "a weak and hungry God, waiting desperately for the next sacrifice to fill his belly,"[86] God presents himself in a consuming fire (v. 3) and as a ravenous lion (v. 22).[87] When seen as a whole, the psalm itself offers a picture of ironic reversal in that YHWH—who does not eat Israel's household beasts (v. 13)—just might devour you (v. 3, 22).[88]

Psalm 74

As one turns to the Asaph Collection in Book 3 (Pss 73–83), Psalm 74 is the first psalm that employs food language. The psalm can be classified

"goats" (עתודים). The logical referent here in v. 9 is "bull" and is thus translated this way to avoid confusion. The term אבירים is also used in Ps 78:25, but here the referent is manna: "each one ate the bread of the mighty" (לחם אבירים אכל איש).

82. Unlike the larger Asaph Collection, Psalm 50 lacks any reference to sheep (צון)—an animal also considered as an acceptable sacrifice.

83. Regarding this scene, Craigie notes: "Not to repent would lead to the risk of being 'torn apart' (v 22b); the metaphorical language is that of God as the fierce lion who would tear apart evildoers (cf. Hos 5:14)." Craigie and Tate, *Psalms 1–50*, 367.

84. Craigie and Tate, *Psalms 1–50*, 365–66.

85. Kraus, *Psalm 1–59*, 494.

86. Craigie and Tate, *Psalms 1–50*, 366.

87. It is notable that in both examples God is personified, not anthropomorphized.

88. This metaphorical image of God as a lion with its prey reminds the audience that unlike their barnyard creatures, God cannot be domesticated.

broadly as a communal lament[89] and can be broken into three sections: lament (vv. 1–11), hymnic praise (vv. 12–17), and a series of petitions (vv. 18–23).[90] Zenger associates this lament with the national distress over the destruction of the Jerusalem Temple.[91] The psalm is framed as a plea for God[92] to remember (זכר, vv. 2, 18, 22 // "not forget," אל שכח, vv. 19, 23) his people and to respond to their distress.[93]

Food language appears three times (vv. 1, 14, 19),[94] occurring within each of the three sections of the psalm. The psalm opens with the identification of the congregation as God's "flock" (צאן) and a plea that God would show concern for the animals that dwell within his domain (מרעיתך): "Why have you rejected us forever? Why does your anger smolder against the sheep of your pastures?"[95] Within the hymnic section, the psalmist recalls in v. 14 how God subdued Leviathan and gave it as "food" (מאכל) for "the creatures of the desert" (לעם לציים).[96] The final

89. Tate notes: "The language of vv 1–11 and vv 18–23 is clearly that of a communal lament, a prayer voiced for the people because of the great distress they have experienced. . . . The fourth section (vv 12–17) is different, however; it is hymnic in nature, describing in a glorifying way the cosmic actions of God." Tate, *Psalms 51–100*, 246.

90. Hossfeld and Zenger, *Psalms 3*, 241–42.

91. There is disagreement among scholars as to which national crisis this psalm is referencing. While many scholars (Kraus, Tate, Mays) follow Zenger in associating the psalm with the Babylonian invasion of 586/7 BCE, Weber offers a contrary view and assumes an eighth-century date for the psalm. Weber, "Zer Datierung der Asaph-Psalmen 74 und 79," 521–32. For a sixth-century date, see Kraus, *Psalms 60–150*, 97; Tate, *Psalms 51–100*, 246–47; Mays, *Psalms*, 244.

92. Psalms 73–83 are part of the so-called Elohistic Psalter. However, the divine name YHWH appears within a variety of the psalms considered in this discussion (e.g., Pss 74, 75, 78, 79, 81). In light of the Asaph Collection's preference for the term אלהים, I will primarily use the term "God" but will also use "YHWH" for the sake of literary variety. For a helpful chart of divine epithets used in the Asaph Collection, see K. N. Jacobson, *Memories of Asaph*, 178.

93. As Tanner observes: "The psalm is an extended plea for God to act . . . shaped as an argument that will motivate God to reappear and set this horrible event right." DeClaissé-Walford et al., *Book of Psalms*, 594.

94. Within the central hymnic section (vv. 12–17), the psalmist celebrates YHWH's sovereign power in the cosmic and created order. Besides the reference to the ordering of day/night, the psalmist mentions the seasonal ordering of creation—summer and winter (קיץ וחרף). While agricultural process relies on these seasonal changes, Psalm 74 lacks an explicit attempt to make this link. Cf. Gen 8:22, which includes both summer and winter (קיץ וחרף) and seed/harvest (זרע וקציר) in its list of binary pairs.

95. The expression "sheep of your pasture" (צאן מרעיתך) occurs again at the close of Psalm 79, another psalm associated with the national distress of the Babylonian destruction of the temple.

96. Determining the identity of the recipients of this meal is problematic. Various proposals have been offered, including Ethiopians, ships, sharks, and animals of the

food reference (v. 19) occurs within a series of petitions as the psalmist pleads with God not to deliver the soul of "your turtledove" (תורך) to the wild animals (לחית).

The psalmist draws on food language as a powerful rhetorical tool to persuade God to act in Israel's present helplessness like he did in the cosmic past. The psalm draws on two images from the animal world to paint a picture of Israel's defenseless plight against its aggressors. The psalm opens with a picture of unattended sheep (v. 1)[97] followed by a reference to the roaring (שאג)[98] of the enemy as they destroy the sanctuary (v. 4). The psalm draws to a close with a picture of Israel as a small bird in the context of wild beasts (v. 19). Both images picture Israel as a defenseless creature that could easily become prey (i.e., dinner) within the animal kingdom. Each image is an implicit plea for God to act and intervene in light of an imminent threat.

In contrast, the center hymn depicts a moment of divine cosmic intervention in the world. In v. 14, Leviathan—the embodiment of chaos and destruction—is defeated by God and becomes food for the creatures of the wilderness.[99] When considered in the context of the chaos depicted previously in the psalm, Tanner observes: "The hymn section praises God's mastery over chaos in the ancient past and serves as a further motivation to come and conquer chaos once again."[100] This instance of cosmic food reversal, as chaos is served for dinner, is a powerful image offering hope to a people who feel abandoned and helpless in their current plight.[101]

---

desert. See Tanner for a discussion of the options proposed. DeClaissé-Walford et al., *Book of Psalms*, 596n13. What remains clear is the fact that Leviathan becomes a food source.

97. Regarding this image, Tanner notes: "It reminds God that the king-shepherd's purpose is to care for the *sheep*. The people are merely poor sheep in need of protection and guidance of the great King, which makes the abandonment all the more offensive." DeClaissé-Walford et al., *Book of Psalms*, 597–98.

98. The verb שאג is associated with the roaring of lions (cf. Pss 22:14; 104:21), here used figuratively to refer to Israel's enemies.

99. In the following verse (v. 15), there is language of water in the wilderness, but no mention of anyone benefiting from this divine act. This psalm seems to converge images of creation, flood, and wilderness events into one recital. Kraus, *Psalms 60–150*, 99.

100. DeClaissé-Walford et al., *Book of Psalms*, 599.

101. Zenger notes the tension created by these two competing pictures. In Psalm 74, the psalmist holds fast to "a confession of the saving God even though everything speaks against the 'truth' of that confession." Hossfeld and Zenger, *Psalms 2*, 242.

Psalm 75

Psalm 75 is a difficult psalm to classify.[102] It begins like a communal hymn (v. 2) but quickly moves into divine speech (vv. 3–4), prophetic proclamation of judgment (vv. 5–9), and a concluding response of praise (v. 10–11). The theme of God's judgment pervades the psalm[103] and offers a fitting conclusion to the petitions of Psalm 74.[104]

Psalm 75 employs a single food-based image but develops it at length. In v. 9, the psalmist proclaims: "For in the hand of YHWH there is a cup with foaming wine (יין),[105] well mixed; he will pour a draught from it, and all the wicked of the earth shall drain it down to the dregs." Zenger notes the striking detail of the depiction with "the unusually concrete description of the contents of the cup: foaming wine mixed with spices, dregs/yeast."[106] Two aspects of this image make the wine less than appetizing. First, the wine is pictured as "foaming" (חמר)—referring possibly to low-quality wine at the beginning of fermentation or wine that has gone "off" because of contamination by mold or bacteria.[107] Second, the wicked are forced to drink the wine down to its "dregs" (שמר).[108] Unlike

102. Hossfeld and Zenger, *Psalms 2*, 253. Tate observes: "This psalm does not fit easily into any of the traditional psalm types (hymn, lament, royal psalm, etc). It has been classified as a communal thanksgiving, but this interpretation ignores some aspects of the psalm. It contains a traditional hymnic introduction, an oracle and pronouncement of judgment, and a response of praise." Tate, *Psalms 51–100*, 257.

103. Regarding this justice theme, Tate concludes: "YHWH who created and sustains the world and all that is in it can be depended upon to establish justice upon it in good time." Tate, *Psalms 51–100*, 259. He finds that the psalmist draws on three key metaphors to establish this idea: the earth set on firm pillars (v. 3), YHWH cutting off the horns of the wicked (v. 4, 5, 10), and a cup of wine in the hand of YHWH (v. 9). Each of these metaphors presents an image of YHWH's sovereign power over Israel's enemies.

104. As Tanner observes: "Psalm 74 spoke of a catastrophic situation where enemies were invading and God was not to be found. Psalm 75 provides an answer and thus completes the crisis of the previous psalm." DeClaissé-Walford et al., *Book of Psalms*, 606.

105. The word used here for wine (יין) occurs only 4x in the Psalter. It is twice associated with divine judgment (60:5 [ET 3]; 75:9), once with divine provision (104:15), and once for divine inactivity (78:65).

106. Hossfeld and Zenger, *Psalms 2*, 257. Zenger notes that a cup of judgment is an image frequently employed by the exilic prophets. For close parallels, see Isa 51:17; Jer 25:15–28; Ezek 23:31–34; Hab 2:15–16; cf. Lam 4:21.

107. For an explanation of the chemistry involved in fermentation, see Walsh, *Fruit of the Vine*, 187–90.

108. The term "dregs" (שמר) appears only 5x in the MT (Isa 25:6 [2x]; Jer 48:11; Zeph 1:12; Ps 75:8).

modern wines that are processed to remove sediment, wine in the ancient world was typically fermented and stored with the sediment, which eventually settled at the bottom of the storage jug.[109] Here in Psalm 75, the wicked are forced to consume not only the wine but also its unappealing dregs.

This use of food language to describe divine judgment possesses a rhetorical power that Psalm 75's other images of God's sovereign rule of the world do not match.[110] Namely, it is able to "personalize and dramatize" judgment.[111] This image of a cup of wine in the hand of YHWH pulls from all five dimensions of food. Drinking wine—a component of the Mediterranean triad—would have been a familiar experience, but the thought of drinking down to the dregs would shock anyone's food sensibilities. Barker notes that "the dregs which remained in wine were typically so bitter that most individuals would have refused to drink them."[112] Judgment here becomes a visceral experience and a reversal of expectations, where instead of experiencing life in community, the cup of wine brings distress and death.[113] This image also calls to mind the patterned world of a festive banquet with host and guests. Here God is pictured making his guests drink down judgment from the cup in his hand, turning this scene of hospitality into a context of hostility. Commenting on this image of a cup of wrath in the hand of God, Paul Raabe notes: "The metaphor offers a 'from below' depiction of divine judgment. . . . The wrath of Yahweh is a rather intangible concept that cannot easily be described in a straightforward and literal manner."[114] But here in Psalm 75, the audience can not only picture this image of judgment but also figuratively taste and feel it.

109. This sediment would often be strained through a serving vessel before the wine was consumed.

110. The psalmist also describes God as holding the pillars of the earth (v. 3) and cutting off the "horns" of all the wicked (v. 10; cf. vv. 4–5).

111. Mays, *Psalms*, 249.

112. Barker, "Wine Production in Ancient Israel," 272.

113. As Tate observes: "At first it may seem to be a cup for a festival crowd ready to celebrate and enjoy blessings received. But it is not." Tate, *Psalm 51–100*, 260. In the Hebrew Bible, wine is often associated with community celebration, but here this cup brings distress for some of YHWH's guests—which in turn brings celebration for others.

114. Raabe, *Obadiah*, 236–37.

Psalm 79

Psalm 79 is a communal lament[115] that reflects on the devastation following the invasion and destruction of Jerusalem.[116] The psalm begins with a description of the distress (vv. 1–4), followed by pleas and petitions to God (vv. 5–12), and ends with a vow of praise (v. 13).[117] Here in Psalm 79, Israel's plea for divine compassion (רחמים) is rooted in a call for divine forgetfulness (אל־תזכר) of past sins (v. 8).[118]

The psalmist uses food language in each of the three sections of the psalm (vv. 2, 7, 13). In v. 2, the carnage of war is depicted in the language of a feast. Here Israel's fallen become a meal (מאכל) set before the birds of the heavens (עוף השמים) and the wild animals of the earth (חיתו־ארץ). In v. 7, the psalmist petitions God to rescue Israel and pour out his wrath on the nations that have "devoured" (אכל) Jacob (v. 7). The psalm closes with a vow of praise as the congregation self-identifies as God's people and "the sheep of your pasture" (צאן מרעיתך; cf. Ps 74:1).[119]

Here in Psalm 79, the psalmist utilizes food language to picture a world first out of—then moving into—order. The psalm opens with a world out of order where Israel's enemies play the host for a macabre banquet in Jerusalem as the bird of the heavens and the beasts of the fields are provided with food (מאכל), in this case, the flesh (בשר) of Israel's fallen (v. 2). This horrific memory compels the psalmist to petition for a reversal of this reality. Cole argues that this petition takes place through the use of lexical reversals. He observes: "Strophe 1 [vv. 1–5] begins with a reference to the nations (v. 1, גוים), that have made Israel food to be consumed (v. 2, מאכל), while strophe II [vv. 6–12] opens with a request that divine anger be poured out on those same nations (v. 6, גוים) that have consumed

115. Tate, *Psalms 51–100*, 298.

116. Mays notes: "The scope of the disaster sketched in verses 1–4, 7 and 11 points to the fall of Jerusalem to the Babylonians in 587 B.C. (II Kings 25). The holy temple has been defiled by the intrusion and uses of foreigners. Jerusalem is in ruins. The population has been slaughtered, its land devastated." Mays, *Psalms*, 260. For a similar view, see Kraus, *Psalms 60–150*, 134.

117. DeClaissé-Walford et al., *Book of Psalms*, 626.

118. Mays notes: "Psalm 79 is the only corporate prayer for help that includes a confession of sin." Mays, *Psalms*, 261.

119. Tate notes: "The last verse in the psalm foresees an end to this nightmare period of death, confusion, and isolation. In confidence the people assert that Israel is Yahweh's people, his flock, and that when his redemption comes they will recount his praise for generations. It is worth noting that the last word in the psalm is 'praise'—hardly expected at the beginning of the psalm." Tate, *Psalm 51–100*, 301.

Jacob (v. 7, אכל)."[120] The psalm closes with an equally unexpected turn. In v. 13, the congregation moves from desperate pleas to hopeful praise, as they self-identify as "the sheep of your pasture" (צאן מרעיתך).[121] Thus here in Psalm 79, we find that Israel moves backward through the food cycle, beginning with the reality of death and becoming food and ending with the hope of protection and the preservation of life.

Psalm 80

Psalm 80 is a communal lament[122] that can be divided into three stanzas, each ending with a refrain: invocation and petition (vv. 2–4), lamentation (vv. 5–8), and the parable of the vine (vv. 9–20).[123] The psalm is an appeal for God to act again on Israel's behalf like he did in their past.

In each of the three stanzas, the psalmist uses a different image drawn from the arena of food. The psalm opens with a plea to "the Shepherd of Israel" (רעה ישראל)[124] who leads Israel like "a flock" (צאן) to listen and come and save them (v. 2–3). In the second stanza, the psalmist laments that while God has fed (אכל) his people (v. 6), their diet has consisted of "the bread of tears" (לחם דמעה)[125] and "tears in large measure" (בדמעות שליש).[126] In the third stanza, the psalmist describes Israel as a transplanted vine (גפן)[127] that has been abandoned by its vigneron.

120. Cole, *Shape and Message of Book 3*, 78.

121. Regarding this turn, Tanner observes: "In this moment of suffering, a new situation can barely be imagined. However, Israel's long history with God tells a story that even in the darkest of days, there is a future with God for his people." DeClaissé-Walford et al., *Book of Psalms*, 629.

122. Curtis, *Psalms*, 168.

123. Tate, *Psalms 51–100*, 308. Zenger divides the "parable of the vine" into two sections (vv. 9–14, 15–20). Hossfeld and Zenger, *Psalms 2*, 309.

124. Curtis notes: "This is the only occurrence of this actual title, but the concept of God as 'shepherd' and the people as his 'flock' are familiar, and are a recurring theme in this part of the Psalter (see Pss 77:20; 78:52–53; 79:13), perhaps in part explaining the juxtaposition of these psalms." Curtis, *Psalms*, 169.

125. Kraus observes: "The bread of tears makes us think of a disaster that lasts a long time and not an acute threat." Kraus, *Psalms 60–150*, 142.

126. The word שליש means "a third." Tanner translates the phrase "to drink tears in triple," recognizing that here it seems that God is increasing sorrows, not diminishing them. DeClaissé-Walford et al., *Book of Psalms*, 631. Possibly in light of Gunkel's translation "a great stein" of drink, Tate opts for "by the keg." Tate, *Psalms 51–100*, 306n6a. To acknowledge the lack of clarity in the image, I follow the trend of Kraus, who translates it "with a full measure." Kraus, *Psalms 60–150*, 137.

127. The imagery of Israel as a vine is common in the Hebrew Bible (e.g., Isa 5:1–7; 27:2–6; Jer 2:21; 12:10; Ezek 15:1–8; 19:10–14).

Without the maintenance of the boundary walls, the produce of the vines is plucked (ארה) by those who pass by (v. 13) and ravaged (כרסם) and devoured (רעה) by the creatures of the field (v. 14).

Each of the food images in Psalm 80 depicts God as provider and sustainer of Israel with standard images of protection (e.g., shepherd, host, vigneron). But in each instance, the relationship is pictured in disarray. Psalm 80 begins where Psalm 79 ended—in the pasture of Israel's shepherd (80:2; cf. 79:13). Now instead of voicing praise, the congregation is calling out to an absent Shepherd to come and save them (v. 3). In the second stanza (vv. 5–8), the congregation again reflects on God's neglect of their basic needs,[128] for here Israel is given an abundant but nutrition-deficient diet—"bread of tears" (לחם דמעה) and tears in "large measure" (בדמעות שליש).[129] Lastly, the image of an untended vine offers a picture of contrast and contradiction between what God had done in the past and their present reality.[130] Here the only ones being well fed are Israel's enemies.[131]

The connection of Psalm 80's food references to Israel's experience in the wilderness is unmistakable. By repurposing the traditions of the past, the psalmist heightens the disjunction between God's care in the past and their present experience. The reference to God as the Shepherd of Israel (v. 2) calls to mind God's care for his people in the exodus from Egypt into the wilderness (cf. Pss 77:20; 78:52–53). Tate notes a link between Israel's current tear-filled diet and their wilderness experience: "God's neglect is being deliberately contrasted with his care in the

128. Zenger notes: "The lament intensifies in vv. 6–7 to accusation, reproaching YHWH with the utter contradictoriness and absurdity of his behavior, through the contrastive development of the shepherd imagery: Israel now experiences him as a bad, even a wicked shepherd. . . . YHWH has given over his flock, Israel, to continuing and uninterrupted misery, suffering, and danger of death." Hossfeld and Zenger, *Psalms 2*, 315.

129. God's active involvement in the provision of this saltwater diet (האכלתם, hif perfect 2ms) is a rhetorically charged statement, especially when compared with the psalmist's tearful exclamation of personal distress in Ps 42:4 [ET 3]: "My tears have been my food both day and night" (היתה לי דמעתי לחם יומם ולילה).

130. Mays notes: "Like the flock, the vine and vineyard represented a basic and familiar possession that was owned, cared for, and prized as a primary good of life. . . . The psalm's parable introduces the anguish and bewilderment of the people over the contrast and contradiction between what God began and what he now has done." Mays, *Psalms*, 263.

131. Regarding the irony of this situation, McCann observes: "The word 'feed' (רעה *rā ʿâ*, v. 13) is particularly poignant as it recalls v. 1, where the word 'shepherd' (רעה *rō ʿēh*) is literally translated 'feeder.' God, who traditionally has been the one to feed Israel, is allowing Israel to be devoured." McCann, "Book of Psalms," 1000.

wilderness where the people dined on manna and quail and had fresh water provided from rocks."[132] Finally, Psalm 80's parable of an uprooted and transplanted vine draws its life from Israel's own exodus from Egypt and entry into the land.

Psalm 81

Many scholars consider Psalm 81 a Festival Psalm, possibly associated with an autumn festival or Passover.[133] Regarding the structure of the psalm, Mays observes "a summons to the celebration of a festival (vv. 1–5 [ET])" followed by "an address to the people of God composed in divine first person style (vv. 6–16 [ET])."[134] The psalm presents itself as a sermon, a summons to Israel "to decide anew whether they will continue the story of their past recalcitrance or will listen to YHWH and walk in his ways."[135]

Psalm 81 presents three food-related images in the divine speech (vv. 8, 11, 17). Verse 7 refers to God's testing (בחן) of Israel at the "waters of Meribah" (מי מריבה), although here—like Ps 106:32—there is no mention of the associated provision of water (cf. Num 20). In v. 11, "the unknown voice" of v. 6 declares: "I am YHWH your God who brought you up out of Egypt. Open wide your mouth (פה) and I will fill (מלא) it."[136] In v. 17, this voice announces the resulting bounty if God's people listen and obey: "But you would be fed (אכל) with the finest of wheat (חלב חטה); with honey (דבש) from the rock (צור) I would satisfy you (שבע)."[137]

132. Tate, *Psalms 51–100*, 314.

133. Kraus, *Psalms 60–120*, 147.

134. Mays, *Psalms*, 265.

135. Mays, *Psalms*, 268.

136. Although there is debate about what would be put into Israel's mouth—food or God's word—the final verse of the psalm leads one in the direction of food. Tanner contends: "It is just as likely that this line refers to the wilderness events where God did fill the people's mouths with food and drink." DeClaissé-Walford et al., *Book of Psalms*, 639. This view is contrary to Tate, who notes: "the varied forms of the expressions for 'putting' or 'filling' the mouth in the OT are used mostly of putting words of speech in the mouth: e.g., Exod 4:15; Num 22:38; 23:5, 12, 16; Deut 18:18; 31:19; 2 Sam 14:3, 19; Isa 30:27; 59:21; Jer 1:9; 5:14; Pss 10:4; 71:8; 126:2; Job 8:21; 23:4, Prov 20:18. . . . But the predominance of filling the mouth and opening the mouth to receive and express speech tilts the meaning strongly in that direction." Tate, *Psalms 51–100*, 325.

137. Regarding this surprising source for honey, Tate notes: "Honey may be found at times in the clefts of rocky cliffs, but the primary meaning is probably that of rich and valuable food produced from any naturally barren sources." Tate, *Psalms 51–100*, 326.

These references draw the audience back to the wilderness experience. While the language of divine testing (בחן)—instead of provision—is associated with the waters of Meribah (v. 7), the remaining two examples (vv. 11, 17) are invitations for Israel to dine. Psalm 81 draws the present audience into the reality of divine provision of the past by reissuing an invitation to be filled (מלא, v. 11), to feed (אכל, v. 17), and to be satisfied (שבע, v. 17).[138]

Psalm 78 in the Midst of the Asaph Collection

When one views Psalm 78 in the midst of the other psalms in the Asaph Collection that employ food language, one finds a variety of similar food features. The collection shows strong literary artistry, with a variety of food references drawn from the arenas of food production and consumption. Food language is also used to develop key themes in the collection. In addition, food language seems to play a role on a compositional level. Food language is used across whole compositions, appears at key junctures in the psalms, and serves as a means of drawing psalms together (i.e., Pss 78–81).

One of the most overlooked aspects of the Asaph Collection (Pss 50, 73–83) is its literary artistry, especially in relation to food language. The Asaph Collection contains a diverse variety of food items served, including abundant wine (Pss 75; cf. 78), a turtledove and a sea monster (Ps 74), human corpses (Ps 79), "bread of tears" (Ps 80), and "the finest wheat" and "honey" (Ps 81). Psalm 78 adds "the bread of the mighty," "grain from heaven," and meat/winged birds. This list also includes lots and lots of sheep (Pss 74, 77, 78, 79, 80). In the Asaph Collection, God is pictured in a variety of food-related roles. God is depicted as game warden (Ps 50), chef de cuisine (Ps 74; cf. 78), sommelier (Ps 75), table host (Ps 79), shepherd (Pss 80; cf. 78),[139] and vigneron (Ps 80).

138. The verbal pair "eat" (אכל) and "be satisfied" (שבע) occurs 25x in the MT, including in the manna/quail accounts in Exod 16:8, 12, as well as in Ps 78:29.

139. Reflected in the literature of the ANE, kings and deities often took the title of "Shepherd." Tanner highlights some notable occurrences in ANE texts of the title "Shepherd" used for the gods in their function as king: "The Sumerian god Enlil is referred to as 'God Enlil, faithful Shepherd, Master of all countries, [faithful] Shepherd, . . . the lord who drew the outline of his land.' Marduk is also referred to as a shepherd of humans: 'Most exalted be the Son, our avenger; let his sovereignty be surpassing, having no rival. May he shepherd the blackheaded ones, his creatures'; and in his victory over Tiamat, 'who the corpse of Tiamat carried off with his weapon; who directs the

The Asaph Collection also draws readily from images related to both food production—particularly agriculture, viticulture, and animal husbandry—and food consumption. In Psalm 80 Israel is depicted as a metaphorical vine planted and tended by God in the land of Canaan. Psalm 78 describes in detail the destruction of agricultural supplies in Egypt as locusts and hail decimate their crops. Images of animal husbandry are not limited to just sheep (Pss 74:1; 77:21; 78:52, 71; 79:13; 80:2) but expand to other domesticated animals. Psalm 50 challenges Israel's mistaken assumption that God actually eats their bulls and goats. Psalm 78 offers a picture of the complete destruction of livestock and cattle in the Egyptian plagues.

The consumption of food—by humans, animals, and God—also dominates the Asaph psalms. In Psalm 75, the wicked are forced to drink a cup of foaming wine down to its dregs. In Psalm 80, Israel is made to eat bread of tears and drink tears in great measure. In Psalm 81, God invites Israel to dine on the finest of wheat and honey from a rock. Psalm 78 offers its own version of divinely provided sustenance, in this case water from a "rock," "grain from heaven," and "bread of the mighty," as well as "meat" in the form of winged birds. The animal kingdom is seen eating in these psalms as well. The corpse of Leviathan is served to the desert creatures (Ps 74). Unburied human carcasses left on the battlefield become the dinner for birds/beasts (Ps 79). In Psalm 78, locusts gorge themselves on Egypt's agricultural bounty. In addition, one finds wild animals metaphorically "feeding" on Israel. In Psalm 74, Israel is pictured as a turtledove threatened by wild beasts.[140] In Psalm 80, Israel is a grapevine ravaged by wild animals, its grapes consumed by all who pass by. The images of Israel as an abandoned flock hint at the idea that they may quickly become food/prey if the shepherd does not return to stand guard (Pss 74, 80). While Psalm 50 refutes the notion that God eats the flesh of bulls or drinks the blood of goats, Psalm 78 likens God's unexpected involvement in events to a warrior waking from wine.

Within the Asaph psalms, food language is used to emphasize key themes in the collection. First, food language is used to describe Israel's

land—their faithful shepherd'; and in his rule over the other gods, 'May he shepherd all the gods like sheep . . . . Because he created the spaces and fashioned the ground, Father Enlil called his name "Lord of the Lands."'" Tanner, "King Yahweh as the Good Shepherd," 272.

140. There is a movement between Ps 74 where Israel is afraid of becoming prey for wild beasts to Ps 79 where in fact their carcasses have become food for the beasts/birds.

present helplessness. Whether this is as a flock that needs to be fed and protected (Pss 74, 80)[141] or as a vineyard that needs to be tended and maintained (Ps 80), these images speak of the need for YHWH's sustaining care. Second, there is a focus on divine inattention and a plea for God to intervene. This theme is present in the image of the absent shepherd in Psalms 74 and 80. In Psalm 79, the psalmist's depiction of the human carnage of war and Jacob being "devoured" by enemies are both attempts to capture the attention of a seemingly distant God. Psalm 80's image of surviving on saltwater rations provides a rhetorically charged plea for intervention. The collection also uses food language to instill hope for the present through remembrance of God's acts of reversal in the past. In Psalm 74, chaos—here pictured as Leviathan—becomes dinner. In Psalm 78, YHWH awakes from wine to bring reproach on Israel's enemies. Finally, there is a renewed hope for divine justice and future provisions. In Psalm 75, Israel's enemies are promised a cup of wine that will lead to their demise. In Psalm 81, God promises extravagant provisions of finest wheat and honey from a rock, echoing back to wilderness plenty (Psalm 78).

One also finds that food language plays a role on a compositional level. In five of the seven psalms considered above, food language is used as a consistent rhetorical device across the psalm. In Psalms 50, 74, 78, 79, and 80, food language appears within each of the main sections of the psalm. In addition, food language appears within individual psalms at key junctures, particularly in the opening and closing lines. Food language occurs at the close of Psalm 50 (v. 22), the opening verse of Psalm 74 (v. 1), the closing verse of Psalm 79 (v. 13), the opening verse of Psalm 80 (v. 2 [ET 1]), and the closing verse of Psalm 81 (v. 17).

Finally, food language serves to draw adjacent psalms together (i.e., Pss 78–81). Pavan notes the increased presence of eating and drinking language within Psalms 78–81. In his study of Book 3, he identifies the presence of common motifs among two or three adjacent psalms. Of particular significance to this study is his recognition of the motif of "food and drink" that unites Psalms 78–81.[142] Across these psalms one finds a sustained use of shepherding language (Pss 78:52–53a, 70–72;

141. It may be possible to view the confidence of the psalmist at the close of Ps 79:13 as a renewed hope rooted in the picture of the divine shepherd's care and protection in Ps 78:53b.

142. Pavan identifies this motif in 78:16, 18, 20, 24, 25, 29, 30, 44, 45, 63; 79:2, 7; 80:6; 81:17 (cf. 75:9). He finds a sustained pastoral motif across the collection (Pss 77:21; 78:14, 52, 53, 70, 71, 72; 79:13; 80:2, 14; cf. 73:24; 74:1; 83:13). Pavan, *He Remembered That They Were But Flesh*, 125–26.

79:13; 80:2). Psalm 78 presents God as Israel's shepherd in the wilderness (78:52–53a) and ends with a striking picture of David—taken from tending a literal flock to now shepherding Israel/Judah (vv. 70–72). Psalm 79 also concludes with a word of hope that once again Israel who identifies as the sheep of God's pastures would be able to praise God (v. 13). Psalm 80 picks up this identification and pleads that God, the Shepherd of Israel, would intervene in their crisis (80:2). This consistent use of sheep/shepherding imagery at the opening and/or closing of Psalms 78–80 offers a strong sense of literary shaping.

Across this smaller collection (Pss 78–81) and present in the Asaph Collection as a whole is a concern for history, particularly the Exodus and wilderness accounts. As one moves from Psalm 78 to Psalm 81, there is a progression from a focus on the past to a consideration of the present, to a look to a future hope. Remembrance is a key theme in Psalm 78 as the recollection of the food "wonders" in the wilderness reminds Israel of divine provision in unexpected places from unexpected sources. Even the destruction of food supplies in Egypt stresses the reality of God's sovereignty over the created order. Psalms 79 and 80 are both reflections on the psalmist's present reality. Psalm 79 mourns the destruction of Jerusalem and the carnage of war where carrion feasts on human flesh. Psalm 80 draws on the language of food scarcity ("bread of tears") and the destruction of food supplies (here Israel is compared to a ravaged vineyard) to challenge God to once again shine forth, to persuade God to intervene. Psalm 81 looks to a future where God would once again feed Israel. These psalms seem to be selected and arranged to respond to a crisis on a national level. McCann argues that this alternating pattern of hope (Ps 78), lament (Pss 79, 80), hope (Ps 81) reflects a community coming to terms with the disorienting reality of exile and the need for a reoriented hope.[143] In the situation of the postexilic community, God's sovereignty surely would have been in question. Gillingham suggests that the presence of the exodus story in the postexilic period functioned "to

143. McCann observes that Book 3 alternates between expressions of hope and lament. He contends that Book 3 displays a purposeful arrangement that "serves to assist the community not only to face squarely the disorienting reality of exile . . . but also reach a reorientation based on the rejection of the Davidic/Zion theology that had formerly been Judah's primary grounds for hope." McCann, "Books I–III and the Editorial Purpose," 99. With the rejection of the traditional basis for hope, McCann argues that new expressions of hope emerge in Book 3 with psalms that "look to God as judge of all the earth and that rehearse God's past deeds on Israel's behalf despite Israel's faithlessness" (100).

encourage the despondent community that the God of the Exodus still offers a future and a hope."[144] Thus when the present world seemed unstable, the psalmists looked to the past for hope for the present.

Divine provision of food is also seen across this smaller collection (Pss 78–81). In Psalm 78, YHWH provides water from a rock, "grain from heaven"/"bread of the mighty," and meat/winged birds. In Psalm 80, Israel is fed "bread of tears" and "tears in large measure." In Psalm 81, Israel is promised the "finest of grain" and "honey from a rock." When viewed together, Psalms 78–81 exhibit repetition and reversals of ideas. In Psalm 78, Israel is a guest at God's wilderness "table" where Israel is supplied with water from a "rock" and served "grain of heaven"/"bread of the mighty" and meat/winged birds. In Psalm 79, we find a world out of order where now Israel's enemies play the host in Jerusalem and now it is the birds of the heavens and the beasts of the fields that are given the corpses of Israel's fallen as "food." In Psalm 80, instead of "bread of the mighty," Israel is given "bread of tears." Instead of abundant water from a rock, Israel is given tears to drink in abundant measure. As Jones notes: "The bread of tears and drink from the deep are reminiscent of God's provisions in the wilderness, but God's present inactivity/activity is in harsh contrast with God's care in the wilderness."[145] And yet in Psalm 81, we find a hope for a future meal scene where Israel is invited to dine before God and eat the finest of wheat and be satisfied with honey from a rock.

In Israel's postexilic reality, the importance of food comes into clearer focus. In this period of uncertainty (politically, religiously, socially), this uncertainty spills over into economic instability as well (Neh 9:36–37). The recital of YHWH's provision in uncertain circumstances (i.e., the wilderness) offers a reminder of YHWH's sovereignty over the natural world and his ability to provide. In Psalm 78, Israel questions: "Can YHWH set a table in the wilderness?" The Asaph Collection seems to be considering a similar question: Can God set a table in the uncertainty of a postexilic reality? Psalm 81 answers this question with a resounding "yes." For here, YHWH once again issues an invitation . . ."open wide your mouth and I will fill it" (v. 11).

144. Gillingham, "Exodus Tradition and Israelite Psalmody," 25.

145. Jones, "Psalms of Asaph," 97.

Psalm 78 in Light of the Asaph Collection

As shown in the discussion above, Psalm 78's use of food language fits comfortably within the larger Asaph Collection. Psalm 78's sheer length sets it apart from the other psalms within the Asaph Collection. Yet, even factoring in the size of Israel's recital, the psalmist shows a remarkable concern for celebrating the divine provision of food in Israel's history. In addition, here in Psalm 78 YHWH is presented as directly present in Israel's story. YHWH is a God who acts—both in divine provision and in divine judgment. Because of this, Psalm 78 itself is a unique statement of confident trust in the midst of the Asaphic laments. Psalm 79:8 petitions: "Do not remember (אל־תזכר) against us the iniquities (עון) of our ancestors; let your compassion (רחם) come speedily to meet us, for we are brought very low." Psalm 78 provides a hope that God will in fact engage with Israel and forgive again.[146] For in the midst of Israel's rebellion in the wilderness, the psalmist notes: "Yet he, being compassionate (רחום), forgave their iniquity (עון), and did not destroy them. . . . He remembered (זכר) that they were but flesh, a wind that passes and does not return" (vv. 38a, 39). Thus we find that Psalm 78 not only calls Israel to a posture of confident trust (v. 7) but becomes the means for instilling this trust as well.

CONCLUSION

In this chapter I have demonstrated Psalm 78's sustained use of food language across the entire historical recital. In these two sections ("wilderness frame" [vv. 13–53] and land section [vv. 54–72]), there are similarities in how Israel's experience and YHWH's response are described, providing literary scaffolding that draws the two locational experiences of Israel's journey together.

By viewing Psalm 78 in the midst of the historical psalms (Pss 105, 106, 135, 136), one finds a variety of similar rhetorical tendencies across these psalms sharing a common content, i.e., historical recital. The theme of reversal undergirds Psalms 78, 105, and 106. The physical and locational dimensions of food are consistently used for rhetorical effect in

146. McCann observes Psalm 79's theological and lexical connection to Psalm 78: "The words 'mercy'/'merciful' (רחום *raḥûm*) and 'forgive' (כפר *kipper*) also occur together in Ps 78:38, which rehearses at length 'the iniquities of our ancestors' (79:8). That is to say, the good news of God's faithfulness and forgiveness proclaimed in Psalm 78 is also the basis of appeal in Psalm 79." McCann, "Book of Psalms," 995.

Psalms 78, 105, 106, 136. Food language is employed for divine provision (Pss 78, 105, 136) and divine judgment (Pss 78, 106), and the themes of divine remembrance and divine engagement on Israel's behalf mark these psalms (Pss 78, 105, 106, 136).

When seen in the context of the historical psalms, Psalm 78 shows a marked concern for the wilderness food events, especially God's extravagant provision in an unlikely setting. One finds a unique emphasis in Psalm 78's recital on both the wilderness food events and the Egyptian plagues (contra Psalm 105's diminished interest in the wilderness food events). Compared with the other historical recitals, Psalm 78 utilizes food language across the composition and employs the dimensionality of food with the most variety.

The study of Psalm 78 in the midst of the Asaph Collection reveals a variety of similarities within the psalms that employ food language. These similarities include the use of food language for the artistic construal of human experience and divine engagement, its use in the development of key themes across the collection, and its use in creating compositional cohesion within individual psalms and adjacent psalms.

When viewed in light of the Asaph Collection, Psalm 78 shows a remarkable concern for celebrating divine provision and divine engagement in Israel's story. For in this extended recital of divine attentiveness, the psalmist both invites (v. 7) and invokes this trust through the language of food.

7

Conclusion

In his study of Psalm 78, Greenstein notes: "How we choose to read matters."[1] In Psalm 78, the psalmist's chronicle of Israel's history is about more than reciting a series of formative events from the past; instead, as Greenstein contends, it is "an exercise in rhetoric."[2] As this study has shown, the psalmist reminds the audience of the past and yet creatively rearranges and re-construes these traditions. Wilder observes that this technique is the mark of a good story in that it "maintains its sway over the imagination by a combination of surprise (novelty) and familiarity (recognition)."[3] As one considers Psalm 78, these dynamics of familiarity and surprise play out repeatedly in the psalmist's favorite rhetorical arena, the language of food. This study has shown that the psalmist's use of food language in the recital of Israel's past is a rhetorically driven means to instill confident trust in the possibility of YHWH's renewed intervention in the present.

As seen in this study, Psalm 78 presents itself as a "riddle" (v. 2) and, as seen in chapter 2, remains a conundrum to biblical scholars. And one of the most overlooked aspects of this psalm by scholars through the years is its "wilderness frame" (vv. 13–53) and its concern with two major events within this literary frame that focus on food, namely the recounting of the Egyptian plagues (vv. 15–31) and the wilderness food events (vv. 44–51). One of the reasons that these events are often overlooked or

1. Greenstein, "Mixing Memory and Design," 197.
2. Greenstein, "Mixing Memory and Design," 197.
3. Wilder, "Story and Story-World," 358.

understudied is the lack of a robust methodology for considering food and its rhetorical potential—a lacuna addressed in chapter 3 through the establishment of categories for considering the multidimensionality of food as a foundational aspect of its rhetorical power. With this lens for understanding food's rhetorical possibilities, chapters 4 and 5 considered these two food-based events through a literary and rhetorical study. Chapter 4 demonstrated how Psalm 78's portrayal of these food events (water from a rock/manna/quail) provides a picture of YHWH's gracious care for Israel's needs, even in the midst of their doubt and rebellion. Here the psalmist uniquely emphasizes the abundance of the food provision, as well as YHWH's active involvement and sovereign power over the created order. In the psalmist's recounting of these events, no human agents appear in the account; instead, the natural world serves as an obedient participant in this provision. In this recital of YHWH's wilderness wonders, the psalmist exploits the rhetorical force of food language in order to capture the attention and instill hope in the audience. Chapter 5 considered the psalmist's depiction of the Egyptian plagues (vv. 44–51) in the context of parallel accounts of this event across the Hebrew Bible. When viewed in the context of the recital itself, one finds that the psalmist's selection and arrangement the Egyptian plagues mirrors the psalmist's earlier presentation of the wilderness food events. Psalm 78's plague account begins with the destruction of Egypt's water supplies (v. 44; cf. YHWH's provision of wilderness water, vv. 15–16), then agriculture (vv. 46–47; cf. YHWH's provision of grain/bread in the wilderness, vv. 23–25), then livestock/meat sources (v. 48; cf. YHWH's provision of meat/winged birds in the wilderness, vv. 26–28). This rhetorically motivated presentation of events now depicts the destruction of Egypt's food supplies as an antithesis of YHWH's provision of food in the wilderness. By beginning with the wilderness food account, the psalmist starts the psalm with a celebration of God's act of gracious care for Israel. By closing the wilderness frame with God's systematic dismantling of food supplies in Egypt, the psalmist invites the audience to evaluate Israel's wilderness rebellion, now in light of YHWH's sovereign power over food in Egypt. By placing the Egyptian plagues after the wilderness food events, the composer invites the audience to critique Israel's dissatisfaction not only at the end of the wilderness food account but again at the end of the plagues, offering a compounded rhetorical punch. In order to understand the literary and theological contributions of Psalm 78, chapter 6 explored a widening circle of contexts, considering the composition as a whole as well as its contexts within the Psalter. By analyzing the psalmist's uses of food language in the wilderness frame (vv. 13–53) and then the land-based section of the psalm (vv. 54–72), this study demonstrated how the psalmist employs all five dimensions of food language across the entire historical recital. When Psalm 78 was viewed in the midst of the other "historical psalms" (Pss 105, 106, 135, 136), a variety of similar rhetorical strategies employing food was seen across these psalms. Seen against the backdrop of the historical psalms, Psalm 78 shows a heightened concern for recalling the wilderness food events, especially God's extravagant provision in an unlikely setting. When viewed within the Asaph Collection (Pss 50, 73–83), Psalm 78 stands in the company of a variety of psalms that employ the language of food production and food consumption for rhetorical effect (i.e., Pss 50, 74, 75, 79, 80, 81). When considered in light of the Asaph Collection, Psalm 78 shows a unique concern for celebrating divine provision and divine engagement in Israel's past while invoking confident trust in the present.

The title of this work draws from the question posed by Israel: "Can God set a table in the wilderness?" (v. 19b). This rhetorical question is unique to Psalm 78, and with this query, the psalmist captures the heart of Israel's concerns in the wilderness as well as their fears after exile. The psalmist, however, begins the recital with an invitation to a posture not of fear, but one marked by a confident trust in God (v. 7a). When viewed against the backdrop of exile, Psalm 78's portrayal of YHWH's provision in spite of Israel's past rebellion offers the audience the hope that YHWH will remember their current plight and act again with compassion. In order to achieve this intention, the psalmist whets the appetite of his audience by telling his tale through the language of food.

Bibliography

Abernethy, Andrew. *Eating in Isaiah: Approaching Food and Drink in Isaiah's Structure and Message*. BIS 131. Leiden: Brill, 2014.

Alexander, Joseph A. *The Psalms: Translated and Explained*. 1873. Repr., Grand Rapids: Baker, 1975.

Allen, Leslie C. *Psalms 101–150*. WBC 21. Nashville: Nelson, 2002.

Alter, Robert. *The Book of Psalms: A Translation with Commentary*. New York: Norton, 2007.

———. *The David Story: A Translation with Commentary of 1 and 2 Samuel*. New York: Norton, 1999.

Altmann, Peter. *Festive Meals in Ancient Israel: Deuteronomy's Identity Politics in Their Ancient Near Eastern Context*. BZAW 424. Berlin: de Gruyter, 2011.

———. "Food and Food Production." *Oxford Bibliographies Online: Biblical Studies*. Oxford: Oxford University Press, 2012. https://www.oxfordbibliographies.com/display/document/obo-9780195393361/obo-9780195393361-0022.xml.

Altmann, Peter, and Janling Fu, eds. *Feasting in the Archaeology and Texts of the Bible and the Ancient Near East*. Winona Lake, IN: Eisenbrauns, 2014.

Anderson, A. A. *The Book of Psalms*. Vol. 2, *Psalms 73–150*. NCB. London: Oliphants, 1972.

Arnott, Margaret, ed. *Gastronomy: The Anthropology of Food and Food Habits*. The Hague: Mouton, 1975.

Ashley, Timothy R. *The Book of Numbers*. NICOT. Grand Rapids: Eerdmans, 1993.

Avrahami, Yael. *The Senses of Scripture: Sensory Perception in the Hebrew Bible*. LHBOTS 545. New York: T&T Clark, 2012.

Barker, William D. "Wine Production in Ancient Israel and the Meaning of שמרים in the Hebrew Bible." In *Leshon Limmudim: Essays on the Language and Literature of the Hebrew Bible in Honour of A. A. Macintosh*, edited by David A. Baer and Robert P. Gordon, 268–74. London: Bloomsbury, 2013.

Bartchy, S. Scott. "The Historical Jesus and Honor Reversal at the Table." In *The Social Setting of Jesus and the Gospels*, edited by Wolfgang Stegemann et al., 175–83. Minneapolis: Fortress, 2002.

Batto, Bernard F. "The Sleeping God: An Ancient Near Eastern Motif of Divine Sovereignty." *Bib* 68 (1987) 153–77.

Beardsworth, Alan, and Teresa Keil. *Sociology on the Menu: An Invitation to the Study of Food and Society*. New York: Routledge, 1997.

Bellinger, William H., Jr. "Psalm 61: A Rhetorical Analysis." *Perspectives in Religious Studies* 26 (1999) 379–88.

Berlin, Adele. "Interpreting Torah Traditions in Psalm 105." In *Jewish Biblical Interpretation and Cultural Exchange: Comparative Exegesis in Context*, edited by Natalie B. Dohrmann and David Stern, 20–36. Philadelphia: University of Pennsylvania Press, 2008.

———. "Psalms and the Literature of Exile: Psalms 137, 44, 69, and 78." In *The Book of Psalms: Composition and Reception*, edited by Peter W. Flint and Patrick D. Miller, 65–86. VTSup 99. Leiden: Brill, 2005.

———. "The Rhetoric of Psalm 145." In *Biblical and Related Studies Presented to Samuel Iwry*, edited by Ann Kort and Scott Morschauser, 17–22. Winona Lake, IN: Eisenbrauns, 1985.

Berry, Wendell. "The Pleasures of Eating." In *What Are People For? Essays*, 145–52. Berkeley: Counterpoint, 2010.

Bitzer, L. F., and E. Black, eds. *The Prospect of Rhetoric*. Englewood Cliffs, NJ: Prentice-Hall, 1971.

Blomberg, Craig L. *Contagious Holiness: Jesus' Meals with Sinners*. NSBT 19. Leicester: InterVarsity, 2005.

———. "Jesus, Sinners, and Table Fellowship." *BBR* 19 (2009) 35–62.

Boer, Roland. *The Sacred Economy of Ancient Israel*. Louisville: Westminster John Knox, 2015.

Bolyki, János. *Jesu Tischgemeinschaften*. WUNT 2.96. Tübingen: Mohr Siebeck, 1988.

Borowski, Oded. *Agriculture in Iron Age Israel*. Winona Lake, IN: Eisenbrauns, 1987.

———. "Eat, Drink, and Be Merry: The Mediterranean Diet." *Near Eastern Archaeology* 67 (2004) 96–107.

Boyd, Samuel L. "The Rhetoric of Memory and the Formation of Identity in Psalm 78 and Deuteronomy 32." *Biblical Research* 66 (2021) 7–30.

Brenner, Athalya, and Jan Willem van Henten, eds. *Semeia 86: Food and Drink in the Biblical Worlds*. Atlanta: SBL, 1999.

Brettler, Marc Z. "The Poet as Historian: The Plague Tradition in Psalm 105." In *Bringing the Hidden to Light: The Process of Interpretation: Studies in Honor of Stephen A. Geller*, edited by Kathryn F. Kravitz and Diane M. Sharon, 19–28. Winona Lake, IN: Eisenbrauns, 2007.

Briggs, Charles A., and Emilie G. Briggs. *A Critical and Exegetical Commentary on the Book of Psalms*. Vol. 2. ICC. Edinburgh: T&T Clark, 1907.

Broshi, Magen. "The Diet of Palestine in the Roman Period: Introductory Notes." In *Bread, Wine, Walls, and Scrolls*, 121–43. LSTS 36. Sheffield: Sheffield Academic, 2001.

———. "Wine in Ancient Palestine: Introductory Notes." In *Bread, Wine, Walls, and Scrolls*, 144–72. LSTS 36. Sheffield: Sheffield Academic, 2001.

Brothwell, Don R., and Patricia Brothwell. *Food in Antiquity: A Survey of the Diet of Early Peoples*. Exp. ed. Baltimore: Johns Hopkins University Press, 1998.

Brueggemann, Walter. *Abiding Astonishment: Psalms, Modernity, and the Making of History*. Louisville: Westminster John Knox, 1991.

———. *First and Second Samuel*. IBC. Louisville: Westminster John Knox, 1990.

Brueggemann, Walter, and William H. Bellinger Jr. *Psalms*. NCBC. Cambridge: Cambridge University Press, 2014.

Buber, Martin. *Moses: The Revelation and the Covenant*. London: Humanities, 1988.

Campbell, Antony F. *The Ark Narrative (1 Sam 4–6; 2 Sam 6): A Form-Critical and Traditio-Historical Study*. SBLDS 16. Missoula, MT: Scholars, 1975.

———. "Psalm 78: A Contribution to the Theology of Tenth Century Israel." *CBQ* 41 (1979) 51–79.

Capon, Robert Farrar. *The Supper of the Lamb: A Culinary Reflection*. Garden City, NY: Doubleday, 1969.

Carroll, Robert P. "Psalm LXXVIII: Vestiges of a Tribal Polemic." *VT* 21 (1971) 133–50.

———. "The Significance of the Election Traditions of Ancient Israel for the Prophets and Their Development in Jeremiah and the Exilic Prophets." PhD diss., University of Edinburgh, 1967.

———. "YHWH's Sour Grapes: Images of Food and Drink in the Prophetic Discourses of the Hebrew Bible." In *Semeia 86: Food and Drink in the Biblical Worlds*, edited by Athalya Brenner and Jan Willem van Henten, 113–31. Atlanta: SBL, 1999.

Ceresko, Anthony R. "A Poetic Analysis of Ps 105, with Attention to Its Use of Irony." *Bib* 64 (1983) 20–46.

Cheon, Samuel. *The Exodus Story in the Wisdom of Solomon: A Study in Biblical Interpretation*. Sheffield: Sheffield Academic, 1997.

Cheung, Alex T. *Idol Food in Corinth: Jewish Background and Pauline Legacy*. Sheffield: Sheffield Academic, 1999.

Childs, Brevard S. *The Book of Exodus*. OTL. Louisville: Westminster John Knox, 1974.

Claassens, L. Juliana M. *The God Who Provides: Biblical Images of Divine Nourishment*. Nashville: Abingdon, 2004.

Clifford, Richard J. "In Zion and David a New Beginning: An Interpretation of Psalm 78." In *Traditions in Transformation: Turning Points in Biblical Faith*, edited by Baruch Halpern and Jon Levenson, 121–41. Winona Lake, IN: Eisenbrauns, 1981.

———. *Psalms 73–150*. AOTC. Nashville: Abingdon, 2003.

———. "Style and Purpose in Psalm 105." *Bib* 60 (1979) 420–27.

Coats, George W. *Rebellion in the Wilderness: The Murmuring Motif in the Wilderness Traditions of the Old Testament*. Nashville: Abingdon, 1968.

Cohen, A. *The Psalms: Hebrew Text and English Translation with an Introduction and Commentary*. London: Soncino, 1968.

Cole, Robert L. "Rhetorics and Canonical Structure in the Hebrew Psalter Book III (Psalms 73–89)." PhD diss., University of California Los Angeles, 1996.

———. *The Shape and Message of Book 3 (Psalms 73–89)*. JSOTSup 307. Sheffield: Sheffield Academic, 2000.

Cook, Ryan. "Prayers That Form Us: Rhetoric and Psalms Interpretation." *JSOT* 39 (2015) 451–67.

———. *The Rhetoric of Praise: Prayer and Persuasion in the Psalms*. Wilmore, KY: GlossaHouse, 2018.

Corley, Kathleen E. *Private Women, Public Meals: Social Conflict in the Synoptic Tradition*. Peabody, MA: Hendrickson, 1993.

Craigie, Peter C., and Marvin E. Tate. *Psalms 1–50*. 2nd ed. WBC 19. Nashville: Nelson, 2004.

Crossan, John D. "Life of a Mediterranean Jewish Peasant." *The Christian Century* 108 (1991) 1194–200.

Curtis, Adrian. *Psalms*. Epworth Commentaries. Peterborough: Epworth, 2004.

Dalrymple, Sarah. "Royal Lineages: A Study of Psalm 78:59–72 in the Light of the Narrative Traditions." PhD diss., Queen's University Belfast, 2008.

Davies, G. I. "Wilderness Wanderings." In *ABD* 6:912–14.

Davis, Earl Clinton. "The Significance of the Shared Meal in Luke-Acts." ThD diss., The Southern Baptist Theological Seminary, 1967.

Davis, Ellen F. "Propriety and Trespass: The Drama of Eating." *Ex Auditu* 23 (2007) 74–86.

———. *Scripture, Culture, and Agriculture: An Agrarian Reading of the Bible*. Cambridge: Cambridge University Press, 2009.

———. *Who Are You, My Daughter? Reading Ruth Through Image and Text*. Louisville: Westminster John Knox, 2003.

DeClaissé-Walford, Nancy L., et al. *The Book of Psalms*. NICOT. Grand Rapids: Eerdmans, 2014.

Delitzsch, Franz. *Biblical Commentary on the Psalms*. Vol. 2. Translated by David Eaton. 2nd ed. London: Hodder and Stoughton, 1902.

———. *Commentar über den Psalter*. Leipzig: Dorffling und Franke, 1859.

Douglas, Mary. "Deciphering a Meal." In *Implicit Meanings: Essays in Anthropology*, 249–75. London: Routledge & Paul, 1975.

———. "Food as a System of Communication." In *In the Active Voice*, 82–124. London: Routledge & Paul, 1982.

Dunn, James D. G. "The Incident at Antioch (Gal 2:11–18)." *JSNT* 18 (1983) 3–57.

Durham, John I. *Exodus*. WBC 3. Nashville: Nelson, 1987.

Ebeling, Jennie. "Grains, Bread, and Beer." In *T&T Clark Handbook of Food in the Hebrew Bible and Ancient Israel*, edited by Janling Fu et al., 99–112. London: T&T Clark, 2021.

Eidevall, Göran. "Metaphorical Landscapes in the Psalms." In *Metaphors in the Psalms*, edited by Pierre van Hecke and Antje Labahn, 13–21. Leuven: Peeters, 2010.

Eissfeldt, Otto. *Das Lied Moses Deuteronomium 32 1–43 und das Lehrgedicht Asaphs Psalm 78 samt einer Analyse der Umgebung des Mose-Liedes*. Berlin: Akademie-Verlag, 1958.

Emanuel, David. *From Bards to Biblical Exegetes: A Close Reading and Intertextual Analysis of Selected Exodus Psalms*. Eugene, OR: Wipf & Stock, 2012.

———. "The Psalmists' Use of the Exodus Motif: A Close Reading and Intertextual Analysis of Selected Exodus Psalms." PhD diss., Hebrew University, 2007.

Estes, Daniel J. "Psalm 78:1–8 as a Musical Intertext of Torah and Wisdom." *BibSac* 173 (2016) 297–314.

Feeley-Harnik, Gillian. *The Lord's Table: The Meaning of Food in Early Judaism and Christianity*. Washington, DC: Smithsonian Institution, 1994.

Fensham, Frank Charles. "Neh. 9 and Pss. 105, 106, 135 and 136: Post-Exilic Historical Traditions in Poetic Form." *JNSL* 9 (1981) 35–51.

Fernandes, Salvador. *God as Rock in the Psalter*. Frankfurt: Lang, 2013.

Finger, Rita Halteman. *Of Widows and Meals: Communal Meals in the Book of Acts*. Grand Rapids: Eerdmans, 2007.

Firth, David. "Asaph and Sons of Korah." In *Dictionary of the Old Testament: Wisdom, Poetry, and Writings*, edited by Tremper Longman III and Peter Enns, 24–27. Downers Grove, IL: InterVarsity, 2008.

Fishbane, Michael A. *Biblical Interpretation in Ancient Israel*. Oxford: Clarendon, 1985.

———. *Text and Texture: Close Reading of Select Biblical Texts*. New York: Schocken, 1979.

Fokkelman, J. P. *The Psalms in Form: The Hebrew Psalter in Its Poetic Shape*. Leiden: Deo, 2002.

Foster, Robert, and David Howard, eds. *My Words Are Lovely: Studies in the Rhetoric of the Psalms*. LHBOTS 467. New York: T&T Clark, 2008.

Fotopoulos, John. *Food Offered to Idols in Roman Corinth: A Socio-Rhetorical Reconsideration of 1 Corinthians 8:1—11:1*. WUNT 2.151. Tübingen: Mohr Siebeck, 2003.

Fox, Michael V. "The Rhetoric of Ezekiel's Vision of the Valley of the Bones." *HUCA* 51 (1980) 1–15.

Frankel, Rafael. *Wine and Oil Production in Antiquity in Israel and Other Mediterranean Countries*. Sheffield: Sheffield Academic, 1999.

Fretheim, Terence E. "The Plagues as Ecological Signs of Historical Disaster." *JBL* 110 (1991) 385–96.

Frisch, Amos. "Ephraim and Treachery, Loyalty and (the House of) David: The Meaning of a Structural Parallel in Psalm 78." *VT* 59 (2009) 190–98.

Fu, Janling, et al., eds. *T&T Clark Handbook of Food in the Hebrew Bible and Ancient Israel*. New York: Bloomsbury, 2021.

Füglister, Notker. "Psalm LXXXVIII [*sic*]: Der Rätsel Lösung?" In *Congress Volume: Leuven 1989*, edited by J. A. Emerton, 264–97. VTSup 43. Leiden: Brill, 1991.

Fulton, Deirdre N., and Paula Wapnish Hesse. "Underrepresented Taxa: Fish, Birds, and Wild Game." In *T&T Clark Handbook of Food in the Hebrew Bible and Ancient Israel*, edited by Janling Fu et al., 171–82. London: T&T Clark, 2021.

Gärtner, Judith. "From Generation to Generation: Remembered History in Psalm 78." In *Remembering and Forgetting in Early Second Temple Judah*, edited by Ehud Ben Zvi and Christoph Levin, 269–78. Tübingen: Mohr Siebeck, 2012.

———. *Die Geschichtspsalmen: eines Studie zu den Psalmen 78, 105, 106, 135 und 136 als hermeneutische Schlüsseltexte im Psalter*. FAT 84. Tübingen: Mohr Siebeck, 2012.

———. "The Historical Psalms: A Study of Psalms 78; 105; 106; 135, and 136 as Key Hermeneutical Texts in the Psalter." *HeBAI* 4 (2015) 373–99.

Geiger, Michaele, et al., eds. *Essen und Trinken in der Bibel: Ein literarisches Festmahl für Rainer Kessler zum 65. Geburtstag*. Gütersloh: Gütersloher, 2009.

Gillingham, Susan. "The Exodus Tradition and Israelite Psalmody." *SJT* 52 (1999) 19–46.

———. "Psalm 105 and 106 and the Participation in History Through Liturgy." *HeBAI* 4 (2015) 450–75.

Gillmayr-Bucher, Susanne. "How Does Food Shape History? Images of Food in the Historical Review of Psalm 78." *Protokolle zur Bibel* 27 (2018) 85–95.

Girard, Marc. *Les psaumes redécouverts: de la structure au sens, 2, 51–100*. Montréal: Bellarmin, 1994.

Goldingay, John. *Psalms*. Vol. 1, *Psalms 1–41*. BCOTWP. Grand Rapids: Baker, 2006.

———. *Psalms*. Vol. 2, *Psalms 42–89*. BCOTWP. Grand Rapids: Baker, 2007.

Goody, Jack. *Cooking, Cuisine, and Class*. Cambridge: Cambridge University Press, 1982.

Goulder, Michael D. "Asaph's History of Israel (Elohist Press, Bethel, 725 BCE)." *JSOT* 65 (1995) 71–81.

———. *The Psalms of Asaph and the Pentateuch: Studies in the Psalter, III*. JSOTSup 233. Sheffield: Sheffield Academic, 1996.

Greenstein, Edward L. "Mixing Memory and Design: Reading Psalm 78." *Prooftexts* 10 (1990) 197–218.

Greer, Jonathan. *Dinner at Dan: Biblical and Archaeological Evidence for Sacred Feasts at Iron Age II Tel Dan*. CHANE 66. Leiden: Brill, 2013.

Grimm, Veronika E. *From Feasting to Fasting, the Evolution of a Sin: Attitudes to Food in Late Antiquity*. London: Routledge, 1996.

Gudme, Anne Katrine de Hemmer. "'If I Were Hungry, I Would Not Tell You' (Ps 50, 12): Perspectives on the Care and Feeding of the Gods in the Hebrew Bible." *SJOT* 28 (2014) 172–84.

———. "Invitation to Murder: Hospitality and Violence in the Hebrew Bible." *Studia Theologica-Nordic Journal of Theology* 73 (2019) 89–108.

Guillaume, Philippe. *Land, Credit, and Crisis: Agrarian Finance in the Hebrew Bible*. Sheffield: Equinox, 2012.

Gunkel, Hermann. *Die Psalmen*. Handkommentar zum Alten Testament. Göttingen: Vandenhoeck & Ruprecht, 1926.

Gunkel, Hermann, and Joachim Begrich. *An Introduction to the Psalms: The Genres of the Religious Lyric of Israel*. Translated by James D. Nogalski. Macon, GA: Mercer University Press, 1998.

Haglund, Erik. *Historical Motifs in the Psalms*. Coniectanea Biblica, Old Testament Series 23. Uppsala: CWK Gleerup, 1984.

Hakham, Amos. *The Bible: The Psalms with the Jerusalem Commentary, Volumes 1–3*. Jerusalem: Mosad Harav Kook, 2003.

Harris, Marvin. *Good to Eat: Riddles of Food and Culture*. New York: Simon and Schuster, 1985.

Hawk, L. Daniel. *Joshua*. Berit Olam. Collegeville, MN: Liturgical, 2000.

Hays, Rebecca W. Poe. "Trauma, Remembrance, and Healing: The Meeting of Wisdom and History in Psalm 78." *JSOT* 41 (2016) 183–204.

Heil, John Paul. *The Meal Scenes in Luke-Acts: An Audience-Oriented Approach*. SBLMS 52. Atlanta: SBL, 1999.

Herman, Judith. *Trauma and Recovery*. New York: Basic, 1997.

Hiebert, Paula Sharpe. "Psalm 78: Its Place in Israelite Literature and History." ThD diss., Harvard University, 1992.

Hill, Andrew. "אבן." In *NIDOTTE*, edited by Willem A. VanGemeren, 1:248–50. Grand Rapids: Zondervan, 1996.

Hobbs, T. R. "Hospitality in the First Testament and the 'Teleological Fallacy.'" *JSOT* 95 (2001) 3–30.

Hofbauer, J. "Psalm 77/78: ein 'politisch Lied.'" *ZKTh* 89 (1967) 41–50.

Hoffmeier, James K. "Egypt, Plagues in." In *ABD* 2:374–78.

Holm-Nielsen, Svend. "The Exodus Traditions in Psalm 105." *ASTI* 11 (1978) 22–30.

Hossfeld, Frank-Lothar, and Erich Zenger. *Psalms 2: A Commentary on Psalm 51–100*. Translated by Linda M. Maloney. Hermeneia. Minneapolis: Fortress, 2005.

———. *Psalms 3: A Commentary on Psalm 101–150*. Translated by Linda M. Maloney. Hermeneia. Minneapolis: Fortress, 2011.

Houtman, Cornelis. *Exodus*. Vol. 2, *(Chapters 7:14–19:25)*. Translated by Sierd Woudstra. HCOT. Kampden: KOK, 1996.

Howard, David M., Jr. "Recent Trends in Psalms Study." In *The Face of Old Testament Study: A Survey of Contemporary Approaches*, edited by David Baker and Bill T. Arnold, 329–68. Leicester: Apollos, 1999.

Hubbard, Robert L., Jr. *Joshua*. NIVAC. Grand Rapids: Zondervan, 2009.

Illman, Karl-Johan. *Thema und Tradition in den Asaf-Psalmen*. Åbo: Åbo Akademi, 1976.

Jacobson, Karl N. *Memories of Asaph: Mnemohistory and the Psalms of Asaph*. Minneapolis: Fortress, 2017.

———. "Perhaps YHWH Is Sleeping: 'Contend' and 'Awake' in the Book of Psalms." In *The Shape and Shaping of the Book of Psalms: The Current State of Scholarship*, edited by Nancy L. Declaissé-Walford, 129–45. Atlanta: SBL, 2014.

Jacobson, Rolf A. *"Many Are Saying": The Function of Direct Discourse in the Hebrew Psalter*. LHBOTS 178. London: T&T Clark, 2004.

Jacquet, Louis. *Les Psaumes et le coeur de l'homme: étude textuelle, littéraire et doctrinale, 42 à 100*. Gembloux: Duculot, 1977.

Jasper, F. N. "Early Israelite Traditions and the Psalter." *VT* 17 (1967) 50–59.

Jewett, Robert. "Gospel and Commensality: Social and Theological Implications of Galatians 2:14." In *Gospel in Paul: Studies in Corinthians, Galatians, and Romans for Richard N. Longenecker*, edited by L. Ann Jervis and Peter Richardson, 240–52. Sheffield: Sheffield Academic, 1994.

Jones, Christine Brown. "Lessons Learned: Applying a Hermeneutic of Curiosity to Psalm 78." *Perspectives in Religious Studies* 44 (2017) 173–83.

———. "The Message of the Asaph Collection and Its Role in the Psalter." In *The Shape and Shaping of the Book of Psalms: The Current State of Scholarship*, edited by Nancy L. Declaissé-Walford, 71–85. Atlanta: SBL, 2014.

———. "The Psalms of Asaph: A Study of the Function of a Psalms Collection." PhD diss., Baylor University, 2009.

Junker, H. "Die Entstehungszeit des Ps. 78 und des Deuteronomiums." *Bib* 34 (1953) 487–500.

Kass, Leon. *The Hungry Soul: Eating and the Perfection of Our Nature*. New York: Free Press, 1994.

Katz, Solomon H., ed. *Encyclopedia of Food and Culture*. 3 vols. New York: Scribner's, 2003.

Kidner, Derek. *Psalm 73–150*. TOTC. Downers Grove, IL: InterVarsity, 1975.

Kim, Yeol, and H. F. van Rooy. "Reading Psalm 78 Multidimensionally: The Authorial Dimension." *Scriptura* 84 (2003) 468–84.

———. "Reading Psalm 78 Multidimensionally: The Dimension of the Reader." *Scriptura* 88 (2005) 101–17.

———. "Reading Psalm 78 Multidimensionally: The Dimension of the Text." *Scriptura* 74 (2000) 285–98.

King, Philip J., and Lawrence E. Stager. *Life in Biblical Israel*. Louisville: Westminster John Knox, 2001.

Kirkpatrick, A. F. *Psalms 1–41*. Bk. 1 of *The Book of Psalms*. Cambridge: Cambridge University Press, 1892.

———. *Psalms 42–89*. Bks. 2 and 3 of *The Book of Psalms*. Cambridge: Cambridge University Press, 1898.

Klein, Anja. *Geschichte und Gebet: Die Rezeption der biblischen Geschichte in den Psalmen des Alten Testaments*. Tübingen: Mohr Siebeck, 2014.

———. "Praying Biblical History: The Phenomenon of History in the Psalms." *HeBAI* 4 (2015) 400–426.

Klein, Lillian R. *The Triumph of Irony in the Book of Judges*. JSOTSup 68. Sheffield: Almond, 1988.

Klinghardt, Matthias. *Gemeinschaftsmahl und Mahlgemeinschaft: Soziologie und Liturgie frühchristlicher Mahlfeiern*. Tübingen: Francke, 1996.

Klosinski, Lee E. "The Meals in Mark." PhD diss., Claremont Graduate School, 1988.

Knierim, Rolf P. "Cosmos and History in Israel's Theology." In *The Task of Old Testament Theology: Substance, Method, and Cases: Essays*, 171–224. Grand Rapids: Eerdmans, 1995.

———. "Food, Land, and Justice." In *The Task of Old Testament Theology: Substance, Method, and Cases: Essays*, 225–43. Grand Rapids: Eerdmans, 1995.

Koehler, Ludwig, and Walter Baumgartner. *The Hebrew and Aramaic Lexicon of the Old Testament*. Vol. 3. Leiden: Brill, 1996.

Kok, Johnson Lim Teng. *The Sin of Moses and the Staff of God*. Assen: Van Gorcum, 1997.

Kollman, Bernd. *Ursprung und Gestalt in der frühchristlichen Mahlfeier*. Göttingen: Vandenhoeck & Ruprecht, 1990.

Koopmans, William T. "Psalm 78, Canto D: A Response." *UF* 20 (1988) 121–23.

Korpel, Marjo C. A., and Johannes C. de Moor. "Fundamentals of Ugaritic and Hebrew Poetry." In *The Structural Analysis of Biblical and Canaanite Poetry*, edited by Willem van der Meer and Johannes C. de Moor, 1–61. JSOTSup 74. Sheffield: Sheffield Academic, 1988.

Kraus, Hans-Joachim. *Psalms 1–59*. Translated by Hilton C. Oswald. CC. Minneapolis: Fortress, 1989.

———. *Psalms 60–150*. Translated by Hilton C. Oswald. CC. Minneapolis: Fortress, 1993.

Kugler, Gili. "Not Moses, but David: Theology and Politics in Psalm 78." *SJT* 73 (2020) 126–36.

Kungu, Dickson J. N. "A Dialogical Study of Psalm 78 and Isaiah 1." PhD diss., Westminster Theological Seminary, 2013.

Lee, Archie C. C. "The Context and Function of Historical Recitation in Ancient Israel: A Study of the Historical Psalms, 78, 105, and 106." PhD diss., University of Edinburgh, 1980.

———. "The Context and Function of the Plagues Tradition in Psalm 78." *JSOT* 48 (1990) 83–89.

———. "Genesis I and the Plagues Tradition in Psalm CV." *VT* 40 (1990) 257–63.

Leonard, Jeffrey M. "Historical Traditions in Psalm 78." PhD diss., Brandeis University, 2006.

———. "Identifying Inner-Biblical Allusions: Psalm 78 as a Test Case." *JBL* 127 (2008) 241–65.

Leonard, P. E. "Luke's Account of the Lord's Supper Against the Background of Meals in the Ancient Semitic World and More Particularly Meals in the Gospel of Luke." PhD diss., University of Manchester, 1976.

Leuchter, Mark. "The Reference to Shiloh in Psalm 78." *HUCA* 77 (2006) 1–31.

Levine, Baruch A. *Leviticus*. JPSTC. Philadelphia: JPS, 1989.

MacBeth, Helen M. *Food Preferences and Taste: Continuity and Change*. New York: Berghahn, 1997.

MacDonald, Nathan. "'The Eyes of All Look to You': The Generosity of the Divine King." In *Decisive Meals: Table Politics in Biblical Literature*, edited by Nathan MacDonald et al., 1–14. London: T&T Clark, 2012.

———. *Not Bread Alone: The Uses of Food in the Old Testament*. Oxford: Oxford University Press, 2008.

———. *What Did the Ancient Israelites Eat? Diet in Biblical Times*. Grand Rapids: Eerdmans, 2008.

Malina, Bruce. "The Received View and What It Cannot Do: III John and Hospitality." *Semeia* 35 (1986) 171–94.

Mann, Thomas W. "Not by Word Alone: Food in the Hebrew Bible." *Int* 67 (2013) 351–62.

Marlow, Hilary. "The Lament over the River Nile: Isaiah xix 5–10 in Its Wider Context." *VT* 57 (2007) 229–42.

Matthews, Victor H. "Hospitality and Hostility in Genesis 19 and Judges 19." *BTB* 22 (1992) 3–11.

———. "Hospitality and Hostility in Judges 4." *BTB* 21 (1991) 13–21.

Mays, James L. *Psalms*. IBC. Louisville: John Knox, 1994.

McCann, J. Clinton, Jr. "The Book of Psalms: Introduction, Commentary and Reflections." In *The New Interpreter's Bible*, 4:641–1280. Nashville: Abingdon, 1994.

———. "Books I–III and the Editorial Purpose of the Hebrew Psalter." In *The Shape and Shaping of the Psalter*, edited by J. Clinton McCann Jr., 93–107. JSOTSup 159. Sheffield: Sheffield Academic, 1993.

———. "Bread for the World: Toward an Agrarian Reading of the Psalter (or, Reading the Christ 'Psalmologically')." *Review and Expositor* 112 (2015) 303–10.

———. *A Theological Introduction to the Book of Psalms: The Psalms as Torah*. Nashville: Abingdon, 1993.

McCarter, P. Kyle, Jr. *II Samuel: A New Translation with Introduction, Notes, and Commentary*. AB 9. Garden City, NY: Doubleday, 1984.

McConville, Gordon. *Deuteronomy*. ACOT 5. Downers Grove, IL: InterVarsity, 2002.

McKinlay, Judith E. *Gendering Wisdom the Host: Biblical Invitations to Eat and Drink*. JSOTSup 216. Sheffield: Sheffield Academic, 1996.

McLain, Charles Earl. "An Investigation of Psalm 78 as Political Accession Justification for the Davidic Dynasty." PhD diss., Westminster Theological Seminary, 1996.

McMahan, Craig T. "Meals as Type-Scenes in the Gospel of Luke." PhD diss., The Southern Baptist Theological Seminary, 1987.

Mennell, Stephen, et al. *The Sociology of Food: Eating, Diet, and Culture*. London: Sage, 1993.

Meyers, Carol. *Exodus*. NCBC. Cambridge: Cambridge University Press, 2005.

———. "Food in the First Family: A Socioeconomic Perspective." In *The Book of Genesis: Composition, Reception, and Interpretation*, edited by Craig A. Evans et al., 137–57. Leiden: Brill, 2012.

———. "From Field Crops to Food: Attributing Gender and Meaning to Bread Production in Iron Age Israel." In *The Archaeology of Difference: Gender, Ethnicity, Class, and the "Other" in Antiquity: Studies in Honor of Eric M. Meyers*, edited by D. R. Edwards and C. T. McCollough, 67–84. Boston: American Schools of Oriental Research, 2007.

Milgrom, Jacob. *Leviticus*. CC. Minneapolis: Augsburg Fortress, 2004.

———. *Leviticus 1–16: A New Translation with Introduction and Commentary*. AB 3. New York: Doubleday, 1991.

Miller, Patrick D. "Prayer as Persuasion: The Rhetoric and Intention of Prayer." *Word and World* 4 (1993) 356–62.

Mintz, Sidney W., and Christine M. Du Bois. "The Anthropology of Food and Eating." *Annual Review of Anthropology* 31 (2003) 99–119.

Mowinckel, Sigmund. "Psalms and Wisdom." In *Wisdom in Israel and in the Ancient Near East*, edited by Martin Noth and D. Winton Thomas, 205–24. VTSup 3. Leiden: Brill, 1955.

Mrozek, Andrzej. "The Motif of the Sleeping Deity." *Bib* 80 (1999) 415–19.

Muilenburg, James. "Form Criticism and Beyond." *JBL* 89 (1969) 1–18.

Nasuti, Harry P. *Tradition History and the Psalms of Asaph*. Atlanta: Scholars, 1988.

Nelson, Richard. *Deuteronomy: A Commentary*. OTL. Louisville: Westminster John Knox, 2002.

Neyrey, Jerome H. "Ceremonies in Luke-Acts: The Case of Meals and Table-Fellowship." In *The Social World of Luke-Acts: Model for Interpretation*, edited by Jerome H. Neyrey, 361–87. Peabody, MA: Hendrickson, 1991.

———. "Meals, Food, and Table Fellowship." In *The Social Sciences and New Testament Interpretation*, edited by Richard L. Rohrbaugh, 159–82. Peabody, MA: Hendrickson, 1996.

Noth, Martin. *A History of Pentateuchal Traditions*. Translated by Bernhard W. Anderson. Atlanta: Scholars, 1981.

Olson, Dennis T. *Numbers*. ICB. Louisville: Westminster John Knox, 1996.

Pavan, Marco. *He Remembered That They Were But Flesh, A Breath That Passes and Does Not Return (Ps 78,39): The Theme of Memory and Forgetting in the Third Book of the Psalter (Pss 73–89)*. New York: Lang, 2014.

Peters, Kurtis. *Hebrew Lexical Semantics and Daily Life in Ancient Israel: What's Cooking in Biblical Hebrew?* Biblical Interpretation Series 146. Leiden: Brill, 2016.

Pitt-Rivers, Julian. "The Stranger, the Guest, and the Hostile Host: An Introduction to the Study of the Laws of Hospitality." In *Contributions to Mediterranean Sociology: Mediterranean Rural Communities and Social Change*, edited by J. G. Peristiany, 13–30. Paris: Mouton, 1968.

Pritchard, James B., ed. *Ancient Near Eastern Texts Relating to the Old Testament*. Princeton: Princeton University Press, 1969.

Raabe, Paul R. *Obadiah: A New Translation with Introduction and Commentary*. AB 24D. New York: Doubleday, 1996.

Ramond, Sophie. "The Growth of the Scriptural Corpus by Successive Rewritings: The Case of the So-Called 'Historical Psalms.'" *HeBAI* 4 (2015) 427–49.

———. *Les leçons et les enigmes du passé: une exégèse intra-biblique des psaumes historiques*. Berlin: de Gruyter, 2014.

Ray, David. "Who Did What to Whom? Reassessing God's Activity in Psalm 78." *Colloquim* 52 (2020) 65–84.

Reed, Stephen. "Food in the Psalms." PhD diss., Claremont Graduate School, 1987.

Ryken, Leland, et al. *Dictionary of Biblical Imagery*. Leicester: InterVarsity, 1998.

Sarna, Nahum M. *Exodus*. JPSTC. Philadelphia: JPS, 1991.

Schmitt, Eleanore. *Das Essen in der Bibel: Literaturethnologische Aspekte des Alltäglichen*. Studien zur Kulturanthropologie 2. Münster: Lit Verlag, 1994.

Seybold, Klaus. *Introducing the Psalms*. Translated by R. Graeme Dunphy. Edinburgh: T&T Clark, 1990.

———. *Die Psalmen*. Tübingen: Mohr Siebeck, 1996.

Shafer-Elliott, Cynthia. *Food in Ancient Judah: Domestic Cooking in the Time of the Hebrew Bible*. Sheffield: Equinox, 2012.

Sharon, Diane M. *Patterns of Destiny: Narrative Structures of Foundation and Doom in the Hebrew Bible*. Winona Lake, IN: Eisenbrauns, 2002.

———. "When Fathers Refuse to Eat: The Trope of Rejecting Food and Drink in Biblical Narrative." In *Semeia 86: Food and Drink in the Biblical Worlds*, edited by Athalya Brenner and Jan Willem van Henten, 135–48. Atlanta: SBL, 1999.

Smend, Rudolf. "Essen und Trinken: ein Stück Weltlichkeit des Alten Testaments." In *Beiträge zur alttestamentlichen Theologie: Festschrift für Walther Zimmerli zum 70 Geburtstag*, edited by Herbert Donner et al., 447–59. Göttingen: Vandenhoeck & Ruprecht, 1977.

Smit, Peter-Ben. *Fellowship and Food in the Kingdom: Eschatological Meals and Scenes of Utopian Abundance in the New Testament*. WUNT 2.234. Tübingen: Mohr Siebeck, 2008.

Smith, Dennis E. *From Symposium to Eucharist: The Banquet in the Early Christian World*. Minneapolis: Fortress, 2003.

Spero, Shubert. "Was Psalm 50 Misplaced?" *JBQ* 30 (2002) 26–31.

Stager, Lawrence E. "First Fruits of Civilization." In *Palestine in the Bronze and Iron Age: Papers in Honour of Olga Tufnell*, edited by J. N. Tubb, 172–87. London: Institute of Archaeology, 1985.

Steele, E. Spring. "Jesus' Table-Fellowship with Pharisees: An Editorial Analysis of Luke 7:36–50, 11:37–54, and 14:1–24." PhD diss., University of Notre Dame, 1981.

Steffen, Daniel S. "The Messianic Banquet as a Paradigm for Israel-Gentile Salvation in Matthew." PhD diss., Dallas Theological Seminary, 2001.

Stinson, Michelle A. "Dining in the Kingdom: Jesus and Table Fellowship in the Gospel of Luke." MA thesis, Denver Seminary, 2000.

———. "The Parable of the Sensible Farmer." *The Big Picture* 13 (2025) 10–11.

———. "Praise the LORD, the (un)Creator of Heaven and Earth: Psalm 105's Depiction of YHWH's Sovereignty in the Egyptian Plagues." In *For Us, but Not to Us: Essays on Creation, Covenant, and Context in Honor of John H. Walton*, edited by Adam E. Miglio et al., 99–109. Eugene, OR: Pickwick, 2020.

———. "Sourdough and Bitter Tears: Food and Communal Laments in the Time of COVID-19." *Word and World* 41 (2021) 177–84.

———. "Summer and Winter, Seedtime and Harvest: Re-Considering the Psalter's Agrarian Hope in a Season of Covid." *BN* 198 (2023) 55–65.

———. "Turning Tables in Israel's History: Food Language and Reversals in Psalms 105 and 106." *CBQ* 83 (2021) 588–98.

Strawn, Brent A. "Manna." In *Dictionary of the Old Testament: Pentateuch*, edited by T. Desmond Alexander and David W. Baker, 560–62. Downers Grove, IL: InterVarsity, 2003.

Stulac, Daniel J. *History and Hope: The Agrarian Wisdom of Isaiah 28–35*. Siphrut 24. University Park, PA: Eisenbruans, 2018.

Talmon, Shemaryahu. "Prophetic Rhetoric and Agricultural Metaphora." In *Storia e tradizioni di Israele*, 267–80. Brescia: Paideia Editrice, 1991.

Tammuz, Oded. "Psalm 78: A Case Study in Redaction as Propaganda." *CBQ* 79 (2017) 205–21.

Tanner, Beth LaNeel. "King Yahweh as the Good Shepherd: Taking Another Look at the Image of God in Psalm 23." In *David and Zion: Biblical Studies in Honor of J. J. M. Roberts*, edited by Bernard F. Batto and Kathryn L. Roberts, 267–84. Winona Lake, IN: Eisenbrauns, 2004.

Tate, Marvin E. *Psalms 51–100*. WBC 20. Waco, TX: Word, 1990.

Trible, Phyllis. *Rhetorical Criticism: Context, Method, and the Book of Jonah.* Minneapolis: Fortress, 1994.

Tull, Patricia K. "Persistent Vegetative States: People as Plants and Plants as People in Isaiah." In *The Desert Will Bloom: Poetic Visions in Isaiah*, edited by A. Joseph Everson and Hyun Chul Paul Kim, 17–34. Atlanta: SBL, 2009.

Vancil, Jack W. "Sheep, Shepherd." In *ABD*, edited by David Noel Freedman, 5:1187–90. New York: Doubleday, 1992.

Vesco, Jean-Luc. *Le psautier de David traduit et commenté I.* Paris: Cerf, 2006.

———. *Le psautier de David traduit et commenté II.* Paris: Cerf, 2006.

Visser, Margaret. *Much Depends on Dinner: The Extraordinary History and Mythology, Allure and Obsessions, Perils and Taboos, of an Ordinary Meal.* New York: Grove, 1986.

———. *The Rituals of Dinner: The Origins, Evolutions, Eccentricities, and Meaning of Table Manners.* New York: Penguin, 1992.

Wagner, Thomas. "Recounting חידות מני־קדם in Psalm 78: What Are the 'Riddles' About?" *Journal of Hebrew Scriptures* 14 (2014) 1–21.

Walsh, Carey. *The Fruit of the Vine: Viticulture in Ancient Israel.* Winona Lake, IN: Eisenbrauns, 2000.

Warren, Tish Harrison. *Liturgy of the Ordinary: Sacred Practices in Everyday Life.* Downers Grove, IL: InterVarsity, 2016.

Watson, Wilfred G. E. *Classical Hebrew Poetry: A Guide to Its Techniques.* JSOTSup 26. Sheffield: JSOT, 1984.

Weber, Beat. "Der Asaph-Psalter-eine Skizze." In *Prophetie und Psalmen, Festschrift für K. Seybold*, 117–41. AOAT 280. Münster: Ugarit-Verlag, 2001.

———. "Psalm 78: Geschichte mit Geschichte deuten." *Theologische Zeitschrift* 56 (2000) 193–214.

———. "Zer Datierung der Asaph-Psalmen 74 und 79." *Bib* 81 (2000) 521–32.

Webster, Jane S. *Ingesting Jesus: Eating and Drinking in the Gospel of John.* ABib 6. Atlanta: SBL, 2003.

Weiser, Artur. *The Psalms.* OTL. Philadelphia: Westminster, 1962.

Welton, Rebekah. "Ethnographic and Biblical Studies: 'A Land Flowing with Milk and Honey' as a Case Study for Re-contextualising a Familiar Phrase." *Biblical Interpretation* 30 (2022) 1–20.

———. *"He Is a Drunkard and a Glutton": Deviant Consumption in the Hebrew Bible.* Leiden: Brill, 2020.

Wenham, Gordon J. *Genesis 16–50.* WBC 2. Nashville: Nelson, 1987.

———. *Story as Torah: Reading Old Testament Narrative Ethically.* Grand Rapids: Baker Academic, 2004.

Westermann, Claus. "The 'Re-Presentation' of History in the Psalms." In *Praise and Lament in the Psalms*, translated by Keith R. Crim and Richard N. Soulen, 214–49. Edinburgh: T&T Clark, 1981.

Wiggins, Steve A. "Tempestuous Wind Doing YHWH's Will: Perceptions of the Wind in the Psalms." *SJOT* 13 (1999) 3–23.

Wilder, Amos N. "Story and Story-World." *Int* 37 (1983) 353–64.

Wilson, Carol Bakker. *For I Was Hungry and You Gave Me Food: Pragmatics of Food Access in the Gospel of Matthew.* Eugene, OR: Pickwick, 2014.

Wilson, Gerald H. *The Editing of the Hebrew Psalter.* SBLDS 76. Chico, CA: Scholars, 1985.

Witte, Markus. "From Exodus to David—History and Historiography in Psalm 78." In *History and Identity: How Israel's Later Authors Viewed Its Earlier History*, edited by Núria Calduch-Benages and Jan Liesen, 21–42. New York: de Gruyter, 2006.

———. *Von Ewigkeit zu Ewigkeit: Weisheit und Geschichte in den Psalmen*. Neukirchen-Vluyn: Neukirchener Verlag, 2014.

Woudstra, Marten H. *The Book of Joshua*. NICOT. Grand Rapids: Eerdmans, 1981.

York, John. *The Last Shall Be First: The Rhetoric of Reversal in Luke*. Sheffield: Sheffield Academic, 1991.

Zakovitch, Yair. "'He Did Choose the Tribe of Judah . . . He Chose David His Servant'—Ps 78: Sources, Meaning and Message." In *David King of Israel Alive and Enduring?*, edited by Herzelia Baron and Ora Lipschitz, 117–202. Jerusalem: Simor, 1997.

Ancient Document Index

OLD TESTAMENT

Genesis

Exodus

Exodus (continued)

Leviticus

Numbers

Ruth

1 Samuel

2 Samuel

1 Kings

2 Kings

1 Chronicles

2 Chronicles

Job

Psalms

Psalms (continued)

Psalms (continued)

Psalms (continued)

Proverbs

Ecclesiastes

Song of Songs

Isaiah

Jeremiah

Ezekiel

Hosea

Joel

www.ingramcontent.com/pod-product-compliance
Lightning Source LLC
LaVergne TN
LVHW050621100826
845148LV00011B/1671

* 9 7 9 8 3 8 5 2 6 2 2 8 1 *